FORBIDDEN
FRUIT

FORBIDDEN FRUIT

LOVE STORIES FROM THE UNDERGROUND RAILROAD

★ ★ ★

BETTY DeRAMUS

Slave couples who ran away together, a white woman who escaped with her slaves and an Underground Railroad that sometimes ran in reverse

ATRIA BOOKS

NEW YORK LONDON TORONTO SYDNEY

1230 Avenue of the Americas
New York, NY 10020

ISBN-13: 978-0-7434-8263-9
ISBN-10: 0-7434-8263-8
ISBN-13: 978-0-7434-8264-6 (Pbk)
ISBN-10: 0-7434-8264-6 (Pbk)

This Atria Books trade paperback edition February 2006

10 9 8 7 6 5 4 3 2 1

Manufactured in the United States of America

For information regarding special discounts for bulk purchases, please contact Simon & Schuster Special Sales at 1-800-456-6798 or business@simonandschuster.com

To my mother, Lucille Richardson DeRamus, and my father, Jim (cq) Louis DeRamus, who, during thirty-three years and nine months of marriage, stayed in love

Acknowledgments

I owe many thanks to Rita Rosenkranz, my agent, who believed in me even when I didn't; my patient editor, Malaika Adero; researchers Dale Rich, Camille Killens and Cathy Dekker of Detroit and Berkley; Katharine C. Dale, Iowa City, Iowa; Linda Worstell of Sandy, Utah; Tom Gorden, Boston; Russell Magnaghi and Darlene Walch, Northern Michigan University, Marquette, Michigan; Brigitte Burkett of Richmond, Virginia; Martina Kunnecke, director of exhibits and technology, Kentucky Center for African American Heritage, Louisville, Kentucky; Dr. Ronald Palmer, professor emeritus, George Washington University, Washington, D.C.; Dr. Norman McRae, historian, Detroit; Arthur La Brew, musicologist and historian, Detroit; Bryan Prince, historian, Buxton, Ontario, Canada; Alice Torriente, Baltimore, Maryland; Joanne McNamarra, Louise Dougher and Deanne Rathke, Greenlawn-Centerport Historical Society, Greenlawn, New York; Louis Hunsinger Jr. and Mamie Diggs, Williamsport, Pennsylvania; Mary Neilsen, North Fairfield Museum, Ohio; Bonnie Mead, Huron County Historical Society, Ohio; Amy Wilson, acting director, and Jason Harmon, education coordinator, Chemung County Historical Association, Elmira, New York; Ralph Clayton, Enoch Pratt Free Library, Baltimore, Maryland; Pete Lesher, Chesapeake Bay Maritime Museum, St. Michaels, Maryland; Jeanne Willoz-Egnor, Mariners' Museum, Newport News, Virginia; Clarence Still Jr., Linda Waller and C. Joyce Fowler of the Lawnside Historical Society, Lawnside, New Jersey; Mary Davidson and Margo Brown of the Salt Spring Historical Society, Saltspring Island, British Columbia, Canada; Calvin Murphy, Bear Lake, Michigan, and Shelley Murphy, Charlottesville, Virginia, for information about their cousin, Calvin Clark Davis; Bennie J. McRae Jr., Trotwood, Ohio; Larry O. Simmons, Detroit, Michigan; Ronald Stephenson, Detroit, Michigan; Professor Kimberly Davis, Adrian, Michigan; Sharon Rucker, Grand Rapids, Michigan, a descendant of Molly Welsh and Bannaka; Marie Berry Cross and Jim Cross, Mecosta County, Michigan; the late Marguerite Berry Jackson and Raymond Pointer, Morley, Michigan, descendants of Isaac and Lucy Berry; and Berenice Easton, Greenlawn, New York, granddaughter of Samuel and Rebecca Ballton.

Permissions

The author is grateful to those listed below for granting her permission to use the following material. All possible care has been taken to trace ownership of material and to make full acknowledgment. If any errors or omissions have occurred, they will be corrected in subsequent editions if notification is sent to the publisher.

The Chemung County Historical Society for permission to use excerpts from the *Chemung Historical Journal*, June 1960 issue, pages 710–11.

Wayne State University Press for permission to use excerpts from *Copper Country Journal: The Diary of Schoolmaster Henry Hobart, 1863–1864*, ed. Philip P. Mason, © 1991 Wayne State University Press.

Ginalie Swaim, editor, the *Iowa Heritage Illustrated*, for permission to use excerpts from "The Desire for Freedom," May 1929 issue of *The Palimpsest*, now known as the *Iowa Heritage Illustrated.*

Mark Silverman, publisher, the *Detroit News*, for permission to use excerpts from the *Detroit News*, "Black Pioneers Tackle Northern Wilderness" (February 15, 2000) and "Duty, Not Race, Defined War Hero" (February 5, 2002).

Marie Loretta Berry Cross and Jim Cross for permission to use material written by family members.

Introduction

This is a collection of love stories about slavery-era couples, some enslaved, some free, most black, but a few interracial, who fought mobs, wolves, bloodhounds, bounty hunters, bullets and social taboos to preserve their relationships. For both the black couples and the interracial ones, lasting love was the forbidden fruit, the apple no one was supposed to bite. Yet all of these couples insisted on leaping at life and love, no matter what price they had to pay.

Many of these couples received help from the Underground Railroad, as it is commonly known, a sometimes organized, sometimes informal and sometimes spontaneously assembled network of people and places that sheltered fugitives. However, in most cases they began their journeys alone or created their own networks, finding help whenever and wherever they could.

I began collecting these stories after visiting a central Michigan town where I first heard the story of a twenty-year-old white woman named Lucy Millard and a twenty-six-year-old slave named Isaac Berry. In 1858, they ran away separately so they could meet and marry in Canada. He traveled on foot and on the Underground Railroad while she rode a real train.

In this collection you'll also meet a young slave girl who travels inside a wooden chest to meet her fiancé, a Canadian runaway who outlives five wives, a man who literally carries his wife to freedom and a black man who trades his freedom for love.

These, however, are not simply stories about the past. Each one contains a lesson for the present—a reminder of what once sustained people, what armored their spirits, what preserved their communities and what inspired them to push on. A couple of these stories, in fact, have the sweep of an epic, tracing the influence of a family tradition, story or person through several generations.

My sources include descendants of runaway slave couples, unpublished memoirs, unpublished school curriculum outlines, nineteenth-century newspaper articles, family reunion publications and videotapes, slave narratives, Civil War pension records, census data, slave schedules, books, magazine articles, photo exhibits, cookbooks and historical museum monuments.

This is a book about people pursuing love and achievement in a time of hate and severely limited opportunities. Though not all of these true tales end in triumph, they all include hope, passion and the pursuit of joy.

Contents

Book I **The Rebels**

Book II **Crossing the Color Line**

Book III **Free at Last**

Book I

THE REBELS

★

The bridegroom wears a Union army uniform in this 1866 *Harper's Weekly* illustration reflecting the eagerness of many former slaves for legal marriages.

1

LOVE IN A TIME OF HATE

Joseph Antoine would have found the twenty-first century as baffling as ballet is to a bulldog. He wouldn't have understood married couples who split up before their wedding flowers wilt or their new woks and washing machines lose their showroom shine. He wouldn't have understood why black marriage, as an institution, began dwindling so drastically after 1940. He wouldn't have understood why black children, who once could count on honorary "aunts" and "uncles" on every plantation, now, in some cases, boil their own oatmeal and tuck themselves into bed. Most of all he wouldn't have understood why, for some men, falling in love became a fatal flaw, the crack in a man's smooth chocolate-ice-cream cool.

For the love of a woman, Joseph Antoine sat in a jail cell, churning out letters that explained how he wound up in the trap baited, set and sprung by his wife's owner.

For the love of a woman, Joseph Antoine stood on an auction block to be sold like a keg of bourbon or a hog.

For the love of a woman, Joseph Antoine signed away his freedom and became an indentured servant, or temporary slave, for seven and a half years. His court petitions and records document his struggle to hold on to his wife, no matter how large or even deadly a price he was required to pay. However, his story of commitment to a slave-era marriage is hardly unique.

But why would a free black man in the early 1800s open his heart so totally to a woman he couldn't legally marry? Wouldn't a man born in one slave society and living in another have learned to keep his emotions on ice, his affections scattered, his love chopped and diced into small, easily swallowed chunks? Some slave owners certainly believed this. In fact, many justified splitting up plantation couples by claiming that slaves felt little pain at losing a mate and cared nothing about lasting relationships. "Not one in a thousand, I suppose, of those poor creatures have any conception whatever of the sanctity of marriage," wrote the wife of an Alabama minister. American-style slavery did indeed promote serial relationships, sex without commitment and the wholesale production of babies for sale. All the same, slave families valued their kin and often longed for the stability of legal relationships and families. In fact, during the Civil War and immediately afterward, freedmen rushed to get married, round up lost relatives and bring their women home from the fields. Between 1890 and 1940, a slightly higher percentage of black adults than whites married.

Still, full-fledged romantic love—the kind of love Joseph Antoine felt—could lead to heartbreak, particularly if a man had to stand by and watch his woman insulted, beaten, overworked, raped, starved or sold away. In Louisiana, a slave named Hosea Bidell was separated from his mate after twenty-five years of togetherness, and others could tell similar stories. As a freeman informally married to a Southern slave woman, Joseph Antoine was especially vulnerable, yet he never put any fences around his heart.

He had been born a slave on the hilly green main island of Cuba. It was a land where gold-seeking Spanish conquerors armed with muskets, cannons, armor and steel swords had nearly wiped out the native population with diseases, beatings, torture and harsh work. They then brought in African slaves to work the plantations. Once the sugar cane and tobacco industries based on slave labor took over the island's economy, black Cubans, slave and free, multiplied. However, despite the harshness of life on strength-sapping sugar cane plantations and the deadly punishments for runaway slaves, Cuban blacks made up a large part of both the skilled and unskilled labor pool on the island. By the mid-eighteenth century, free black people, known as *negros horros*, were most of the island's shoemakers, plumbers, tailors, carpenters and other tradesmen. Moreover, slaves had certain basic rights, including the right to marry, stay with their families, embrace the Catholic Church and receive religious instruction.

In the late 1700s, Joseph Antoine's owner freed him. It's not known why his owner did this or even who his owner was. However, a Cuban slave could be freed for all kinds of reasons, including identifying counterfeiters, exposing treason, denouncing a virgin's rape, avenging his owner's murder or simply because his master wanted to let him go. As a result, 41 percent of Cuba's blacks were free by 1774.

In 1792, Joseph Antoine left Cuba, a land with dry and wet seasons, mahogany, ebony and royal palm forests, and moved to Virginia, which, until at least 1860, was the oldest and largest slave society in North America. Antoine was twenty-seven years old, could read and write and carried papers that proclaimed his freedom. He never explained why he decided to come to America—perhaps the smell of adventure drew him or perhaps he simply wanted to start his life as a freeman in a place where he had never been branded a slave.

It was the kind of mistake anyone could make.

Like Cuba, Virginia had thick forests, but there were no easily caught hogs or cattle, no wild fruits to pinch from trees and, for someone like Joseph Antoine, little that felt or tasted like freedom. In his native land, slaves had the right to personal safety and the right to marry. In eighteenth-century Virginia, a man could kill his slave without being guilty of a felony, slave marriages had no legal standing and a host of laws squeezed, hemmed in and whittled away at the rights of free blacks. Many whites, in fact, considered free blacks good for nothing except making slaves think too much of themselves or inspiring them to run.

Until 1782, Virginia law made it nearly impossible for anyone to free a slave. Once those restrictions fell, the number of free blacks in the state leaped from fewer than three thousand to nearly thirteen thousand by 1790. Slaveholder Joseph Hill was one of those who decided he wanted to free his slaves. In 1783, he wrote a will giving his bondsmen their freedom upon his death because, he said, he felt that freedom was the natural condition of mankind. Inspired by the Declaration of Independence, others followed his lead. However, a year after Joseph Antoine's arrival, Virginia began turning off the tap. It passed a whole series of laws that set traps for free blacks and slung nooses around their necks.

In 1793, Virginia prohibited free blacks from moving into the state. In 1800, it made those who were there register. In 1806, newly freed blacks were ordered to leave the state within twelve months or return to slavery. In 1819, the Virginia General Assembly ruled that freedmen and slaves couldn't meet in groups for educational purposes. In 1832, a year after Nat Turner's bloody, Bible-bolstered raiders spread terror across the countryside, the Virginia legislature clamped more restrictions on free blacks, forbidding anyone to teach them to read and write. Black ministers lost their voices, too: they could no longer preach in Virginia or help run a church. Under an 1838 law, any free Negro who left the state to get an education couldn't return to Virginia. Frances Pelham, a free black Virginia wife and mother, once threatened to scald with boiling water an official who came to snatch her family's dog. Under Virginia law, whites and slaves could own dogs, but free blacks couldn't.

These were just a few of the traps and snares waiting for Joseph Antoine when he landed in his new home, sweet Virginia, also known as the Old Dominion. Did he understand at once the hurdles he faced? Or did it take a while for him to size up his situation and realize its scope? Actually, despite Virginia's hostility toward free blacks—much of it springing from white fears that free blacks and slave laborers were stealing their jobs—Joseph Antoine still might have led a fairly low-key, friction-free life.

The woman changed everything. Oh yes, she did.

She was a slave owned by a man named Jonathon Purcell, who was born in 1754 in Hampshire, Virginia, now West Virginia. Antoine married her—or what passed for marriage in American slave societies. Her name is not known, and no pictures of her or Antoine survive. Maybe she was a black beauty with the kind of high-riding hips that could support a bundle or rock a baby, Africa oozing from every pore. Or maybe she was a pale woman with a slant to her eyes and a whisper of silk and cinnamon in her hair. Or perhaps Antoine just looked into eyes the color of morning coffee and saw something that told him that in this far-off place called Virginia he'd managed to find a home.

Joseph Antoine didn't know it, but his love for his enslaved wife put him in all kinds of danger, including the danger of giving her master a button he could push. Around 1796, Jonathon Purcell decided to do just that. He was about to move to the frontier post at Fort Vincennes, Indiana, in the Northwest Territory. In 1787, the U.S. Congress had established the Northwest Territory as free and declared that slavery there "save in punishment for crime" would be prohibited. The territory included land that would later be divided into the states of Ohio, Indiana, Illinois, Wisconsin and Michigan. However, some slavery still lingered in the region in 1796 and even later. In 1830, the village of Vincennes, the oldest town in Indiana, contained 768 white males, 639 white females, 63 free black men, 63 free black females, 12 slave men and 20 slave females. Still, Jonathon Purcell would have been fully aware that moving to free territory would eventually deprive him of the services of Joseph Antoine's wife. So he took out an insurance policy guaranteed to keep her in bondage and make sure she wouldn't run: he appealed to her husband's heart.

Antoine already had decided to accompany his wife to Vincennes. Knowing how much Antoine loved his wife, her owner threatened to sell the woman in Spanish territory unless Antoine, a freeman, signed papers making him an indentured servant for seven and a half years. Purcell also demanded that Antoine's wife sign an identical contract. Indentured servitude was the seventeenth-century solution to America's scarce labor problem. Before sailing to America, immigrants signed contracts that spelled out the terms of their service and their freedom dues. Skilled workers rarely served more than three years, and others agreed to four or five. Seven was usually the maximum number of years served. Typically, at the end of his term, an indentured servant received freedom dues that might include tools, clothes, a gun and, in the first half of the seventeenth century, fifty acres of land. The earliest blacks who came to America were indentured servants, not slaves, pledging to work free for a specific period of time to cover the cost of their transportation to this country. They were treated more or less like poor whites bound by the same contracts and received money at the end of their service. There is no record that Antoine and his wife were promised freedom dues, land or any other compensation besides the right to stay together.

At first, Antoine refused to sign the indenture papers. Purcell forced the couple into a room and locked the door. He promised that both Antoine and his wife would be free at the end of their service. Finally, the couple agreed to sign the papers and accompany Purcell to Vincennes, in the Indiana Territory, on the east bank of the Wabash River among vineyards and peach, cherry and apple trees. Purcell's brothers, William and Edward, and their families came along, too, all of them Revolutionary War veterans. Purcell became a prominent man in the Indiana Territory: in 1800, he was appointed a justice of the Court of General Quarter Sessions of the Peace for Knox County, Indiana, and a justice of the Court of Common Pleas.

Meanwhile, for seven years, Joseph Antoine and his wife labored on the Indiana frontier, dreaming of a free future. Around 1803, as the couple neared the end of their service, Antoine reminded Purcell of his promise. That's when Purcell informed the Antoines that they had misunderstood the agreement. Their term of service was for fifteen years each, not seven and a half.

Before Antoine could absorb this shock, he heard a rumor that Purcell planned to sell him and his wife to Manuel Lacey, a slave trader from St. Louis. The rumor hardened into fact. Lacey took Antoine and his wife straight to the slave market in New Orleans and sold them as slaves for life. Antoine managed to obtain an audience with Manuel Juan de Salcedo, the last Spanish governor of

Louisiana, who served until the territory was transferred to France on November 30, 1803. After Antoine showed the governor his freedom papers from Cuba, the governor, usually portrayed as a corrupt official who tried to squeeze profits from his post, did the right thing. He released Joseph Antoine and his wife from the sale. However, they feared that, under the law, Antoine's wife would remain a slave until the two of them had served out the full fifteen-year terms of their indenture.

A legal noose still encircled their necks and they couldn't seem to shake it off. Lacey assured the couple he would treat them kindly while they served out the final years of their contract. However, on the trip to St. Louis, they quickly saw that they had, once again, stumbled into a trap. Lacey treated them so badly that the couple decided they had only one move left—they would run. In 1804, they fled into Kentucky, Antoine taking the name Ben. No doubt they hoped to reach Ohio or some other free territory. However, Antoine's wife, drained and exhausted, collapsed by the roadside. While cradled in the arms of the man she loved, she died.

Despite what must have been profound grief, Antoine continued on to Louisville but was soon captured by Davis Floyd, a slave driver hired by Lacey. After trying unsuccessfully to sell Antoine, Floyd threw him into the Louisville jail. On September 19, 1804, Antoine presented the first of a series of petitions to the Jefferson County Circuit Court, spelling out his troubles and pleading for help.

In his petitions he referred to himself as "Yr orator." He told the court that he had strong reasons to believe that Davis Floyd planned to strip him of his liberty. He declared that he was a freeman and could "establish this fact to the satisfaction of this . . . Court." He said he worried that Floyd would take him back to St. Louis and turn him over to Lacey, who would turn him into a lifelong slave. He informed the court that he could prove he deserved freedom and that people had conspired to steal it. Finally, in June 1805, the court released Joseph Antoine, then forty. Yet there was no way he could ever shed the image of his wife, the woman he loved more than his freedom, dying in his arms.

Joseph Antoine's story doesn't stand alone. Many black husbands risked their liberty and lives for enslaved wives. They considered freedom a dubious gift, a counterfeit coin, if they couldn't spend it on the people they loved.

After the Virginia legislature decided in 1806 that newly freed blacks must leave the state within a year or be reenslaved, other black Virginia husbands and wives—like Joseph Antoine—prepared themselves to do the unthinkable. They offered to return to slavery rather than leave without their wives or husbands. Told to leave Virginia, a black man named Walker declared that he never would have purchased himself if he'd known he'd have to leave behind his wife and five children. He had bought his freedom from Edward Holladay on August 5, 1833. Robin was another black man who discovered he didn't like the taste of solo freedom. Freed by Benjamin Ferguson, he left for Ohio in 1836 but returned to Culpeper County, Virginia: there, he hoped to spend the rest of his life with his wife. Twenty-four people who knew Robin signed his petition to stay in the state. A former Giles County slave named Dilly also pleaded with the Virginia General Assembly to let her stay with her husband, a slave of Abram Nisewander. Former slave Nelly McIntosh wanted to remain with her relatives and friends, too. So did Armistead Johns, a freedman from Fauquier County, who preferred slavery to separation from his wife.

The records don't show what became of families whose petitions the General Assembly rejected. Free Virginia blacks, however, had another way of keeping their families together, but it was even more controversial than returning to slavery. If they had been freed before 1806, they could stay on in Virginia, buy their own relatives and friends and become slave owners themselves. Some did just that.

Over the years, Samuel Johnson of Fauquier County filed several petitions asking the Commonwealth of Virginia to let his wife, two children and three grandchildren remain in the state. Johnson owned his wife and two children. Peyton Shelton of Fluvanna County purchased and married a slave named Anna and then asked that Anna be allowed to stay in the state. Carter Armistead, forty-five, was freed in September 1844 by Lucinda Armistead, presumably his wife. She had purchased him in 1842 from John Alsop of Spotsylvania. George DeBaptiste of Fredericksburg owned his wife, Maria, whom he set free on March 12, 1823. His son, also named George, would become an Underground Railroad conductor in Cincinnati, Ohio; Madison, Indiana; and Detroit, Michigan.

Others simply left Virginia. This group included Frances Pelham, the free black woman whose dog officials had tried to take, and her husband, Robert, a farmer, mechanic, bricklayer and a "successful contractor in masonry construction."

One of her descendants described Frances as a woman with "an independent and aggressive nature," which "caused a restlessness in the Pelham household which was eventually to cause an upheaval of the family life. This incident of the dog has been given at various times as the principal factor which caused Robert and Frances Pelham to come North. This however was only one incident. In and around Petersburg, the Pelhams had many loyal friends among the liberal minded whites who were urging them to seek some place where there was less race friction and where the explosive nature of Mrs. Pelham was less likely to cause trouble."

The Pelhams left Virginia in 1859, moving first to Columbus, Ohio, where they never unpacked, then on to Philadelphia and, finally, to Detroit, where they settled because the schools seemed superior. Other free black Virginians who joined the exodus to Detroit included a shoemaker and clarinet player named Major Cook; his wife, Priscilla; and their five children, who arrived in 1848; Alexander D. Moore, a barber and musician whose band played for dances on the steamer *Hope*; and John Richards and his sister, Fannie, who became the first black schoolteacher in Detroit.

There are many other stories like this, stories about black men and women who, even during the slavery era, cared as much about the welfare of their mates as they did about their own. Henry Bibb, a Kentucky slave, ran away because he couldn't endure watching his wife and daughter insulted and abused without being able to step in and stop it. However, he couldn't bear the separation and returned to

Kentucky again and again, trying four times to take his slave wife, Malinda, with him. Though he eventually married another woman in Canada, where he became a leader in the antislavery movement, a newspaper publisher and Underground Railroad supporter, it's not likely Henry Bibb ever forgot his first love.

Dangerfield Newby, quite literally, died for love. The free black Virginian had raised enough money to buy his wife out of slavery, but her master either pushed up the price or turned him down. Meanwhile, Newby, a blacksmith with a smoldering temper, had received a letter from his wife, Harriet, begging him to rescue her before she was sold. The letter was no passive slip of paper. It spoke to Dangerfield, sang to him, pleaded with him and poked him in all of the places where he hurt. Spurred by that letter and other "Dear Dangerfield" letters from Harriet, Newby joined John Brown in the doomed raid on the federal armory at Harper's Ferry, Virginia (now Harpers Ferry, West Virginia), where two mighty rivers, the Potomac and the Shenandoah, rush into each other's arms and flow together to the sea. Like John Brown, he believed the raid would trigger a black uprising. He also hoped it would be the first step in his rescue of Harriet and his children. "Newby joined John Brown out of desperation," according to Ronald Palmer, who may be a descendant of Harriet Newby's parents. One of five black raiders, Dangerfield Newby became the first of the Harper's Ferry attackers to die. He was gunned down on October 17, 1859, about noon while trying to escape from local militia coming across the Potomac River Bridge. It was not an easy dying, a gentle swooning into darkness. A spike from a gun tore open his throat, people stabbed his corpse, souvenir hunters ran off with his ears and hogs partially ate his body. But some say Newby's ghost still prowls the area, roaming the grounds in baggy pants and an old slouch hat, the gash across his throat as bloody as ever. Nothing can comfort him, goes the story, because he failed to rescue Harriet and their children.

Joseph Antoine would have understood Dangerfield Newby's and Henry Bibb's desperate attempts to rescue their wives and children. He probably wouldn't have understood why, between 1970 and

1990, the proportion of black women married by age twenty-four plunged from 56 percent to 23 percent as more black men shambled into prisons, died young or found it difficult to imagine making enough money to support a family. Joseph Antoine's largely forgotten story survives only in his barely legible petitions to Kentucky's Jefferson County Court, but it is a powerful reminder of how far some black men and women once went to determine who and how they would love.

Some slaves followed the North Star all the way to free territory despite the obstacles they faced, including slave catchers. Quilt square and photo courtesy of Virginia Handy.

2

A LOVE WORTH WAITING FOR

The woman's face looked as familiar as a burlap sack waiting for someone to stuff its mouth with Georgia cotton. Oh yes, sweet Jesus, James Smith knew that face. The woman's face seemed as much a part of James Smith's past as the taste of hoecakes snatched from ashes and the high tenor saxophone wail of hounds. The woman's face might have seemed as familiar as that jail cell in Richmond where a branding iron had seared James Smith's face and neck, his skin hissing and sputtering like salt flung on flames and then surrendering, Lord God, to the pain.

But was this really the wife he had left behind in Virginia with a short kiss and a long prayer? Was this the face he'd imagined each time he crossed a river whose name he didn't know or outran a bounty hunter too slowed down by whiskey and rage to catch him?

Smith would tell reporters later that his legs trembled on an October day in 1850 as he neared a house in Sandwich, Ontario. It was the home of a woman who could have been the wife for whom he'd longed, prayed and searched for seventeen years. Finally, he gathered all of his strength into one ball and tossed it to the woman, whispering the name that he'd been waiting so long to say: "Fanny?" And, according to newspaper accounts, she answered, "Yes," and greeted Smith as her "beloved husband."

In 1852, antislavery newspaper editor Henry Bibb described this reunion between two fugitive slaves calling themselves James and Fanny Smith in a five-part series in *Voice of the Fugitive*, a Canadian antislavery newspaper. The series described one of the most incredible love stories ever plucked from the pages of the Underground Railroad, the sometimes organized and sometimes improvised slave-aiding network that gave fugitives food, transportation, directions and, sometimes, information about safe havens and the slave hunters tracking them. Yet James Smith's story is more than the tale of a man punished for praying and more than the saga of a couple who wouldn't turn their love loose.

It's a story about faith.

Not the puny, soft-fleshed kind of faith that people embrace when they're in the mood for a Sunday-morning stroll with God. There was no flab in James Smith's faith. No weak or neglected spots. He had the kind of faith that was muscular enough to withstand beatings and endure jail terms. He had the kind of faith that kept pace with him as he shambled away from his family in chains. He had the sort of faith that made him pray out loud when silent prayers would have saved him from torture.

His ordeal began around 1833, when Smith—probably not his real name—decided he wanted to join his owner's Baptist church, one of the denominations that especially appealed to blacks longing for emotional and expressive religion. The desire for religious expression was strong among people from a continent where the gods, some good, some evil, lived inside everything and gave things their special qualities. Some slaves would go out into midnight fields and pray in ditches or cover their heads with iron pots to muffle the sound of their prayers. Meanwhile, the slave preacher became magician, healer, preacher, politician and, sometimes, martyr. "There were black ministers before there were black churches," Dr. Stacy Williams declared in a 1980 lecture before Detroit's Council of Baptist Pastors. ". . . Some were even preaching to their slave masters. The black minister had to sing, pray and preach under conditions which many times brought lashes to his back. But his image as a leader and as God's man had been established. There developed a craving in the hearts of the Black-slave subjects for a meeting place of their own where they could serve God according to the dictates of their consciences."

However, joining an organized church was a large ambition for a slave. Organized religion was a prize many slave owners kept locked up in their own kitchens, serving only thin, carefully cut slices to religion-hungry servants. Some slaves went to church with whites and sat in rear pews or balconies, listening to white preachers tell them that whites were superior, that God sanctioned slavery and they'd go to heaven if they obeyed their masters and mistresses and stopped stealing chickens. Others attended their own churches, where trusted white observers watched the services and made sure they stressed the joys of the afterlife and the need to accept one's fate. Yet many people feared that slave religion—like reading and writing—fueled rebellions. Nat Turner, the Virginian whose band plundered plantations and beat, beheaded and killed more than fifty white men, women and children in 1831, had been a preacher, claiming biblical signs and omens urged him to strike. After Nat's rebellion, all nighttime religious meetings were prohibited and no blacks, free or slave, could hear colored preachers or ministers. They could only listen to white preachers and only during the daytime. Twenty-four-year-old Gabriel Prosser—who, like Smith, lived in Henrico County, Virginia—had been hanged in 1800 for his plot to march on the city of Richmond, seize the arsenal, strike down the whites and liberate slaves. He, too, had won followers by predicting God would strengthen the hand of rebels.

So James Smith's request to join any church, even the church his Richmond, Virginia, area master attended, was no small matter. The church's minister said he would have to talk it over with "William Wright," the name Smith coined for his master in his newspaper interview. Smith's master eventually gave him permission to join the church, but Smith had to assure him that he would be a good and faithful servant and would work harder, if possible. However, no one foresaw how seriously James Smith would take his faith or how it would consume him.

He became a man who could stay up all night after sweating in fields all day, a man who roamed his plantation telling other slaves to plead for light and beg for release from the God who could free any spirit. Though he still worked as hard as ever, Smith's devotion troubled his master, who worried that his fervor might spread and disturb the daily patterns of plantation life. To discourage Smith, his master sometimes kept him tied up all day on Sundays or had him whipped until blood dripped down his back. Yet he continued converting slaves. Finally, his owner sold James Smith to a slave trader from Georgia, warning his new master of Smith's passion for wading in religion and urging other slaves to join him in its waters.

"I can soon break him of that practice when I have him staked down with his face to the ground and his back striped and checked with the lash—with salt and red pepper well rubbed into the gashes, he will give up and forget his religion," his new master, Mr. White, said, according to the story Smith told the *Voice of the Fugitive.*

As he bundled up his clothing for the last time and said good-bye to his wife and two children, Smith felt "as if my poor heart would break with grief." The family prayed together one last time, and then Smith's new master took him in chains, his ankles chafing from the shackles tying him to the slave caravan. He wound up at a cotton plantation with at least three hundred slaves. He lived in a hovel with ten people and was strictly forbidden from holding religious meetings. However, he soon began singing and praying, and others joined in. The slave driver reported him to the overseer, who ordered a hundred lashes for Smith. When the driver brought Smith to the cotton gin house for his beating, he demanded to know why the man prayed. He even offered to stop beating Smith if he would promise not to pray again. Smith refused the man's offer and took his whipping. The next night he ran away, but the tracking dogs quickly found him, and the search party dragged him back to the plantation.

He now worked with a heavy chain and a clog of iron trailing him; at night, he was yoked to a block of wood. For slaves with a history of running, such restraints were common. Other instruments of torture sometimes used on runaways included thumb screws, billy clubs and the speculum oris, a device that allowed plantation officials to force-feed slaves who tried to starve themselves to death.

But the whippings didn't work. Smith would still pour out his feelings and let them fill up all the space in a room. He prayed for his family. He prayed for acquaintances and friends. He prayed for the people who beat him. He prayed for the people who were thinking about beating him. Perhaps he prayed as fervently, as fiercely, as Dr. C. T. Walker, born a slave in Georgia. Dr. Walker preached an entire sermon on "The Second Coming of Jesus Christ," mostly by repeating two words, "He" and "coming," until they became hammer blows, lightning bolts, roaring drums: "He's coming, He's coming, coming, coming, He's coming." Not only did Walker's sermon convert many listeners, some people actually dove under their seats, convinced that Jesus would stride in at any moment, too bright to bear. James Smith must have radiated that kind of power, too.

He was certainly compelling on one particular night. That was the night the plantation slave driver, who was black, heard James Smith praying for both him and the overseer, men who had beaten and bloodied him. In the Old South, black slave drivers or foremen sometimes worked under the slave owner or overseer, disciplining and supervising field hands. Caught between the white and black worlds, some became cruel while others found ways to give their fellow slaves small nuggets of kindness. The slave driver on Smith's plantation was so overwhelmed by Smith's prayers that he unchained him. He asked him to continue praying. He asked for forgiveness for his cruelty. And he urged Smith to run off, promising that he wouldn't try to recapture him. That night, Smith did what so many runaway slaves separated from their families did. He set off for his former home in Virginia, hoping to find his wife.

He traveled for six to eight weeks, hiding during the day and journeying by night. Finally, he found the plantation where he'd last seen his family. Since it was the middle of the night, he did not dare knock at the door for fear of rousing someone who'd start shouting or screaming. Instead, he eased open the door and crept inside, moving toward the corner where his wife used to sleep. Suddenly, a white man wielding a pistol and knife lunged at him, yelling that he would shoot him if he took another step. On orders from the white man, one of the slaves clubbed Smith in the head, knocking him senseless.

The next morning, James Smith awakened swimming in blood, tied with cords and lying in a horse cart driven by the overseer. His captors took him to a Richmond jail, where he spent several months. While in jail, he learned from another slave that his wife had been sold to a trader who took her to Kentucky. He also learned that his sufferings weren't over. One morning, his master flogged him and branded his initials on the side of his face and back of his neck with a hot iron. The devil was real, but Smith still called on God. A few days later, a man named William Graham bought him at a public auction. Smith lived with Graham for about three years, finally deciding it was time to seek that place of refuge, that land of Canaan, he'd heard so much about: Canada.

However, Smith made the mistake of sharing his secret with another slave, who agreed to come with him. Any slave sharing information about a planned escape risked discovering that a supposed friend was really a traitor, ready to turn him in for a few dollars, a few pats on the head or a few slugs of whiskey. Two slaves had spilled Gabriel Prosser's plan to their owner. A house servant also had betrayed Denmark Vesey. Handbills circulated in Kentucky and southern Ohio warned slaves about a black man named Robert Russell, who operated in and around Ripley, Ohio. For a fee, he would help slaves escape to Cincinnati, and for another fee, he would capture and return them to their masters. Despite the existence of such treachery, Smith felt he could trust his friend. But for half a gallon of whiskey and one dollar, his "friend" became his enemy.

White men waited for Smith when he rendezvoused with his friend. They captured and beat Smith and forced him to listen as his supposed friend recited the details of their escape plot. However, Smith's captors drank so much whiskey, they became careless. They sloshed slugs of whiskey down Smith's throat, and he fooled them into believing he was dead drunk, harmless as a log. Certain Smith would be out cold until the next morning, his captors went to bed and left the runaway slave stretched out on the kitchen floor. An hour later, Smith took off, bound for Canada.

The old dog Smith had trained to hunt raccoons and possums followed him, hiding with him beside mossy logs. The dog had helped him hunt at night to avoid starving on the skimpy rations Smith's master doled out. Unfortunately, the animal loved Smith too much for its own good. It kept on following him, yapping at every twitch and tremble, growl and yelp, crackle and rustle in the woods. Fearing the dog would cause his capture, Smith decided to hang it. He looped a rope around its neck and led it to a tree. The dog didn't resist; in fact, Smith later told Henry Bibb that the animal seemed to understand what was happening. Like the biblical Isaac who had calmly watched his father, Abraham, prepare to slit his throat and offer his burning body to God, the dog seemed willing to surrender his life if it would help—or so it seemed to Smith. While he pondered whether or not it was right to sacrifice a loyal friend, Smith heard a sound that made him forget all about his old hunting dog. The bloodhounds were coming now, mournful-looking, sorrow-spreading dogs capable of following a trail more than two weeks old and pursuing it with a relentless stride for more than a hundred miles. If they cornered him, he would be yanked back to a life where he had been beaten and separated from his wife simply for praying. He released his dog and began to run, but the hounds overtook him.

That's when Smith's old hunting dog demonstrated how deep its loyalty and love went.

Three bloodhounds surrounded Smith, who had armed himself with a heavy club. His dog seized one of the hounds by the neck and held on, forcing the other dogs into the fight. Smith battered two of the hounds with his club, and the other one managed to escape. Then Smith and his dog—two old and fast friends—continued north to the Ohio border, guided by the North Star, the brightest star near the Big Dipper and a compass for so many other runaways. He stumbled upon a stream and roamed up and down it, finally noticing a large steamboat. That's when he realized he had found the Ohio River. It was not as broad as it became in modern times when it was widened to create channels that would accommodate big ships. In the mid-nineteenth century, its banks sometimes stretched on for miles, untouched by any trace or whisper of human life.

Because it bordered the slave states of Kentucky and that part of old Virginia that is now West Virginia, the Ohio River became a major highway for escaping slaves, the amen at the end of a fugitive's prayer. After Smith found a skiff tied to a tree, he ferried across the river, leaving his dog behind. But the dog leaped into the stream and crossed it, too, reaching the Ohio shore before Smith. After landing in Ohio, Smith stepped into a forest and met an old man chopping poles. He was an abolitionist who worked for the Underground Railroad. He directed Smith to a friend about thirty miles away, and that friend hired Smith for about five years.

Yet, for fugitives like Smith, Ohio could be both the best and worst of places: a free state containing many supporters of the South. The Northwest Ordinance of 1787 had declared that the whole Northwest Territory, including Ohio, would be composed of free states. However, Ohio, at its first constitutional convention in 1802, missed becoming a slave state by a single vote. Harriet Beecher Stowe lived in Cincinnati and her home served as a station on the Underground Railroad, yet mob violence against blacks erupted again and again in Cincinnati, particularly in August 1829 and September 1841. The first of Ohio's Black Laws, which were passed in 1804, required that all blacks register for a certificate of freedom at a cost of twelve and a half cents for each name. In 1807, blacks settling in Ohio were required to post bonds of five hundred dollars and could not testify in any court case involving whites. As late as 1831, Ohio blacks could not serve in the militia or on juries, or attend public school.

Still, many Ohioans would have reached out to someone like James Smith. Augustus West, an escaped Virginia slave, had arrived in the state in 1837. To raise money for a farm, he and a white abolitionist named Alexander Beaty concocted a bold plan: Beaty sold West three times to Southern slave owners, each time helping him escape and splitting the profits with him. West then purchased land in Fayette County, Ohio, where he built his home near a road known as Abolition Lane. Abolitionists and freed slaves lived along that road. In Albany, John Brown—not the famous one—hid runaways under his general store. Slavery supporters murdered two sons of Thomas and Jemima Woodson, in the all-black community of Berlin Cross Roads, because the two men worked for the Underground Railroad. James and Sophia Clemens, who lived in one of Ohio's earliest black settlements, Longtown in Darke County, were conductors on the Railroad. David Adams, a black barber in Findlay, hid and transported runaways, too. So did John Parker of Ripley, a former slave who had walked shackled with four hundred other slaves from Richmond to Alabama. Once free, he became famous for risky ventures, such as returning to snatch the baby of a slave couple from the arms of the baby girl's sleeping master after already rescuing the baby's parents. He reportedly helped free more than one thousand slaves. The Ripley home of the Reverend John Rankin also became the doorway to freedom for at least four thousand fugitives who crossed the Ohio River. Fugitives who arrived in Cleveland from Ripley often showed up with written messages for a free black man named Bynum Hunt, who found short-term jobs for them around the docks and then put them on a Detroit-bound steamboat.

During five years of farming in Ohio, Smith preached among blacks in the area and probably questioned every Virginian he met about the wife and children he'd last seen in Henrico County, Virginia. He also buried his best friend, his devoted dog. By then, black churches with walls and pulpits and preachers existed, the first one being organized in 1773 in Aiken County, South Carolina, as the Silver Bluff Baptist Church by the Reverend George Lisle. Like James Smith, Lisle began his life as a Virginia slave. Finally, after five years in one spot, Smith moved to Huron County, Ohio, in the state's midsection, a part of what was known as Sufferers Land or Fire Lands. Either name fit. After the British destroyed coastal towns in Connecticut during the Revolutionary War, the state of Connecticut promised to compensate everyone whose land had been burned. All it could offer them were land grants to some five hundred thousand acres on the western part of its reserve, land that ultimately became

Ohio. Chopped up into townships and sections, the Fire Lands drew settlers from Connecticut and other New England states.

Huron County was part flatlands and part winding hills, the natural home of tall prairie grass, oak-hickory savannah, elm, ash, beech and maple forests, marsh wetlands dotted with wildflowers and farms. People raised corn and soybeans, hay, wheat and oats, dairy cows and beef cattle, horses and pigs and, now and then, a little anti-slavery hell. When two men showed up in Savannah, Ohio, looking for a runaway slave, Scottish-born William Sutherland blackened his face and hid himself in a wagon loaded with hay; he poked his head out of the hay so the two men would spot him and follow the wagon. Meanwhile, the real fugitive escaped.

James Smith bought a small farm in Huron County and toiled on it for about seven years, working fertile land wreathed in low, deep animal smells. Ohio had an active rumor mill, the "grapevine telegraph," which circulated information about slaves and slave catchers through churches and homes, talk and letters. There is no evidence during this period that Smith ever picked up his wife's trail, but his faith that he would see her again must have remained strong—he never remarried. Then, in the fall of 1850, a new Fugitive Slave Act was passed, making it a crime for bystanders to refuse to help slave catchers and creating a federal system for recapturing runaways anyplace and at any time. Through the rumor mill, James Smith learned that he was a man with a warrant out for his arrest. That meant that if he did not flee to Canada, where slavery officially ended in August 1834, authorities could seize him anywhere in America and drag him back to Virginia, the source of all his troubles.

He sold his property and moved on to Canada as so many thousands before him had done. He had plenty of company. Fugitives showed up daily in the so-called Promised Land, some traveling alone like Smith and others in groups. Henry Bibb wrote about a group that arrived in Canada West (the southern part of the modern-day province of Ontario) in December 1851 and included "a mother with six children and three men. The next day there came four men, the next day two men arrived and then one came alone." One of the men talked about having had "a warm combat by the way with two slave catchers in which he found it necessary to throw a handful of sand in the eyes of one of them," Bibb added.

However, Canada, as newcomers like Smith soon discovered, was sometimes both antislavery and antiblack, swirling with prejudices such as those expressed in two letters appearing in the *Amherstburg Courier* on December 7, 1850. The letter writers ranted about black inferiority and charged that blacks didn't want to work. Still, in nineteenth-century Canada, blacks enjoyed legal freedom, fair treatment in courts, an absence of racial violence and the security of knowing the government wouldn't ship them back to the United States. As a result, by the middle of the nineteenth century, small black settlements and black enclaves inside larger cities dotted the Canadian landscape, giving James Smith a range of places to put down roots or search for Fanny.

The most famous black enclave was the nine-thousand-acre Elgin Settlement in Kent County, which includes the present-day village of North Buxton. It was organized in 1849 by the Reverend William King of Louisiana and fifteen of his former slaves. King raised the money to purchase land in what was then Raleigh Township and sold the settlers fifty-acre lots for $125—payable over a ten-year period at 6 percent interest. They became the nucleus of a colony of self-sufficient black American fugitives who swore off liquor, soaked up Greek and Latin, planted flower gardens, provided their own tools and raised corn, wheat, tobacco, hemp, maple sugar, cows, sheep and hogs. They also put up picket fences and built homes set back at least thirty-three feet from the road and containing at least four rooms. Tiger lilies were among their favorite plants, perhaps because they, like these black settlers, loved the full sun and could flourish in almost any soil.

The Dawn Settlement near Dresden straddled the Sydenham River and included about 623 acres of rich fertile land, heavy timber and unbroken forests. In the early 1840s, the Reverend Josiah Henson—a fugitive slave and the model for novelist Harriet Beecher Stowe's Uncle Tom—purchased land there with the help of abolitionists. In 1842, Henson and white abolitionist Hiram Wilson established Dawn. It included a school, a sawmill, a brickyard, a rope factory, black walnut orchards and a gristmill. Black communities also sprang up in Sandwich, which organized a Union Sabbath School by February 1851; Windsor, Amherstburg, London, the Queen's Bush, Brantford, Wilberforce (now Lucan), founded in 1829–1830 by blacks from Cincinnati as a New Jerusalem; along the Niagara Peninsula at St. Catharine's, Niagara Falls, Newark (Niagara-on-the-Lake) and Fort Erie; Hamilton and Toronto; and the northern perimeter of Simcoe and Grey Counties, especially in Oro, Collingwood and Owen Sound.

While traveling around the country, James Smith met many fugitive slaves. He told them where he came from and how he had been separated from his wife for praying. One day, he met a man who changed his life. He told Smith about a woman living in Sandwich, now a part of Windsor. This woman, Smith learned, had come from his home near Richmond and had belonged once to a man with the same name as Smith's former owner.

The next day, Smith journeyed to the house in Sandwich where he had been told the woman lived. By 1855, Sandwich had twenty-two black refugee families, according to historian Benjamin Drew. Henry Bibb's wife, Mary, taught twenty-five students in her home. However, James Smith wasn't worried about the size of Sandwich's black population, the extent of its services or even how often slave catchers slipped across the Detroit River to the river-bordering community. His eyes were on the woman at the house, the woman whose face looked like his wife's. He offered her his hand and called her by her old Virginia name.

"Oh, is this my beloved husband whom I never again expected to see?" she answered.

According to Bibb, "her eyes sparkled and flashed like strokes of lightning upon his furrowed cheeks and wrinkled brow."

They embraced, no doubt remembering the last time they'd seen each other—the day Fanny had tried to console him but had collapsed in tears, the day James had been led off to Georgia in chains for the crime of praying too much. Not only had they spent most of their adult lives apart; their children had been scattered, sold here and there, lost. Oh, they had plenty of reasons to weep. But in 1847, Fanny had managed to escape from Kentucky and had lived in Canada some three years. Once again, James Smith's prayers had been answered.

Starting in the eighteenth century, black churches sprang up all over the country, and both freedmen and slave ministers built reputations as powerful preachers. New York's Abyssinian Baptist Church was founded in 1808 after four sailors from Abyssinia, Ethiopia's former name, walked out of a Baptist church that seated them in a slave loft. After a preacher from Boston joined them, they pooled their resources and set up a church. Black churches took shape in every state, including Virginia, Georgia, Kentucky, Massachusetts, New York, Philadelphia and Michigan. In Philadelphia, Richard Allen founded the African Methodist Episcopal Church in what had been a mason's stable. In Richmond, Virginia, the Reverend John Jasper was baptized in 1830 and preached a funeral that same day that made him famous. He had taught himself to read and write, preached in Southern slave dialect and conducted all-day camp meetings, baptizing as many as three hundred people in four hours. After the Civil War, the United States Freedman's Bureau also authorized Mr. Jasper to legalize slave marriages.

In 1851, runaway slaves built Sandwich First Baptist Church, a redbrick church, in Ontario, Canada. According to stories accepted by some historians and disputed by others, a sentry stood outside the door during services, watching out for slave catchers who could easily cross the river to Sandwich. When slave catchers showed up, the minister would stop the singing on a signal from the sentry and begin a solo: "There is a stranger in this house." Then the runaways in the congregation would stand up and run to the stairs leading to the pulpit, moving aside a carpet square covering a trapdoor and descending into a tunnel leading to the river.

Neither James nor Fanny Smith ever used that tunnel.

Or ran again.

3

THE SPECIAL DELIVERY PACKAGE

The box was a temporary tomb, a chamber of strange tortures, a hole leading to hell, but Lear Green climbed inside it just the same. For eighteen hours, it became her world.

Actually, it was an old sailor's chest designed for voyages that might last for hundreds of salt-coated, wind-slapped days. It was meant to hold trousers and shirts, razors and combs, hairbrushes and quilts, paper and pens, tacks and thread, needles and thimbles, woolen stockings and shoes. It was for Bibles and hymnbooks, shaving soap and painkillers, not for a runaway slave girl with an average-sized body and larger-than-average hopes.

It was too short for Lear Green's legs, too narrow for her arms, too smothering for her spirits. She had to curl up inside it like an unborn child waiting to crawl out of sticky darkness and yell at her first glimpse of light. She could doze inside the box but not stretch out, yawn but not cough or sneeze, twitch but not fight off muscle cramps. She could daydream about becoming a free woman and wife but never gulp down enough food or water to silence a complaining stomach. She would have time to worry that someone might kick, shove or knock her box upside down, sending blood and fear rushing to her head. She also would have time to wonder if the love awaiting her was worth such torture.

It was 1857, a year in which the U.S. Supreme Court decided, in the *Dred Scott v. Sandford* case, that blacks weren't citizens, couldn't sue in courts and had no rights anyone couldn't step on or smash. That year, a prime field hand in the South sold for thirteen hundred dollars, but a white North Carolinian named Hinton Helper warned in his book *The Impending Crisis of the South: How to Meet It* that slavery was morally and economically ruining many Southern whites. Meanwhile, the Farmers' Almanac predicted two eclipses of the sun, and the United States moved ever closer to another kind of darkness, one in which men from the North and the South with Bibles in their pockets would kill each other over an idea already coughing and wheezing on its deathbed. In January 1857, at the Worcester, Massachusetts, State Disunion Convention, which favored the peaceful separation of North and South, Boston abolitionist William Lloyd Garrison stood up and declared, "No union with slaveholders." However, attorney and editor George Fitzhugh's book *Cannibals All! or, Slaves Without Masters* challenged the idea that freedom was necessarily better than slavery.

In Baltimore, where men sold their abundant slaves cheaply to men who resold them for more cash in the Deep South, a young house slave named Lear Green settled all these questions for herself. She didn't wait for court rulings, state conventions or the boom of battle cannons. She squeezed herself into a wooden chest, which two men carried down cobblestone streets to the nearby Patapsco River. Luck must have ridden in that chest with Lear because the steamer that would carry her and her box to Philadelphia left Baltimore at 1:00 P.M. in 1854 and 3:00 P.M. in 1861. Instead of slipping off in the shadows, Lear had to escape in the wide, unblinking glare of daylight, possibly meeting her rescuers in the hallway of her dwelling.

The names of the men who helped her carry out this plan aren't known, but Baltimore did have an antislavery movement. Rabbi David Einhorn became so identified with it that he was driven out of the state at the start of the Civil War. The home of black activist William Watkins and his family was an important Underground Railroad station as well. Watkins's niece, Frances Ellen Harper, gained considerable fame by the late 1850s as an antislavery poet, novelist and speaker. According to local legend, Orchard Street Church in Baltimore's Druid Hill section also sheltered slaves traveling to freedom. Famed conductor Harriet Tubman's routes of escape from the Eastern Shore usually led from Cambridge, Maryland, over the big Choptank River bridge to the Delaware towns of Camden, Dover, Smyrna, Odessa and Wilmington.

But Lear Green wasn't escaping from a secluded farm or a sprawling plantation surrounded by woods, streams or swamps. She lived in a row house at 153 South Broadway in the heart of the section of Baltimore known as Fells Point, and her owner, James Noble, ran a butter depot at that address. Married to a woman named Mary and the father of four children, Noble was in his early forties and a man of some wealth: by 1860, he owned three thousand dollars in real estate and five hundred dollars in personal property, owned a male slave and had a female German servant. Noble's butter depot probably sat on the first floor of the house, and Lear Green, most likely, lived in the attic, as children, house slaves and servants usually did in Fells Point. Houses in the area usually stood two and a half stories high with two rooftop dormers.

From her window, Lear could have seen many things that reminded her of how slavery really looked beneath its sometimes loose-fitting city clothes. She could have seen the auctions in which men, women and children were sold along with desks and china. She might have seen prospective buyers pinching and squeezing slaves, fingering their skin in search of broken bones or other flaws. Like young Frederick Douglass, who had escaped from the same neighborhood ten years earlier, she also might have seen a young female slave fighting with pigs for offal—tossed-out animal snouts, shanks, kidneys, spleens, oxhearts, oxtails, bone marrow, pork bellies, intestines, gizzards, cocks' combs, pigs' feet, pigs' brains, bulls' testicles and other meat scraps that poverty and necessity transformed into edible food. All of this would have encouraged her to walk, run, sail, swim or even climb into a wooden box to break from the past.

The men who carried Lear Green to the river would have walked down streets ripe with the mingled smells of whiskey, roasted peanuts, coffee, catfish and perch, and ringing with the shouts of sailors, prostitutes and slave traders. In Baltimore, men bought and sold slaves on ships, in yards, in inns and even on the steps of the penitentiary and courthouse. People also could board slaves in a slave jail for twenty-five cents a day. It was not a neighborhood for anyone who spooked easily. An Irish mob had rioted there after someone stuffed straw into some old clothes to represent St. Patrick and hung it from the mast of an idle schooner. A ship's captain had been tarred and feathered there for lowering a flag, and a man had built his own coffin and kept it in his house for years. It is generally believed that prostitutes were first called hookers when they followed the encampments of hard-drinking Civil War general Joe Hooker, but at least one author suspects the word *hooker* originated in Fells Point. In the middle of the eighteenth century, the area curved into a hook shape and had scores of prostitutes.

Lear Green, however, wasn't fleeing riots or rowdiness. She was running off to meet the man she planned to marry—if she didn't suffocate or swoon inside an old sea chest first. According to a May 26, 1857, *Baltimore Sun* ad offering $150 for her return, she was an attractive young woman with an impressive wardrobe, possibly her own and possibly her mistress's. The ad said she had "a black complexion," was "round-featured, good-looking and ordinary size; she had on and with her when she left, a tan-colored silk bonnet, a dark plaid silk dress, a light mouslin delaine, also one watered silk cape and one tan colored cape." "Mouslin delaine," or, more correctly, mousseline de laine, was a soft, lightweight, high-quality wool dress fabric, usually covered with a pattern. James Noble had inherited Lear from his wife's mother, Mrs. Rachel Howard, when she was just a child. Lear didn't know much about her old mistress, but the young one left a lasting impression, pushing and prodding her and never giving her any space in which to find herself. Yet she bore it until a young man named William Adams stepped into her life and challenged her to change it.

Adams was a barber, but worked mostly in taverns, opening oysters and performing other tasks. Many blacks cut hair, but a black barber with a white clientele needed special qualities, including the ability to keep his own feelings out of the discussions swirling around him and to tell white men what they wanted to hear. When George DeBaptiste, a barber and caterer, worked as an Underground Railroad conductor in Madison, Indiana, slave owners often teased DeBaptiste about being a secret agent for the Underground Railroad. DeBaptiste would just laugh and say he wasn't smart enough for that. However, William Adams, Lear Green's love, apparently wasn't that skilled at disguising his intentions. He stood about five feet ten inches tall, had a four-inch scar running by the corner of his mouth and was described as fast talking. Loose talking might have been a more accurate description. The slave ad for Lear Green noted that people had overheard William Adams saying he was going to marry Lear and move to New York, where his mother, a free black woman, lived. According to James Noble's ad, Adams had been missing for about a week when Lear Green—just like that—disappeared, too.

In Underground Railroad conductor William Still's account of Lear's escape, the young woman decided she needed to be free to "fill the station of a wife and mother." In author Sylvia Dannett's version of this story, Lear was at first afraid to run off with William, but after he left Baltimore, "the ugliness and emptiness" of Lear's life oppressed her. Her mistress kept demanding more and more tasks from her, and the day finally came when Lear felt she could take no more. After learning that William had reached Elmira, she decided to join him. According to Dannett, Lear managed to get word to Baltimore Quakers active in the Underground Railroad, and they concocted the plan to carry her to freedom in a sea chest—probably marching right past slave dealers and slave catchers.

She was, of course, not the only slave who had been stuffed inside a box and shipped to the north as freight or luggage. In 1845, an unnamed "negro servant girl" had been boxed up and mailed to

York, Pennsylvania. This was four years before Henry "Box" Brown became famous for being shipped in a box for a twenty-five-hour journey from Richmond, Virginia, to Philadelphia, traveling upside down most of the time. A relative stuck a Baltimore man named William Peel Jones into a box and sent him to Philadelphia on an Ericsson steamer; Jones nearly gave himself away by coughing inside his container. In the winter of 1857, a young pregnant seamstress clambered into a box lined with straw in Baltimore and spent nearly all of one night in the depot, upside down more than once. When finally freed in Philadelphia, she spent three days struggling to regain her ability to talk with ease. However, escaping in such a dangerous way required considerable courage and meant the eighteen-year-old Lear Green would have to mature overnight. After searching her soul, she apparently decided she had what it took to endure eighteen hours coiled up in a chest, an act that Still compared to "cutting off the right arm or plucking out the right eye."

It only took the men carrying Lear's chest a few minutes to reach Light and Pratt streets on the edge of the river, some three or four blocks from Lear's residence. In the 1850s, this was the spot where the Philadelphia-bound Ericsson Line steamships docked in the Patapsco River, an arm of the Chesapeake Bay. Ericsson steamers were driven by underwater propellers instead of the wider paddle wheels, which steadied ships and made it possible for large steamers to pass through the narrow gated chambers or locks that raised and lowered ships moving through the Chesapeake & Delaware Canal.

Strong ropes fastened the chest, which was stowed with the freight on the steamboat. Lear, of course, had none of the conveniences available to contemporary researchers who retrace the escape routes of fugitive slaves. She had no cell phone for emergencies, no backpack crammed with extra rations, no sports drinks, no protein bars. She brought nothing with her but a quilt, a pillow, a few pieces of clothes, a small amount of food, a bottle of water and a pound or two of courage. Like other slaves who escaped as freight or luggage, she would have abstained from eating and drunk only an occasional sip of water to lessen her need to eliminate waste. To re-create the experiences of fugitives like Lear Green, researcher Anthony Cohen climbed inside a wooden crate in May 2002 and had himself shipped on a train from Philadelphia to New York. During his two-hour ordeal, he sweated so furiously that he stripped down to his boxer shorts, but it didn't help. Moisture condensed on the box's screw plates and dripped from the ceiling. By the time he stepped out of his box, the heat had wrung him dry and he had drained his water bottle. Imagine what might have happened if, like Lear Green, he had stayed in his box for another sixteen hours.

Fortunately, Lear Green's fiancé's mother, a free black woman, came along as a passenger on the boat ferrying Lear to freedom. Like other black passengers, she was assigned to the deck, which put her near the sailor's chest. Once or twice during the night, she untied the ropes circling the chest and lifted the lid, allowing Lear a chance to snatch a lungful of air. The two women later told William Still they had shared a silent prayer that their time of peril would soon end. However, sometime that night, some disturbing thoughts must have stomped around in Lear Green's head. She must have sniffed at least a whiff of raw fear. There must have been at least a moment when she longed to leap out of a chest that looked way too much like a coffin.

Finally, the steamer reached Pier 3, south, the Philadelphia wharf where Ericsson ships docked. After crewmen carried the chest off the boat, it was delivered to a house on Barley Street occupied by friends of William Adams's mother. The chest and its occupants then moved to the home of William Still, who would write about Lear's escape and hundreds of similar adventures in his book *The Underground Railroad.* Finally, Lear Green and Mrs. Adams journeyed on to Elmira, New York, a place allegedly named for a young girl whose father loudly called her name every day. Many runaway slaves called Elmira's name, too.

Elmira was the place where Lear expected to find William Adams waiting for her with a preacher and promises of devotion. It also was the last Underground Railroad stop between Philadelphia and St. Catharine's, Ontario. One historian has estimated that one thousand fugitives passed through Elmira between 1840 and 1860.

The geography of the area is the easiest thing to describe. Elmira just happened to sit smack in the middle of several river valleys. Once the Chemung Canal connecting the Chemung River and Seneca Lake was completed in 1833 and railroad lines in 1850, the city had major connections with much of New York and Pennsylvania. The Elmira route to freedom started in Philadelphia and ran through Harrisburg, Williamsport, Canton, Alba, Elmira and then to St. Catharine's. Some fugitives hiding among the cargo on boats and in railroad baggage cars continued to Canada and others chose to stay in Elmira. Between 1840 and 1850, the city's black population jumped from 60 to 215.

Because some of Elmira's older homes had been built with twelve- and fourteen-inch boards or slabs, the black neighborhood in the center of town became known as Slabtown. Bounded on the north by the Lackawanna Railroad, on the east by Lake Street, on the south by Clinton and on the west by the Chemung Canal, the neighborhood had its own special small-town flavor and feel. In 1860, 243 free blacks lived there, according to Wilson's Elmira Directory, most of them sharing bare single-family homes. However, an observer emphasized that "in its heyday, it could not in any sense be called a slum." Slabtown included a sprinkling of black-owned grocery stores, churches, a meat market and a tiny candy store. Antislavery lectures and other meetings often took place in grocery stores and other public buildings. In 1848, famed abolitionist Frederick Douglass spoke in Elmira, and the Reverend Tabbs Gross, a black minister and the editor and publisher of the *Arkansas Freeman* newspaper, came to the area in 1855.

In the 1840s and 1850s, Slabtown's main streets were Dickinson, Benjamin and Baldwin. According to Wilson's Elmira Directory for 1860, a "colored" laborer named William Adams lived in a house on Baldwin at the corner of Third. The 1861–1862 directory shows a "colored" William Adams boarding at 186 Water Street. After their marriage, Lear Green and William Adams apparently lived right in the thumping, pulsing, laughing, story-sharing, neighbor-helping heart of Slabtown, the kind of community that television, cars, fast food and air-conditioning has all but wiped out. It was a neighborhood where people entertained each other. A neighborhood where people ate food just plucked from their gardens and still tangy with the smell of life. A neighborhood where, in hot weather, a breeze from the river provided the only air-conditioning. A neighborhood where, in winter, people slept under handmade quilts so heavy they pinned you in place. After dark, Slabtown residents, including former slaves like Lear Green and William Adams, sat on their porches, spinning stories from the tangled threads of memories.

Did Lear Green ever tell her neighbors about her escape from Baltimore in a sailor's chest? Did William Adams, a man who didn't always guard his tongue, talk about how he persuaded Lear to follow him to Elmira and become his wife? Or did they remain silent for fear someone might show up and try to collect the reward James Noble had offered for Lear Green's return? They must have chosen silence: neither Lear nor William appears in any histories about old Slabtown. Their neighbors do, though. Oh, how they do.

Mr. and Mrs. Jeremiah George, former slaves, would sit with their neighbors at dusk and tell stories about the old days, some tales triggering tears and others sparking laughter.

"More than half of Mister George's anecdotes were really humorous," one man reminisced in the *Chemung Historical Journal*, "and the laughter of Mr. and Mrs. George themselves was loudest and rang out up and down Dickinson St., a block east or west of Baldwin. His laughs graduated from chuckles into full fledged belly laughs and we children went to bed listening to these happy people."

Another runaway slave who adopted Elmira as his home was a man known as "Uncle John" Smith, who had escaped from a Maryland plantation with five other men and found work with prominent families in the city. He died in 1898 at around one hundred years of age after being attacked and bitten by a vicious dog. Meanwhile, many parents frightened their youngsters to bed by hinting that "Wild Bill" Jackson was on the loose. His claim to fame was a habit of earning drinks on Saturday night by eating ground glass, an activity some people apparently found amusing.

"Eventually, he died of his habits," according to an article in the *Chemung Historical Journal*, "and about everyone in Slabtown attended his funeral. He had never harmed anyone but himself."

However, Lear Green and William Adams's chosen hometown was no untainted Eden free of snakes and sinful urges: like other Northern communities, it had racial discrimination and harassment and limited educational opportunities for blacks. Yet its residents included powerful abolitionists like Jervis Langdon, a wealthy businessman who made his fortune in lumber and coal and spent some of it helping escaped slaves. In December 1858, a year after Lear Green's arrival, a near riot broke out in Elmira as residents tried to prevent an old slave from voluntarily returning to his former master. The man, who had escaped through the Underground, had written asking his owner, John W. Mills, to come to Canada and get him and take him back home. When the man and his master stopped in Elmira on their way back to Calvert County, Maryland, an armed crowd surrounded the pair and tried to rescue the old slave, but the sheriff drove them back. The slave and his master got away only by running for and boarding a train that took them south.

Yet the main reason Lear Green and William Adams would have felt at home in Elmira was because of a black gravedigger named John Walter Jones. He became such a towering figure in the town's history that a museum bearing his name was taking shape in 2003. In 1844, John W. Jones and four other slaves escaped together from a plantation in Leesburg, Virginia. They stuffed their pockets with all the food they could, and one of them carried a pistol and a knife. They walked nearly three hundred miles, with Jones and his four companions fighting off slave hunters in Maryland. In Elmira, Jones first worked as a gardener and laborer and later became sexton of the First Baptist Church. He moved into the yellow house near the church, a house that would shelter hundreds of fugitive slaves in the decade before the Civil War. As the Underground Railroad agent at the Elmira station, he helped more than eight hundred other slaves escape. His allies included a bank president, a college founder, several lumber dealers and a hardware merchant. In 1864–1865, John Jones became a legend for burying and recording personal information about nearly three thousand Confederate soldiers who died in the Elmira Prison Camp, known as the death camp of the North. It was ironic that those dead who had enlisted in the Confederate army to preserve slavery should have been buried by a man who had escaped from slavery and become a symbol of what a free black man could do.

As they had planned, Lear Green and William Adams married in Elmira, but they never moved on to Canada. Something about Elmira—Slabtown's warmth or the presence of William's mother—kept them there. Unfortunately, the happiness Lear purchased with eighteen hours inside a sailor's chest lasted for only a few green summers before death stole it. After only three years in Elmira, surrounded by story-telling neighbors with rich memories and welcoming front porches, Lear Green Adams died. At around the same time, her mother-in-law passed away, too. The causes of their deaths aren't known, but they passed away at a time when people died from everything from cholera to colds. Lear and William never had time to move from the flash of first love to the steady flame of a middle-aged fire. Yet some people can pack a lifetime worth of passion and pleasure into a few years or even days. They can love so much that their memories become like one of those heavy homemade patchwork quilts so popular in Elmira, something they can reach for on chilly days and wrap around their souls. Maybe William Adams took such a quilt of memories with him when he left Elmira. After 1863, his name disappeared from Elmira street directories and he more than likely started over somewhere else.

Yet he is not likely to have forgotten the two women who loved him enough to board a ship together one spring day and sail through dangerous waters. He never saw the box that became his wife's prison for eighteen hours. She left it in Philadelphia, discarding it the way larvae shed worn-out skins so they can sprout wings. However, Lear and William's story is not just another Underground Railroad adventure or another example of those who, wrote William Still, "purchased their liberty by downright bravery, through perils the most hazardous." The story is a warning, familiar yet always urgent, to anyone who hesitates before plucking a handful of happiness and gulping it down. Don't just seize the day, Lear and William's romance reminds us, seize the stormy or sunlit moment: one steamy day in May might be all the summer you'll see.

Baltimore contains no plaques or statues commemorating Lear Green's courage, and the butter depot from which she escaped closed its doors long ago. The space the old depot once occupied has become 504 South Broadway between Eastern Avenue and Fleet Street. In the spring of 2003, it housed a three-story nightclub with green shutters and a Federal roof, a club flanked by shops selling edible underwear, homeopathic medicine, video rentals, tarot cards and neon G-strings. The prostitutes so abundant in old Fells Point might have felt at home. Yet in a neighborhood haunted by the ghosts of famed orator Frederick Douglass, private shipowners authorized to plunder British ships during the War of 1812 and speedy slave ships like the Baltimore clipper, the Federal-roofed building on Broadway only adds more history, more romance. It is easy to visualize Lear Green peering from her attic window at cobblestone streets or descending narrow stairs to run an errand or being shipped from the same port where blacks left the area going to Liberia. There are no monuments to her in Baltimore, or in Elmira, either, but she lives and breathes in the pages of William Still's *The Underground Railroad*, which contains a sketch of the girl he sheltered and aided on her journey. It shows a pretty brown girl peering over the rim of a sailor's chest, and the look on her face tells her whole story, past, present and future: she seems to be asking if, after the longest, steamiest and most uncomfortable day and night of her life, she now can rise up from her box and grab some light and love.

4

THE MAN WHO COULDN'T GROW A BEARD

Danger was everywhere: it lurked inside the slave cabins shrouded by cedar trees, it crept along wagon-rutted, red-clay Georgia roads and it lazed on the porches of plantations, puffing cigars and gulping bourbon. Yet that did not stop two slaves named Ellen and William Craft from slipping off, one by one, to the Macon train station on a December morning in 1848. Ellen, according to an acquaintance, had "hardly a tinge of African blood in her veins," and the couple believed her creamy color would purchase their tickets to freedom: Ellen would pass for an ailing white male planter traveling to Philadelphia for medical treatment, and William would pose as the slave who cut up her meat and warmed her flannels. However, when they reached the train station in the predawn magnolia-perfumed darkness, they found danger waiting there, too.

Before the couple's train could even pull out of the station, William's employer—the cabinetmaker who had hired him from his master—showed up. Suspicious about William's request for a pass to leave home during the Christmas holiday, he stomped through the train searching for his apprentice. Fortunately, the cabinetmaker failed to see past Ellen's dignified cape and distinguished top hat and, just as fortunately, the train left before the man spotted William, curled up in a corner in the black section.

A few minutes later, Ellen faced her first solo test of nerves. An old friend of her master's named Mr. Cray, a man she had known since childhood, sat down next to her. He had just had dinner at her master's house the night before. He kept hammering Ellen with questions, and she kept pretending she couldn't hear him. According to Ellen's memoirs, the man was so determined to be heard that he finally yelled, "It is a very fine morning, sir!"

"Yes," Ellen replied, refusing to say more.

She spent the rest of her journey to Savannah staring through the window, ignoring the man and steeling herself for the other stops and challenges ahead, all of them the price of keeping love.

Ellen had learned what losing love was like while she was enslaved by her first owner, Major James Smith of Clinton, Georgia. There was always trouble at Smith's dinner parties. It was the sort of trouble that clung to the clothes of a whiskey-swilling Georgia planter with two families, one slave, one free, living so close together they could smell each other's troubles and secrets. The trouble would start when one of Smith's guests mistook eleven-year-old Ellen for one of Smith's white children. She actually was his child by a house slave, Maria, a fact that had burned night and day in the head of Smith's wife, never letting her anger lose its head of steam. Every time someone mistook Ellen for a white girl, Mrs. Smith would pound the child with insults and then slap or punch her. However, in the spring of 1837, Mrs. Smith decided it was time to do more than lash out at the face that made her fury bubble. She would rid herself of this young slave who reminded everyone of her husband's backroom betrayals.

She gave Ellen to her daughter, Eliza, as a present—a brown-eyed, silky-haired package—for her April marriage to Dr. Robert Collins of Macon. Macon, with its Japanese cherry trees and green fields of watermelons, was only some fifteen miles from Ellen's birthplace, Clinton, Georgia; however, at a time when traveling a few miles could take hours and slaves couldn't leave plantations without passes, fifteen miles might as well have been one hundred and fifty. Dr. Collins thought he knew a great deal about managing slaves. He even wrote an essay on the subject, advising that slave owners feed their slaves good bacon and strong coffee, give them some space in which to spread out and dress them neatly enough to instill pride. However, he showed the limits of his understanding by insisting that most slaves are happier when punished for breaking rules and "look upon their obligation to each other very lightly."

This was certainly not true of Ellen. Separated from her mother, Ellen made a promise that would one day spur mobs to roam the streets of Boston yelling, "Bloodhounds," and make Ellen so famous people would pay to see her. It was a promise that would touch the lives of a U.S. president, the Queen of England, the widow of a famous English poet and two frustrated Georgia bounty hunters. Yet it was a simple promise—she would have no children while she was a slave. Ellen's previous owner and alleged father, Major Smith, later moved to Macon and became one of its first lawyers and one of the five commissioners who laid out the town. This reunited Ellen with her mother, but didn't spur her to break her vow. She still wanted no babies who might wind up watering cotton fields and auction blocks with their tears or grow up clinging to dwindling memories of lost siblings and parents.

Sleeping on a pallet outside her mistress's door, she tried to sink into the life of a skilled seamstress and lady's maid. By the 1840s, she was allowed to have her own one-room cabin for storing sewing supplies. Compared to the lives of slaves who labored on cotton, hemp or coastal rice plantations and who might be lashed until they bled and then have brick dust or salt rubbed on their sores, Ellen's life wasn't harsh. But a bubble of silent anger bounced around inside of her, ready to burst. Then she met a slave cabinetmaker named William Craft, a tall, broad-backed, bass-voiced man who would later defend himself against slave hunters with firearms and fury.

William enjoyed more independence than most slaves because his owner hired him out to other employers in exchange for an annual fixed sum of two hundred dollars: he could keep the rest of his earnings. However, he would later write that he had never recovered from the anguish of watching members of his family standing on auction blocks, sold off one by one along with kegs of brandy, bales of cotton and chairs. His fourteen-year-old sister, he said, had "large, silent tears trickling down her cheeks" as she was carried away. He also could not forget standing on a block himself at age sixteen and being sold to Ira H. Taylor, a bank cashier who worked for Ellen's owner.

William and Ellen fell in love but postponed marriage because of Ellen's refusal to bear enslaved children. Finally, in 1846, they asked their owners' permission for a slave "marriage" and settled into what, on the surface, looked like the routine life of an enslaved couple. The Reverend Theodore Parker, a Boston abolitionist, would later claim that Ellen had a baby who died while she was forced to leave the ailing child alone and serve dinner to her owners; however, no historians support Parker's story. According to Ellen and William's own account of their story, Ellen did not become pregnant after her marriage, possibly because she used crude birth control devices such as sponges or grapefruit halves. Some slave women induced miscarriages with cotton root or cotton seed, though there is no evidence that Ellen did this. Yet there is plenty of evidence that the Crafts spent much of their time hatching escape plots and planning for the day they could raise a free family. William even built a chest of drawers with a lock and hid his extra earnings so he could afford train tickets and hotels. Finally, in 1848, as workers all over Europe rebelled against their kings and Americans began streaming to California in search of gold, William latched onto an idea he believed would open his own door to freedom. His wife, so often mistaken for white, would pass for white.

Since no Southern white female would travel alone with a male slave, Ellen would have to disguise herself as a white man. She would wear dark glasses to help hide her expressive eyes and a muffler or wrappings to conceal her beardless chin and make her seem to have a toothache. Illiterate and unable to sign hotel registers, Ellen decided she should wear her right arm in a sling. The Crafts also agreed that Ellen should pretend she was hard of hearing to avoid prolonged conversations with Southern planters. William bought pieces of Ellen's disguise in different places and at different times, including a top hat and the handkerchiefs that would swaddle her chin. Ellen sewed a pair of men's trousers and hid them in her little cabin. Then Ellen got a pre-Christmas pass from her mistress, allowing her to be away from the plantation for a few days. William got a similar pass, a necessary thing because slave owners protected each other's property by asking for the passes or freedom papers of black people they saw walking or wandering about.

The Crafts, of course, were not the first slaves or slave couple to run away in disguise. Harriet Tubman plopped a bonnet on the head of a fleeing black man and led him to freedom. The Reverend Calvin Fairbank dressed a girl as a boy, put her on a large log, straddled the log behind her and paddled them both to safety with a piece of board. Frederick Douglass told the story of a slave couple who escaped across the Ohio River, the short, dark man wearing female clothing and posing as the slave of his wife, who, like Ellen Craft, passed for white. The man was the slave of William R. King, president pro tempore of the U.S. Senate and Democratic vice president-elect, and the wife was the mulatto daughter of King's brother. When Underground Railroad conductor John Fairfield decided to help a band of mulattos escape from slavery in Kentucky, he powdered their faces, plopped horsehair wigs on their heads and passed them off as white. William Webb, a free black man from Virginia, was James Bond before Agent 007 had even been imagined. He wore disguises and snooped and spied on slave catchers, eavesdropping on them in taverns where they traded bourbon-soaked secrets. In this way he managed to find out what they knew about slave escape routes and hiding places. In countless other stories, fugitive males don horsehair wigs or widow's veils and fugitive women snip off their hair and slip into trousers.

Yet the Crafts' story is different, in part because the couple traveled so far and in part because people were entranced by the story of how Ellen Craft used her creativity and intelligence as well as men's clothes to transform herself. It is a psychological drama in which an enslaved couple grows up before our eyes, bluffing, bargaining, pleading, playacting and changing with each leg of their journey. It also is the story of a couple who flee not only for freedom but for each other, clinging to love in a system designed to crush it, and confronting constant danger.

Eight days before Christmas, the Crafts began the journey that would change both them and their country. First, William cut Ellen's hair in a square bob. Ellen then donned a black coat, trousers, a cape, a top hat, high-heeled boots and green tinted glasses. She wore her arm in a sling and carried a cane. As a final sign of class, she wore a tassel and plaid tartan cape, a coat of arms for a refined gentleman. William's only disguise was a secondhand white beaver hat.

Once dressed, Ellen cried, collapsing onto William's chest, but she recovered quickly. They took separate routes to the railroad station, William arriving first and Ellen showing up later to buy tickets to Savannah for Mr. William Johnson and his slave. They were beginning a journey full of unknown terrors. They were fleeing from the Deep South rather than from a border state such as Missouri or Kentucky, where slaves could look across rivers and see freedom shining on the other side. Moreover, like most slaves, they probably had been fed a steady diet of horror stories about the North, a place where people reportedly lived in houses made of snow and among Yankees who would, quite literally, eat them. Nineteenth-century historian Wilbur H. Siebert even talked about a slave who didn't want to go to Canada because he'd heard farmers there could raise nothing but black-eyed peas. Still, they caught a train in Macon and rode it to Savannah.

In Savannah, a horse-drawn bus carried the other passengers to a hotel for early-morning tea. William and Ellen stayed on the bus, William bringing a tray to his "master." In another eleven years, free blacks and former slaves would complete Savannah's First African Baptist Church, putting nickel-sized holes in the pine floors to ventilate the hiding space below; that space would hide runaway slaves escaping through a tunnel to the Savannah River. But Ellen and William knew nothing about such things as Southern hiding places for slaves. So they boarded a steamer headed for Charleston, South Carolina. Not wanting close contact with the other passengers on the boat, Ellen immediately went to bed. William explained to the other passengers that his master had rheumatism. He took out Ellen's flannels, warmed them at a stove, and carried them to her berth.

In Charleston, which emerged as the center of the slave trade in the eighteenth century, they stayed in what they would describe as the city's "best hotel." However, in Petersburg, Virginia, danger showed up in a different disguise—this time it wore dresses and oozed concern. While a gentleman quizzed William about his master's prospects, the man's two daughters flirted with and fussed over the mysterious "Mr. Johnson." They insisted that Mr. Johnson, who was, of course, Ellen, use their shawls as pillows and accept their father's rheumatism recipe. Ellen couldn't read the recipe and was afraid to look at it for fear she would hold it upside down, so she immediately put it away.

The chaos and close calls continued. A woman who got on the train at Richmond even mistook William for her runaway slave, Ned. Not until she looked William squarely in the face did she realize she was calling the wrong man.

"I never in my life saw two black pigs more alike than your boy and my Ned," she told Ellen.

However, Ellen and William faced their most serious roadblock when they tried to catch the Philadelphia, Wilmington and Baltimore train at the President Street depot. Ten years earlier, a twenty-one-year-old Baltimore shipyard slave later known as Frederick Douglass had escaped aboard a Philadelphia, Wilmington and Baltimore railcar, using fake seaman's papers to pass as a freeman. Train officials had become more vigilant since then, requiring black people wishing to travel on the trains to bring a white Baltimore resident with them to sign a bond.

This was the trap that had been waiting for the Crafts all along. As soon as the Crafts approached the ticket master, the man informed "Mr. Johnson" that he would have to prove his own identity and also post a bond to take a slave to the North. That was the moment when Ellen reached deep inside herself and tapped something she might not even have known she owned. Speaking in the scorn-wrapped voice of a Southern planter, she declared, "You have no right to detain us here." Fellow passengers from the steamer vouched for Mr. Johnson as well. William then begged the ticket master to let his master go, saying he might die if he didn't receive treatment in Philadelphia soon. When Ellen spoke again in the voice of a young white man raised on mint juleps and money, the ticket master finally yielded, waving her on.

In the Jim Crow section of the train to Philadelphia, William began creating his own Underground Railroad: he asked a free black man for information about Northern slave havens. This was a common first step for fugitives fleeing the Deep South; they sought help not from any established network of people who assisted fugitives, but from the first black person they saw. The free black man gave him the name of a boardinghouse run by abolitionists.

Finally, the Crafts reached Philadelphia, where they could stand on free soil, breathe free air and walk around with a free spirit. At the edge of collapse, Ellen finally broke down and let her tears flow. It was Christmas, and they were in Philadelphia greeting black abolitionist leaders Robert Purvis and William Still, the latter chairman of the Philadelphia Vigilance Committee. When Ellen wore her costume for them, they were stunned at how it changed her. However, Ellen stayed mostly in bed for a few days, recovering from her ordeal. The pair spent three weeks with an antislavery Quaker family, members of a religious group who called themselves Friends of Truth and spoke to each other the way they believed Jesus spoke to his biblical friends. Quakers believed in a personal God who spoke directly to their souls and constantly revealed his truths. Ellen distrusted them and all white people, but the family won her over with warm bowls of soup and kindness. William Wells Brown, a fugitive slave, author and antislavery speaker, also called on them, urging them to join him in speaking out against slavery.

Despite the sheen of adventure that surrounds Underground Railroad sagas, only a small band of citizens actually aided slaves, and not all of them welcomed blacks into their homes or even churches except in segregated "negro seats," as the *American Anti-Slavery Almanac* for 1840 pointed out. Yet many of those who sheltered slaves in Philadelphia and elsewhere truly cared about people of color. In Philadelphia, such friends urged the Crafts to push on to Boston, which was farther north and, perhaps, safer for a couple whose daring escape might spark an intense manhunt. After moving to Boston, the Crafts boarded with Lewis and Harriet Hayden at 66 Phillips Street, a brick brownstone with pine floors, marble fireplaces, an owner who had been a fugitive slave and a top floor that sheltered as many as thirteen runaways at a time. Hayden, a fugitive from Kentucky, had arrived in Boston in 1849, still smarting over the fact that, as he pointed out in his account of his life, his master had swapped him for a pair of horses. Hayden kept two kegs of gunpowder under his front stoop and had threatened to blow up the house rather than let any fugitives be taken from it.

While Ellen sewed and learned upholstery, William Craft, who couldn't find work as a cabinetmaker, opened a secondhand furniture store. Craft's advertisement in the July 27, 1849, edition of the *Liberator* read:

"William Craft. Dealer in New and Second Hand Furniture, No. 62 Federal Street Boston. . . . All kinds of furniture cleaned and repaired with despatch [*sic*] in the most satisfactory manner. The patronage of his friends and the public is respectfully solicited."

The couple remained in Boston for two years and joined the congregation of the Reverend Theodore Parker. The Unitarian minister and social reformer claimed that when writing his sermons he kept a rifle on one side of his desk and a Bible on the other. It didn't take long for the Crafts to need both physical protection and prayers. As they became full-fledged celebrities on the antislavery circuit, they also became tempting targets for the slavery supporters on their trail.

Everywhere they went, they met people who recognized the power of their story as an antislavery tool, a saga of adventure and romance that could touch people's souls. Unlike most fugitives, though, the Crafts used their real names and described real events, real places and real people, anxious to make their stories believable. Runaway slave, writer and antislavery activist William Wells Brown wrote about them in the *Liberator* in January 1849. Other stories soon appeared in the *New York Herald*, the *Newark Daily Mercury*, the *National Slavery Standard* and elsewhere. William and Ellen Craft became America's most notorious fugitive slave couple. However, as was the custom in nineteenth-century America, it was William who did the talking at public meetings while Ellen merely stood onstage, her whiteness forcing whites to identify with her plight. William spoke to swelling crowds at the African Meeting House just off Joy Street on Boston's Beacon Hill in the heart of the black community. It was the first still-standing black church established in America. He also spoke in the Hopedale community in Mendon, Massachusetts, a Christian enclave set on six hundred acres of land. When they toured with William Wells Brown, Brown sometimes charged admission.

Then suddenly, with one stroke of his pen, U.S. president Millard Fillmore changed life for Ellen and William Craft and for thousands of other black and white Americans. On September 18, 1850, he signed the Fugitive Slave Act, passed by Congress as part of the Compromise of 1850.

Like cholera or some other virulent disease, the new federal law would infect thousands of people. It had been gaining strength for months. Henry Clay proposed it in the Senate in January 1850 as part of a compromise package. Under it, California would come into the Union free and citizens of the territory acquired from Mexico could choose whether or not they wanted slavery. To appease the antislavery forces, the slave trade was prohibited in the District of Columbia and California joined the Union as a free state. To satisfy Southern slaveholders weary of having their runaways sheltered by Northern communities, a stricter Fugitive Slave Act made it easier to recover runaway slaves.

The new law was not just tough. It was a slab of stone. It set up a federal system of judges, commissioners and marshals to recapture escaped slaves, even in free states. Anyone claiming to own a runaway slave could take the slave into custody after establishing ownership before a federal commissioner. Any bystander, white or black, could be fined one thousand dollars or jailed for six months for refusing to help a marshal capture a fugitive slave.

"Did those framers of the constitution intend that northern freemen should leave their shops, their plows, their merchandise, to give chase to fugitive slaves?" newspaper editor and runaway slave Henry Bibb sneered in the January 1, 1851, issue of *Voice of the Fugitive.*

Apparently, that was just what framers of the new law expected. Also, special commissioners received ten dollars for each fugitive returned to slavery and only five dollars for those turned loose. Slaves weren't entitled to jury trials or judicial hearings; in fact, they had no chance to defend themselves. That meant free blacks as well as fugitives like the Crafts could be kidnapped and thrown into slavery. So eager were some slave catchers to arrest supposed fugitives that two men seized a fourteen-year-old white girl in Chester County, Pennsylvania, mistaking her for a mulatto. After traveling twelve miles, they put her out of their carriage. Patrick Sneed, a black Niagara Falls waiter, also was briefly arrested on the "pretended charge" of a murder committed in Savannah, Georgia.

The law was supposed to ease tensions between the North and South by discouraging slaves from leaving their masters. Supporters also hoped the law would stop Southern secessionists from threatening to leave the Union. However, the law accomplished just the opposite of what its supporters had hoped—more slaves than ever began running to Canada.

"Almost every day we have men arriving here from the land of slavery," Henry Bibb commented in the May 7, 1851, edition of his Canadian newspaper. Within a week, forty blacks left Boston. In Columbia, Pennsylvania, 487 of its 943 African Americans packed up and left. Sandy Lake, Pennsylvania, a northern Pennsylvania community once dubbed Liberia because it had accepted so many Southern runaways, lost so many people it disappeared from the map.

Or as an antislavery tract issued in 1853 pointed out, "Families were broken up—churches disorganized—joy turned into mourning and laughter into tears." In New Orleans, the situation became so laced with paranoia that a June 24, 1853, edition of the *Liberator* claimed a band of twenty-five hundred heavily armed slaves planned to attack the city. The story was quickly retracted.

Runaways walked through woods, hid in hollow logs and coffins, crawled into unused pig pens and corn cribs and curled up under sacks of grain on ships; they crossed rivers in ships, tubs, gates or even logs; they rubbed their bodies with red pepper, raw onion and the dust from graves to baffle the hound dogs on their trail; and they ate raw meat to avoid setting cooking fires that would attract slave hunters. Some ran to swamps and bayous to live with Indians or as solitary outcasts.

Meanwhile, the Crafts and other members of Boston's antislavery movement began speaking with gruffer, angrier voices.

On October 4, 1850, Boston blacks adopted a resolution to resist until death any attempt to snatch away their freedom. Ten days later, Josiah Quincy, former mayor of Boston, and 340 other white abolitionists, called a meeting to support this resolution. Abolitionist leader Frederick Douglass told the assembly, "We must be prepared should this law be put into operation to see the streets of Boston running with blood."

His words were soon tested.

In mid-October, two slave hunters working for Ellen Craft's owner, Robert Collins, showed up in Boston. John Knight, who once worked with William in a cabinetmaker's shop, was one of the men. The *Federal Union* newspaper of Milledgeville, Georgia, described Knight as "a tall, lank, lean looking fellow, five feet ten or eleven inches high, dark hair, about twenty-eight years old." He sent William a letter, asking him to come see him at the United States Hotel and show him around Boston. Knight tossed in an extra cup of sugar: he offered to take a letter from Ellen back to her mother, Maria.

However, the Crafts learned that Knight was traveling with Willis Hughes, a jailer from Macon. There was nothing even remotely sweet about him. The November 5, 1850, edition of the *Federal Union* called him "a short, rowdyish-looking fellow, five feet two, thirty or forty years of age, sandy hair, red whiskers, black short teeth, chews and smokes." A third professional slave catcher named Alfred Beal from Norfolk was also said to be in the area. He was, according to the newspaper, "a very stout, thick set, coarse looking man, about five feet nine inches high, sandy hair, red whiskers, upper front teeth broken off, about forty-five years of age, known to be on a general hunt."

Knight asked for a warrant for the Crafts' arrest after the couple failed to show up at Knight's hotel. On October 25, he finally found a judge to issue one. William barricaded himself inside a store owned by Lewis Hayden and guarded by blacks and abolitionists. He sat at his bench with a plane and saw and a heavily loaded "horse pistol," prepared to shoot anyone who tried to carry him away. Ellen first stayed with her friend Mrs. Hilliard and then with Ellis Gray Loring, a wealthy Boston lawyer, and finally with Mr. Parker. William hid in Lewis Hayden's home, the house barricaded with double locks and Hayden down in the basement with two kegs of gunpowder, ready to blow up the house if the marshal broke through the guard upstairs. A mob gathered in the streets as Judge Levi Woodbury considered Knight's request for warrants. Judge Woodbury issued the warrants, but they were never served.

Meanwhile, Hughes and Knight found out how it felt to be pursued. They were sworn at, arrested for carrying concealed weapons, jailed for driving too fast and threatened with violence. They also went to jail on a charge of libeling the Crafts. An unknown but wealthy supporter bailed them out each time. In a November 26 letter to the *Federal Union*, Knight said both men had been arrested for calling Craft a slave: and that at one time a crowd had rushed their carriage, "hissed . . . called us bloodhounds and some of them seized upon the horses and attempted to open the doors. Mr. Hughes who was in the carriage laughed at them and made sport of them."

After two weeks of harassment, Knight and Hughes scurried out of town. By then, neither man was laughing.

There was not a speck of humor in Hughes's November 21 letter to the *Federal Union*, only outrage and self-pity. He wrote:

> I went to Boston as an agent to execute a lawful trust, thinking I would be protected and assisted by the laws of my country. But on the contrary, from the first, the laws of the country, instead of providing a protection, were made an engine of cruelty, oppression, injustice and abuse, so that my life was constantly endangered, and this without the first offer of assistance from Government, national, state or city.

Ellen's owner, Dr. Robert Collins, complained directly to President Fillmore about his agents' treatment and local officials' failure to go after the Crafts. He was assured that, if necessary, the federal government would fulfill the law by placing troops at the disposal of state and local authorities. W. S. Derrick, acting secretary of state, answered, saying ". . . [President Fillmore] directs me to assure you that, if, unfortunately . . . the painful necessity should arise, he is resolved to perform his duty. . . ."

William Craft wanted to stand his ground, too, but he and Ellen finally heeded the advice of their friends and prepared to leave for England. The Boston Vigilance Committee gave them two hundred fifty dollars for their trip. On November 7, 1850, their minister, Theodore Parker, legally married them and "presented William with a revolver and a dirk-knife, counseling him to use them manfully . . . if ever an attempt should be made by his owners or anyone else to re-enslave them," according to William Still. The next day, the Reverend Samuel J. May, an Underground Railroad conductor, escorted the couple to Portland, Maine, the first leg of their journey.

Anything that could go wrong did. After ramming another boat, the steamer to Portland, Maine, had to be repaired. They were delayed again in New Brunswick. The stagecoach carrying them to Halifax tipped over. For seven miles, they trudged through icy rain. When they finally reached Halifax, they discovered they had missed their steamship by two hours. Once they crossed the Canadian border, they were safe, but far from secure. Ellen had to pose as white to get a room in Halifax. After seeing William's mahogany face, their landlady asked the Crafts to move out and stay with a black family. By the time the S.S. *Cambria* arrived in late November and carried the Crafts to Liverpool, Ellen was wrestling with what could have been pneumonia.

They survived their trip, though, and lived in England from 1851 to 1869. Now their lives were as different from a slave's as flour sacks are from silk. They met people from all over the country, including Queen Victoria, Prince Albert and Lady Noel Byron, widow of the famed poet Lord Byron. William Wells Brown took them on the antislavery speaking circuit, where, as usual, Ellen's white appearance struck a special chord with white audiences forced to imagine themselves in her place. An observer in Edinburgh called her "a gentle, refined-looking creature of twenty-four years, as fair as most of her British sisters, and in mental qualifications their equal too."

But Ellen and William Craft were no longer the same slavery-shaped couple who had fled Georgia in 1848. After traveling thousands of miles to freedom, they began a series of inner journeys, changing all the while. They finally had children, five of them, and spent two years at the Ockham School near Ripley, Surrey, a trade school for rural youth founded by Lady Byron. At Ockham, they learned to read and write and taught manual skills to fellow students. They also helped raise money to set up a girls' school in Sierra Leone, and their home in Hammersmith became a headquarters for abolitionist activity. Ellen, in particular, began finding her own voice and raising it. In 1852, reports circulated in the press that Ellen had grown tired of living free in a strange and distant land and had asked an American gentleman in London to take her back to her slave family. Ellen, long either silent or saying only a few words at antislavery meetings, wrote a letter to the newspapers explaining that she would "rather starve in England, a free woman, than be a slave for the best man that ever breathed upon the American continent." She also peppered some of the most powerful men in England with questions about their racial beliefs. Once, seated at a dinner next to the famed humorist Artemus Ward, Ellen asked him why he belittled Negroes in his books. Clearly, this woman so often praised for her gentility and refinement had another, rawer side: she had become an iron fist wrapped in velvet. That fist would show itself in 1851, when the Crafts attended the Great Exhibition in the hundred-foot-high Crystal Palace built for the occasion in London. Sponsored by Prince Albert, the exhibition was a display of inventions, fine arts and raw materials from around the world. Ellen, William and other abolitionists showed up when Queen Victoria and members of Parliament were present and turned the exhibit into an antislavery protest. Each black visitor walked around on the arm of a white companion.

William was changing, too. His idea of who he could become grew with each book he read and each titled or substantial person he met. His celebrity status suggested he should do something special, something more than making cabinets or even speaking out against slavery, but who was he, really, and how could he make his mark? Against the advice of friends, he tried to set up a boardinghouse: it failed. He dictated to a British friend the story of his and Ellen's escape from slavery. In 1860, the narrative was published as *Running a Thousand Miles for Freedom.* He also sold boots, raincoats and other items made from newly invented vulcanized rubber. His riskiest venture was traveling to the West African nation of Dahomey, one of the more powerful kingdoms in nineteenth-century West Africa, on behalf of a London business house. He tried to convince the king of Dahomey to give up participating in the slave trade—and provide England with a steady source of affordable cotton at a time when America's Civil War disrupted the flow of cotton overseas. While he may have gained the king's confidence, he lost the financial support of his backers and had little to show for his efforts.

Finally, in the late 1860s, the Crafts found a cause big enough to fulfill them: they decided to help educate and uplift newly freed American blacks. In 1869, now speaking "with a clipped British accent," according to one author, they returned to Boston with three of their children. They then moved to the scarred and still-bleeding

South. William became the partner of a black man who had leased a plantation in Hickory Hill, across the Georgia state line in South Carolina. In 1870, Ellen opened a school there. A man named B. McBride, who had owned the plantation in the 1830s, assured a later owner that he would succeed by following his instructions about planting cotton, corn, potatoes and possibly rice, and making sure his young horses were stabled and salted twice a week. But in a region where old hatreds fed on war defeats, the Crafts' efforts only fueled new fires. One autumn night, masked Ku Klux Klan riders tossed kerosene-coated torches into the Crafts' barns and dwellings. Ellen awakened to the crackle of flames and the smell of their neighbors' resentments. She and her children rushed outside in their nightclothes. One-fourth of their investment flared up in flames.

The Crafts, though, still had some steam left. In January 1874 they tried again. With a loan of twelve thousand dollars, they bought Woodville, a cotton and rice plantation at Ways Station in Bryan County, Georgia, about fifty or so miles from Savannah. They hoped to establish a community modeled after the Ockham School they had attended in Surrey, England, teaching blacks practical skills such as carpentry, elementary housekeeping, mechanics and rudimentary reading and writing. At the school, Ellen banned beatings and taught former female field-workers to sew and keep house and use forks and plates. She also prayed with them, brought them medicine and loaned them money for wedding licenses. She even took in an ailing one-hundred-year-old woman and nursed her until she died. By July 1875, sixteen black families were tilling land at Woodville, and seventy-five boys and girls attended the farm school free of charge.

Meanwhile, William took crops to market in Savannah, ran for the state senate in 1874 and raised money in New York and Boston for the school. But soon the Klan's white-robed envy and rage showed up wearing different clothes. Some of the Crafts' neighbors, white and black, began grumbling against them. They sent letters and spread stories to people in the North that William Craft was a charlatan, that the school didn't exist and that Craft was pocketing the money he raised for it. Hearing the stories, Barthold Schlesinger, the German consul in Boston, inserted a notice in a Boston newspaper calling William a swindler.

The notice, which appeared in the *Boston Daily Advertiser* and other Boston papers on September 26, 1876, said:

> The colored man, William Craft, now here asking for money for his colored school in Bryan County, Georgia, is sailing under false colors. He and his family live on the money he collects every summer, and *not one* cent of it goes to any charitable purpose.
>
> Any person desirous of making further inquiries on this subject can write to any of the following named county officers, and the above will be confirmed:
>
> A.J. Smith, (white) Commissioner of Schools in Bryan county.
>
> Sheriff Bashlor, (white).
>
> James Andrews, (colored) Justice of the Peace.

William sued for libel, asking for ten thousand dollars in damages. In 1878, Ellen went to Boston to testify in her husband's libel case. A June 18, 1878, editorial in *The Macon Telegraph and Messenger* predicted that William "will whip the fight against his Northern persecutors. He is said to have undergone the ordeal of a cross-examination without flinching and successfully."

However, it cost $150 to depose a witness, and the Crafts could afford only one witness at their trial. The couple lost the case and surrendered Woodville, but Ellen kept on working with tenant farmers.

After losing Woodville, Ellen and William Craft left public life, draping their dreams for the future around their children's shoulders. Young Ellen and Alfred attended school in the North, William Jr. lived in England, and Charles and Brougham worked for the U.S. Post Office. Around 1890, Ellen and William moved to Charleston to live with their daughter, Ellen Craft Crum, and her husband, Dr.

William Demosthenes Crum. They were everything William and Ellen had hoped to become. Ellen Crum, a society woman, founded the National Federation of Afro-American Women. In 1910, Dr. Crum became U.S. Minister to Liberia, a post William Craft once craved. A graduate of the Howard University Medical School, Dr. Crum had been a delegate to every Republican National Conference from 1884 to 1904. In 1902, President Theodore Roosevelt made him customs collector of the port of Charlestown (later Charleston) as a signal of hope to Southern blacks. Ellen Craft died about 1897 and was buried under her favorite pine tree on Woodville. William Craft died in Charleston in 1900. Yet the seeds they planted in Georgia, South Carolina, Philadelphia, Boston and England flowered in their descendants, creating a legacy of love and long, green journeys to new shores.

A historical marker in downtown Louisville, Kentucky, commemorates the escape of enslaved Thornton and Lucie (Rutha) Blackburn, who became successful entrepreneurs and antislavery activists in Toronto.

5

EVEN A BLIND HORSE KNOWS THE WAY

Daddy Grace drove his cart into the woods with a runaway slave crouched beside him, chains dangling from the fugitive's arms and legs, and a pistol in his hands. One of the rioters held a sword to Grace's head, urging him to hurry to the river. He pushed his horse harder and harder, outrunning the shouts and screams of a rock-flinging, curse-tossing, anger-spewing, blood-seeking mob. His horse was blind as a wall, as sightless as shoes, but it knew the way to freedom.

Americans have rioted about all sorts of things, including horse stealing, the military draft, taxes, trade policies, racial tensions, umpires' decisions, sports victories, sports losses and the assassinations of heroes. When Presbyterian minister Sylvester Graham urged Americans to shun meat and alcohol and eat only home-baked whole-wheat bread, his advice so angered bakers, butchers and saloon keepers that riots erupted wherever Graham spoke. In New York in 1817, an entertainer's refusal to sing a requested song triggered a riot. In October 1834, forty homes were torched in Philadelphia's black community during riots in support of slavery. In October 1835, famed abolitionist William Lloyd Garrison had to be rescued from a Boston mob angered by his insistence that all men were created equal.

But the four or five hundred blacks who milled around the small Detroit jail on two June days in 1833 didn't bash heads, disable stagecoaches and swing swords because they feared competition from home bakers. They didn't switch identities like the characters in Shakespeare's romantic comedies so they could string up horse thieves or support slavery, either. Nor was it taxes that made them arm themselves with clubs, sticks, pistols and rocks, assault Sheriff John M. Wilson and drain all the courage from his deputy.

The drama that led black Detroiters and Canadians to set fires, go to jail, flee temporarily to Canada and start building the foundations for their own antislavery church began with a love affair between two extraordinary escaped slaves. Their names were Thornton and Rutha Blackburn.

After running away together from Louisville, Kentucky, and marrying along the way, the Blackburns arrived in Detroit in 1831. Neither city was ever quite the same again. Thornton had lived an uncertain life, passing from one pair of hands and one set of possibilities to the next. He had been born in Maysville, Kentucky, around 1813, but became the property of Dr. Gideon Brown in Hardinsburg, Kentucky. When Dr. Brown died in 1829, Thornton became the property of the doctor's wife, Susan Brown, who moved to a farm outside Louisville. In the spring of 1831, Brown hired out Thornton as a porter at Wurts and Reinhard's dry goods store in Louisville, a city where slaves about to be shipped south waited in iron-barred coops and men and women in chains marched up Main Street to board boats. It was common practice to hire out slaves not needed at home in order to produce extra income. Thornton might have carried crates and boxes and helped deliver merchandise to people's homes. However, hiring out slaves fostered independence: away from their masters, slaves' vision of the world widened, along with their knowledge of geography, rivers and escape routes.

As both Thornton and Rutha would have been aware, Kentucky slaves didn't only work in fields and homes. They built bridges and canals, cooked, cleaned and waited tables in restaurants and hotels, delivered products to market, rode and groomed racehorses, occasionally delivered mail and were guides at some tourist attractions, including an artesian well in Louisville. Marion Lucas, author of *A History of Blacks in Kentucky*, even tells the incredible story of a slave in Louisville who worked as a paralegal for his master. When his owner put him up for auction in 1849, the owner advertised him as a "good rough lawyer" who could take depositions, decipher legal writings and interview witnesses.

It is likely that during this time Thornton met Rutha, a light-skinned Creole West Indian slave woman who was nine years older than him and had plenty of sass and style. She had worked as a nurse for George and Charlotte Backus of Backus and Bell Dry Goods Company in Louisville. Both owners had died, and Rutha, like Thornton, had no idea what shape her future might take. After the sale of the Backus estate, Rutha became the property of Virgil McKnight, future president of the Bank of Kentucky.

On July 3, 1831, Thornton Blackburn ran away from Susan Brown, his owner. He took Rutha with him. It's not known why they decided to run at that particular time, but as city slaves they would have heard stories about the free North and about Canada, where, in 1793, the government had stopped allowing slaves to be brought into the country. Perhaps Rutha was upset at being sold away from family and friends. Perhaps Thornton, having sipped a small glass of freedom in downtown Louisville, longed for a full bottle. Or perhaps one or both of them had reason to fear being "sold down the river" to the slave markets of Natchez or New Orleans and ending up on a cotton or cane plantation, where their lives would be toil filled and probably short. Whatever the reason, on the day before Independence Day, Thornton and Rutha declared themselves both free and independent: they left Louisville together. You couldn't really call it running away. They had too much confidence in themselves to skulk in the woods or sneak across rivers in skiffs. On July 3, 1831, they took a ferry across the Ohio River to Jeffersonville, Indiana, a river town famous for steamboats and shipyards and the place where Methodist preacher Calvin Fairbank would be arrested twenty years later for taking a slave named Tamar across the Ohio. In Jeffersonville, Thornton and Rutha flagged down the *Versailles*, a steamboat built in Cincinnati in 1831; it was just leaving Louisville for Cincinnati. Though they were fugitive slaves and though Kentucky law forbade taking slaves from the shores of the Ohio River opposite Kentucky, they had no trouble boarding the ship. They also had no trouble dazzling the captain and crew.

They were, by all accounts, two of a kind. They both had perfect manners and a sheen of elegance, and Rutha, a head-turning beauty, swished around in a black silk dress. Thornton also carried himself like a man with a sense of importance. This was noted in the runaway slave ad his owner ran for him. The July 7, 1831, fugitive slave notice published in the *Louisville Public Defender* offered a twenty-five-dollar reward for "a colored man, named Thornton," who stood about five feet nine or ten inches, was stout, had a yellow complexion and light eyes. He had left wearing a blue cloth coat, boots, pantaloons and a black hat and was said to be of "good address," meaning he carried himself well and knew how to impress people.

The officers of the *Versailles* took the pair for free blacks and let them aboard while the boat was floating in the Ohio, a short distance above Jeffersonville. Years later, they would pay for that slip: for helping the Blackburns escape, the steamboat company owners and the ship's master were forced to pay Virgil McKnight and Susan Brown four hundred dollars each. The owners of the ferry boat that took them to Jeffersonville were found to have violated an 1824 statute; a witness swore that he saw the slaves on the boat before it left the Kentucky shore and another witness swore that he had since seen the slaves in Canada. However, when the Blackburns escaped in 1831, Susan Brown's nephew, William Oldham, immediately began tracking them, catching the next steamboat for Cincinnati. He found the Blackburns' names on a logbook for the stagecoach to Sandusky, but gave up the chase, figuring they would beat him to their likely destination, Canada. Ohio members of the Underground Railroad likely advised them about which coaches to take on the road to freedom, according to historian Karolyn Smardz. After reaching Sandusky, they boarded another coach for Detroit, then capital of the Michigan Territory. As a Michigan city, it was part of the Northwest Territory, which, under the ordinance of 1787, prohibited slavery.

The couple arrived in Detroit on July 18, and Thornton soon found work with the local stonemason, Thomas Coquillard. They fit right into a black community that was still very small. In 1830, a year before their arrival, there were only 261 free blacks in the entire Michigan Territory and 32 slaves, holdovers from the days when the area was British ruled. An estimated 50 black families or 250 black individuals lived in the city of Detroit. The Blackburns moved within this small, tight circle, attending church and creating friends. No doubt they learned that they were not the only fugitive slaves to pass through or remain in Detroit, a city that would become the end of the line for thousands of runaways and become known on the Underground Railroad by the code name Midnight. However, in the fall of 1831 the Blackburns' free life became endangered. Thomas J. Rogers, a friend of Susan Brown's, visited Detroit and ran into Thornton Blackburn. He talked with the fugitive and learned that his wife was with him. For unknown reasons, Rogers waited two years before reporting his discovery to authorities in Kentucky. Once the Blackburns' whereabouts were revealed, though, Susan Brown and Virgil McKnight hired Benjamin G. Weir and Talbot Oldham as agents to recover the pair and return them to Kentucky.

On June 14 and 15, 1833, Weir and Oldham appeared before Henry Chipman, justice of the peace for Wayne County, Michigan, with proof that the Blackburns were fugitive slaves. Chipman issued warrants for their arrests, and Sheriff John M. Wilson placed them in the county jail, then on Gratiot Street for safekeeping. They sat in separate cells, waiting for their free lives and, most likely, their lives together to end. Under the Fugitive Slave Act of 1793 and the Territorial Act of 1827, Michigan had to send any proven runaways back to their Southern owners. Also, Wilson and his deputy allegedly were promised fifty dollars each for bringing the Blackburns to the dock.

However, Detroit's black community had different plans for the couple.

They did not see Weir and Oldham as respected representatives of authority. They saw them as slave catchers, their sworn enemies and their worst fears brought to life. Whether fugitives or freeborn blacks, they identified with the Blackburns on a level almost too deep for words, realizing they, too, could easily wind up in jail or on a South-bound ship. Detroit was free territory, but the number of advertisements for fugitive slaves in the *Detroit Gazette* had climbed during the early 1820s, a constant reminder of the fate that might await fugitives. Also, in April 1827, a law to regulate blacks and mulattos and to punish persons who kidnapped them had been enacted. Under this law, every black or mulatto who came into the territory after January 1, 1828, was supposed to post a bond with the clerk of the county court for five hundred dollars. Few, if any, blacks posted this bond, but the law made it possible to force out of the territory any black person considered undesirable. No wonder a steady and angry hum of protests rose from the section of the courtroom occupied by blacks during the Blackburn hearings.

On the evening of June 15, 1833, several black Detroiters decided to take matters into their own hands. They met at the home of Benjamin Willoughby, a real estate speculator, financier and owner of a lumber business, who probably came to Detroit from Kentucky between 1817 and 1830. He had worked as a laborer and acquired some money, often lending it to others. At his home, participants hatched a plot to free the Blackburns; the plan put Willoughby's own property and even life at risk.

Sheriff Wilson allowed Mrs. Caroline French and Mrs. Tabitha Lightfoot into the jail to visit Rutha Blackburn. The trio remained together until near dusk. Caroline French was the wife of George French, and Tabitha Lightfoot was married to Madison Lightfoot: both men were either porters or waiters at Detroit's Steamboat Hotel at the corner of Randolph and Woodbridge streets near the Detroit River. The men held positions that gave them access to the city's power brokers. Madison Lightfoot had married Tabitha Smith at St.

Paul's Protestant Episcopal Church in 1831, the same year that the Blackburns arrived in Detroit. Caroline French had powerful connections as well. Her father was Cornelius Leonard Lenox, who had come to Detroit from Newton, Massachusetts, with Governor William Hull and bought a farm from the family of John Askin, an English loyalist who made a fortune that he partly abandoned when he moved to Canada and began living on the banks of the Detroit River. According to historian Arthur LaBrew, Caroline French also was the cousin of Boston activist Charles Lenox Remond, the first African-American to appear as a regular lecturer for the Massachusetts Anti-Slavery Society and the man who, in 1842, appeared before the legislative committee of the Massachusetts House of Representatives to support people protesting segregation in travel accommodations. By the following year, the segregation had stopped. With all this history sitting on her shoulders, Caroline French was prepared to become the city's first black heroine. She changed clothes with Rutha Blackburn, who walked out of the jail with Tabitha Lightfoot. The three women wept as they parted. Friends then whisked the disguised Rutha Blackburn across the Detroit River to Canada.

While taking breakfast to the prisoners, the deputy sheriff discovered the switch. He rushed over to the Steamboat Hotel to inform George French and Madison Lightfoot of the trick their wives had played. They were "a parcel of hell cats," the deputy sheriff said. The two men denied knowing anything about it. When Sheriff Wilson heard about Rutha Blackburn's escape, he threatened to send Caroline French to Kentucky as a substitute. It was no empty threat.

People in Louisville would have crowded the public square for a chance to watch Mrs. French sold as Rutha's stand-in. Had such a sale taken place, it might have resembled a nineteenth-century lynching with thousands of spectators yelling for blood or at least signs of fear. However, Caroline French's father, Cornelius Leonard Lenox, a free black man with land and political ties, threatened to intervene. Meanwhile, George French was able to appeal to General Charles Larned and obtain a writ of habeas corpus to halt Caroline

French's transfer to Kentucky. While out on bail, she fled to Canada and spent several months there. In the meantime, the Kentucky slave catchers shifted their attention to Thornton Blackburn, figuring it was better to take home half a prize than nothing.

On Monday, June 17, 1833, Thornton Blackburn stood at the door of the Detroit jail in leg irons, guarded by Sheriff Wilson and his deputy as he waited for transportation to the steamboat docks. He was scheduled to sail aboard the steamship *Ohio* to Cleveland at 4:00 P.M. from the Howard and Waterman's dock at the foot of Randolph Street. The sheriff had been warned that black Detroiters planned to rescue Thornton, but he held up his riding whip and announced that he could "scare every Nigger that would be there with this."

That afternoon, a crowd of blacks and mulattos armed with sticks, clubs, knives, pistols, swords and other weapons gathered around the jail on Gratiot Street between Farmer and Farrar, later the site of the downtown branch of the Detroit Public Library. They demanded Blackburn's release. Trying to cool their fire, Sheriff Wilson walked outside three times to talk to the mob, but they continued to hurl threats and brandish weapons. Blackburn then showed the same wiliness and boldness that had allowed him to escape from slavery. He volunteered to talk to the crowd, saying it wasn't worth having so much trouble on his account. The sheriff agreed and Blackburn strode to the front steps of the jail, where someone handed him a pistol. He pointed the cocked weapon at the deputy sheriff and cried: "Stand back, God damn you, or I will blow you through."

The deputy sheriff retreated into the jail, leaving the sheriff to face the mob alone. While Blackburn struggled with the sheriff for Blackburn's gun, the crowd shouted: "Shoot him, blow him through."

Blacks rushed from their hiding places, carrying clubs, knives, bayonets, pistols and swords. The leader was reportedly a one-armed "boss barber" named John Cook, a boss barber being a man who cut the hair of both blacks and whites. Some women carried stones in their handkerchiefs.

Some four hundred people, more than the entire black population of the Michigan territory, moved toward the jail. The *Detroit Courier* claimed that a large contingent of blacks had come over from Canada to take part in the uprising, including members of the "negro settlement near Malden, composed almost exclusively of fugitive slaves." An elderly woman carrying a stake wrapped with a white rag led the charge.

Lewis Austin half carried and half dragged Blackburn into the stagecoach that had been brought to the jail to transport Weir, Blackburn and the sheriff to the dock. As had probably been planned at the meeting at Willoughby's home, some women had removed the linchpin from the vehicle to disable it. Blackburn hid inside the disabled stagecoach. During the melee, an elderly black man called Daddy Grace in some accounts and Daddy Walker in others was forced to back his horse-drawn cart up to the jail steps. An elderly black woman known as Sleepy Polly, who had never before shown a flicker of life, grabbed Blackburn and dragged him into the cart. Meanwhile, the sheriff's teeth were knocked out and his skull fractured with a large stone. As the sheriff fell, he fired his pistol and someone clubbed him in the head, knocking him unconscious. In about a year, Sheriff Wilson died, apparently never recovering from his wounds.

The horse-drawn cart carrying Blackburn disappeared into the nearby woods. His escorts were Austin, Prince Williams, Peter Sands, Alexander Butler, John Lloyd and Madison Mason. The fugitives and his conspirators stopped in the woods long enough to remove Blackburn's leg irons and then rode on to the Detroit River. Just as Blackburn climbed into the boat at the Detroit River, someone gave him a gold watch so he could pay the boatman. He crossed the river to Canada where, in 1793, the government of Upper Canada, which mostly consisted of Ontario, had begun the process of freeing its slaves. It ruled that while those enslaved would remain so, any slave who entered the territory would become free. Within a decade, Lower Canada, including Quebec and the Maritimes, would pass similar legislation.

The Blackburns' escapes had repercussions that flowed on into the twentieth century, tearing apart old ways of life and creating new ones. In Canada, the Blackburn incident became the first test of an extradition treaty Upper Canada and the United States had signed in February 1833. Since escaping slavery was not a crime in Canada, other charges had to be brought against the Blackburns. They were accused of inciting a riot and arrested and jailed in Sandwich. The Territory of Michigan moved swiftly to extradite them. Acting governor Stevens T. Mason, born in Virginia and only twenty-two years old in 1833, sent all of the relevant documents to Sir John Colborne, lieutenant governor of the province of Upper Canada. The Canadian government refused to extradite Thornton and Rutha Blackburn. Lieutenant Governor Colborne argued that they had committed no crime punishable under Canadian law.

After their release from jail in Sandwich, the Blackburns decided to stay in Canada, where freedom was already on its feet and walking about. For a short time, they lived in Amherstburg on the Canadian side of the Detroit River, a well-known haven for fugitives. By the 1850s, in fact, Amherstburg would have such a large fugitive slave population that a longtime resident would compare them to the plague of frogs that rained on Egypt in Bible stories. However, in 1834, the year slavery officially ended in Canada, the Blackburns left Amherstburg. Given the notoriety of their case and the persistence of their Kentucky owners and pursuers, they must have realized they remained in danger in a riverfront community. Detroit steamboat owner Sylvester Atwood could have told them all about that. In the 1840s, slave catchers fooled Atwood, who was white, into taking them on a Detroit River cruise to Amherstburg, supposedly so they could lap up some sunshine. When he discovered they were hunting slaves, Atwood became so riled that he placed an advertisement in a newspaper describing how he had been hoodwinked. He also joined the antislavery movement. John "Daddy" Hall was another former slave who knew from personal experience that Amherstburg wasn't always safe. Slave catchers had stolen him from his home in Amherstburg and sold him in Kentucky. In the 1840s, he escaped to

Canada but didn't stop until he reached Owen Sound, one hundred miles northwest of Toronto.

The Blackburns headed for Toronto, a center of black culture in Canada West until the 1850s. Toronto's black community supported church-related groups, literary societies, temperance groups, the Upper Canada Anti-Slavery Society and the *Provincial Freeman*, a militant black abolitionist newspaper. Moreover, many black immigrants had houses and businesses. Neither Thornton nor Rutha could write their names, but they still had plenty of hustle and shine. Thornton became a waiter at Osgoode Hall, and the couple built a small frame house and a barn on the outskirts of town on what would become the front playground of Sackville Street School. The area was just marshland then and a forest with a few streets snaking through it and a garden west of the house. The very poor Irish would move to this area later, but the Blackburns preceded them, moving there in 1834, the year the city was incorporated. In 1836, Thornton came up with an idea that would make him wealthy. He had noticed public transportation in cities such as Montreal and believed Toronto would embrace it. He got the pattern for a cab from Montreal and had a carriage built, painting it red and yellow and turning it into a cab for hire. It became the first cab company in Upper Canada, but others soon sprang up. Thornton parked his wooden carriage drawn by a single horse near St. James Cathedral at Church and Trinity. In a city where masses of mud often clogged the streets and where only the rich owned carriages and horses, the idea of renting a cab quickly caught on.

On the surface the Blackburns lived what looked like a conventional life, but their Detroit adventures left an indelible mark on both Thornton and Rutha, who changed her name to Lucie in Canada. The experience of being a fugitive slave marked for shipment back to Kentucky was not something they could shrug off or put behind them. Not when hundreds of people had risked their businesses and lives for them. Not when blood had spurted and fires had flared up in their names. When their taxi business succeeded, they remained in the same small frame house, buying the land it sat on and building a small barn for their cab and horse. They lived simply, gardening, hunting, fishing and pouring much of their company's profits into black self-help movements. When the North American Convention against slavery met at St. Lawrence Hall in downtown Toronto in September 1851, Thornton Blackburn attended it as a delegate. The city directories in Toronto for the years 1862 to 1890 call Thornton a "gentleman," suggesting he no longer had to work for a living. He had retired from the taxi business in the 1860s. However, the cool nerve he had displayed during the Detroit uprisings never left him. In the 1840s, he reportedly returned to Kentucky to rescue his mother, an almost unbelievable event considering the circumstances surrounding his own dramatic escape from Kentucky slavers. Yet, according to historian Karolyn Smardz, the family plot in Toronto contains the remains of a woman named Libby Blackburn, who was eighty when she died in 1855.

When Thornton Blackburn died in 1890, he left his wife not only his property, but seventeen thousand dollars. He was buried in the Toronto Necropolis Cemetery, and his monument bears the inscription: "Blessed are the dead which die in the Lord." His wife sold their home and moved to another part of the city. By the time the woman known as Lucie Blackburn died in 1895, the Blackburn money was gone. And for many years, Canada forgot all about this childless couple who couldn't write their own names but had traveled so far and achieved so much. However, their legacy came to light in 1985 when a group of professional and amateur archeologists, many of them schoolchildren, dug up the schoolyard at the corner of Eastern Avenue and Sumach Street on the edge of central Toronto, searching for remnants of the Blackburns' house. By that time, stories about the Blackburns had appeared in Detroit magazines and newspapers. The excavation on the grounds of the Sackville Street School in Toronto where the Blackburns' home once stood turned up no fancy silver or other glittery artifacts, no sign that the couple had spent any time hosting dinner parties and sampling the high life. Ironically, historical markers in Louisville, the city from which the Blackburns escaped, now honor them. (Similar markers in Louisville also claim that "Slave traders were often social outcasts avoided by all but fellow traders.")

Meanwhile, in Detroit, the passions and protests roused by the Blackburn riots produced lasting results. White mobs rioted all over America in the 1830s, but the Blackburn riot was Detroit's first black uprising. It seemed to go on and on. On July 11, 1833, someone set the Detroit jail on fire, but it was quickly extinguished. Four days later, the stables adjacent to the jail burned down and a hundred fifty dollars' worth of horses were destroyed. On July 25, Marshall Chapin, mayor of Detroit, asked Secretary of War Lewis Cass to send a detachment of troops to Detroit "until the excitement has subsided." A citizens committee appointed to investigate the Blackburn riot recommended, among other things, a 9:00 P.M. curfew, the maintaining of city guards and the establishment of an efficient police force. However, the city didn't really improve its police force until after the infamous Faulkner riots of 1863. In that case, a black man named William Faulkner was tried and convicted of raping two girls, one white, one black, and sentenced to life in prison. When a white mob tried to lynch him, police fired into the crowd, killing one and wounding six others. The mob then swept into the near east side, attacking blacks at random and burning buildings. Two victims of the violence later died. Several whites tried to disperse the mob, but it took federal troops to end the violence. In 1870, Faulkner was finally released when his accusers admitted they had lied.

However, after the Blackburn riots, patrols kept watch on Detroit and rounded up all blacks on the streets and in the woods. Black people weren't even allowed to dock their boats. Some thirty were imprisoned. Some had to leave Detroit and others worked off their sentences by repairing the streets. Daddy Grace worked for six months. Accused of knowing who gave Blackburn a pistol, Madison Lightfoot spent three days in jail but refused to talk. George French headed for Windsor, Ontario, and Tabitha Lightfoot was fined for being a prime mover in the riot. Many others sought sanctuary in Canada until it was safe to return. Some Detroit employers who had previously hired black men and women refused to do so. Historian Norman McRae called it "Negrophobia." When a citizens' commission issued its report on the incident, it noted, "Neither [black Detroiters'] habits, nor their morals, with a few exceptions, make them a safe or desirable addition to our population."

In many ways, though, the Blackburn riots, like the fires in a foundry, welded Detroit's fledgling black community into something stronger and steelier. In a sense, the riot created the cohesion, the sense of coming together, that makes a community. Three years after the riot, Tabitha and Madison Lightfoot, Caroline and George French and other participants in that disturbance helped found Second Baptist Church of Detroit, the oldest black Baptist church in the state and the city's major stop on the Underground Railroad. Originally, Second Baptist's founders belonged to the mostly white First Baptist Church of Detroit, established by Baptist missionaries from New York State. Blacks had joined First Baptist as early as 1832, when William Butler was baptized two days after becoming a member. However, black members grew weary of such indignities as being confined to the balcony rather than being allowed to sit downstairs and of not being allowed to vote in the business meetings of the church. Madison Lightfoot, later ordained as an elder in Zion Baptist Church, was the chief spokesman when blacks confronted First Baptist's elders and told them black members wished to leave. In 1836, thirteen black Detroiters asked for letters of dismissal from First Baptist Church so they could organize their own church. They also submitted a petition to the state legislature to form the Society of Second Baptist Church, formally organized in 1839. In 1839, the church established the first school for African-American children and its first pastor, the Reverend William Monroe, became known as an antislavery activist. Second Baptist also would spawn thirty or more other black churches, including St. Matthew's Episcopal, founded by Reverend Monroe, and Zion Baptist, where George French became a deacon.

In the next three decades, a cadre of black leaders willing to risk their lives to help escaping fugitives would emerge in Detroit, all of them heirs to the Blackburns' legacy. They would include Monroe; Benjamin Willoughby, at whose house the Blackburn plot was hatched; his son-in-law, William Lambert, a free black man from New Jersey; George DeBaptiste, a Virginian who had run an Underground Railroad station in Madison, Indiana, and who owned a ship, the *T. Whitney;* William Webb, a light-skinned black man who passed for white to spy on slave catchers in taverns and pass on information to the Underground Railroad; and Obadiah Wood, a barber from New York.

Others, black and white, Detroiters and Canadians, would join the struggle, including Seymour Finney, a white abolitionist who arrived in Detroit from western New York in 1834. He owned a hotel and livery stable. According to legend, he hid fugitives in his stable while entertaining the men pursuing them in his hotel.

Just as the Blackburns remained antislavery activists after moving to Toronto, Second Baptist remained a major force in the struggle for equal rights long after slavery ended. After the Civil War, the church played a key role in helping freed slaves find jobs and homes in Detroit.

And in a February 1957 letter to the Reverend A. A. Banks Jr., then pastor of the church, civil rights leader Dr. Martin Luther King Jr. wrote: "On returning to my office I found your letter with the enclosed check of one thousand five hundred fifty-seven dollars and thirty-six cents ($1,557.36) from Second Baptist Church on my desk. Words are inadequate for me to express my appreciation and the appreciation of the whole Negro citizenry of Montgomery for this great contribution. It comes at a time of real financial need. I think I am correct in saying that Second Baptist Church has contributed more to the work of the Montgomery Improvement Association than any single church in America. You can never know what this means to us. . . ."

Americans have rioted for all kinds of reasons, including winning or losing a sports game, drunkenness, rumors of rape and racial incidents. Unlike those incidents, the riot triggered by Thornton and Rutha Blackburn's imminent return to slavery did more than ignite fires and fights. It changed the Blackburns' lives and the lives of people in at least two cities, establishing an enduring tradition of black self-help and struggle.

6

THE SLAVE WHO KNEW HIS NAME

Hope wasn't just alive, it was green and growing, spreading ripples of springtime joy. A white Underground Railroad conductor, a man who'd single-handedly stopped two lynchings, had set out for Alabama to rescue the enslaved family of a black man called Peter. But all too quickly, green hope died on crackly, dried-up vines. Seth Concklin, Peter's supposed savior, was dead.

Concklin's body had washed up on the shores of the Cumberland River near Paducah, Kentucky, his head bashed in and chains still gripping his arms and legs. It looked like a plain case of murder served up raw and bloody on a cold plate. Meanwhile, Peter's family had been carried back to Alabama, sailing down the same rivers they'd just rowed up. His wife, Vina, was back in the hands of the men who'd tried to rape her and who had whipped her until it damaged her brain. His three children were back in the place where eight of their siblings had died. And the man who owned the family celebrated the return of his slaves by declaring that a slave stealer like Concklin had gotten just what he deserved.

Yet Peter belonged to a black family that had clung to its history, nourished by the belief that they were special. Because of that belief, his father had purchased freedom, his mother had chased it until she caught it and Peter had gained his own liberty through a daring combination of bravery, hard work and trickery. He was not just a former slave, not just a man once known as Peter Gist and Peter Friedman. His name, he had just discovered, was Peter Still, and that made all the difference. He would restore his family's hopes himself. That was what people with proud names did.

Enslaved blacks usually bore the names of the people who owned them, trading one label, one brand, for another. Depriving people of lasting names made it easier to see them as things, as impersonal as plates or spoons. In the beginning, runaway slave advertisements identified fugitive slaves by tribes: they were Congo people, Mandingo people, Ashantis, members of the Poulard nation, Ibos. But after a time, most were known simply as Cuffy or Hercules, Peter or Celia, Tom or Sal, sometimes followed by a last name and sometimes not.

Africans became jigs and jigaboos, darkies and negars, niggers and Negroes. They became Black Sambos and coloreds, maroons and Melungeons, creoles, Geechees and Gullahs. They were Redbones and high yellows, high-browns and shines, coons and spooks, bucks and boys. They were spades and mammies, Griffs and Moors, mulattos and quadroons, octoroons and Carmel Indians. They were the Ethiopians in the woodpile, the Abyssinians in the chimney, the pickaninnies in the watermelon patch, tragic mulattos or black as the ace of spades. But they were invisible men and invisible women, people whose names, according to writer James Baldwin, nobody knew.

But Peter Still had a name that it had taken him forty years to find, a name that suggested slow-moving streams and calm spirits. It showed up in countless stories about men and women who ran for freedom, who sheltered runaways, who healed the sick with sassafras and snakeroot, who thrilled crowds with their words and music. The name didn't really come from Africa, but the people who wore it claimed an African prince had handed them the garment centuries ago. He wanted them to wrap it around them so they'd remember to walk like kings and queens in their new home.

According to family legends and some records, the Stills trace their roots back to the early seventeenth century, when a prince from Guinea, West Africa, and his clan came up the Delaware River to Cooper's Landing in South Jersey. At that time, Guinea referred to the area extending from modern Ghana to Nigeria. Between 1670 and 1700 large numbers of slaves came to America from this region, which was torn by infighting and religious revolts. The prince, according to the story, was an indentured servant, which meant he would be freed after working off the price of his passage for a certain number of years. He came ashore near where Gloucester City now stands in a section of Camden County known as Guineatown. Freed slaves of the Hugg family had established it on land provided by their former masters. The Guinea prince and his clan worked off their indebtedness and mixed and intermarried with the Lenape Indians in South Jersey and the surrounding areas. In the late eighteenth century, the clan became slaves. "After the Revolutionary War, that's when they made us slaves," says Clarence Still Jr., the family historian.

The Guinea prince's descendants were scattered, some taken to Maryland, some kept in the New Jersey area near the Delaware River. But the prince supposedly gave his people something no one could strip away, a sense of shared history and a last name that sounded like Steel but, according to some sources, later became Still. No one knows why he chose that name, but the story and its power endured. Over the years, it would be murmured, spoken, shouted, embraced, celebrated thousands of times and engraved on just as many granite headstones.

Because of that name and the history attached to it, Peter's father, Levin Still, found it impossible to hold back his feelings the day his owner, Saunders Griffin, asked if he were happy.

"I will die before I submit to the yoke," Levin allegedly answered.

Griffin agreed to let his high-stepping slave go free for "a small sum" of money rather than possibly spread rebellion among the other slaves. By working on Sundays, holidays and rest periods, Levin gradually saved several hundred dollars. In 1804, New Jersey governor Joseph Bloomfield signed an act making every child born of a slave free, but such a child must remain a servant of the mother's master until age twenty-five for boys or twenty-one for girls. Levin and his wife, Sidney, vowed to go there after hearing this news through the slave rumor mill. However, after buying his way out of freedom, Levin had no money left to free his wife and children. But Sidney loved him too much to let him leave without her. She had been born and raised by her mother on a plantation near the Eastern shore of the Chesapeake Bay in Maryland. As a young girl she'd watched her drunken slave master shoot her father through the head. Right then, she'd known that, no matter what it took, she would not die a slave either. And now, as Levin's wife, she, too, had a name coated with power, a name that meant something.

The first time Sidney ran away to join her husband, she took all of her children with her, dragging, pushing, shushing and coaxing them through forests and swamps, foraging for berries, heading for South Jersey. However, within a month after a family in Greenwich took the family to Levin, slave catchers snatched her and her young ones from their cabin one night while Levin was away. After that, her owner put Sidney under careful watch, locking her in a garret, where she sewed. Sidney sang her way out of her cage. She filled the small room with her rich, thick, come-to-Jesus contralto, singing loud enough to storm heaven. She sang one praise-God Methodist song after another until her owner finally became convinced she'd gotten over the urge to follow Levin. Once her master unlocked her prison, Sidney sent word along the Underground Railroad that she was ready to run again. This time, she left her sons behind, believing her husband could arrange to steal them later.

Her boys, Peter and Levin, were just six and eight years old, respectively, on that day in 1804 when Sidney bent over their bed for one final nighttime kiss, a kiss they couldn't feel and wouldn't remember unless it somehow floated into their dreams. She left them in the care of her mother, also a slave. She took her daughters with her, fearing what might happen to girls left alone on a plantation. Her husband, Levin, had sent her a message with instructions telling her where to join him in South Jersey.

During the day, Sidney and her children hid in high grass or in grain fields, living on whatever they could pluck or scoop up. At last they reached an Underground Railroad station near Smyrna, Delaware. In the dark of night, they most likely boarded a boat that carried a blue light above a yellow light as identification. In the middle of the Delaware Bay they probably were transferred to a New Jersey boat lit in the same way. They made the turbulent thirty-mile trip across the wide waters of the Delaware Bay to the shore town of Greenwich, an old Quaker village of twisted and snarled buttonwood trees and docks bordering the Cohansey River. From there, they traveled to a black settlement called Springtown, where men clutching rifles patrolled many entrances to the town. From Springtown, Sidney and her daughter Mahala made it to the Pine Barrens of Burlington County, New Jersey, Levin going back to pick up the ailing Kitturah, who had been left with a family along the way. Sidney changed her name to Charity, and the couple spent the rest of their lives among the swamps, sand and scraggly pines of the Barrens.

But the two boys Sidney had left sleeping in their beds in Maryland awakened to a nightmare. Not understanding slavery or slave escapes, they couldn't figure out why their mother had disappeared. Nor could they understand why, on a hot afternoon in 1804, they were flung into a flatboat traveling to Lexington, Kentucky, a city that revolved around tobacco, horses, hemp, whiskey, lumber and slaves. They were certain they had been kidnapped and for years that was the story they told. Actually, their owner, angry at the boys' runaway mother, had sold them to a slave trader named Kincaid. On the boat, Peter's grandmother took Peter in her arms and told him to tell people at the plantation to which he was traveling that he had been stolen from a free place near the Delaware River.

Peter held on to the old woman's words, and they became his life, his truth. For a long time, he believed he really had been stolen.

For a long time, he longed for a home he had never seen but thought he remembered, Philadelphia, near the Delaware Bay.

Kincaid sold the boys to John Fisher, the owner of a brickyard in Lexington, Kentucky. They worked in pairs, carting off three thousand bricks a day. In 1818, Peter and Levin left Kentucky and became the property of Levi Gist of Bainbridge, Alabama. They were part of Gist's inheritance, along with a bowl and pitcher, ten sacks of coffee, a barrel of sperm oil and a cherry bedspread. As the boys traveled to the Deep South, they saw unprecedented poverty, including white people living in shanties. In spite of his harsh life, Peter decided to discipline himself, abstaining from liquor, tobacco and profanity. And, like his father, he saved every penny he managed to earn on the side.

His brother, Levin, died at age thirty-four, but Peter survived a whole series of owners, some kindly, some brutal. He worked mostly as a hired-out slave, paying his master a fee and putting aside a little money. He was hired by a pastor to take care of a church; hired as a cook at a Whig convention in Nashville; hired to a bookseller in Tuscumbia, Alabama, in 1846, who allowed him to keep some of his earnings; hired to a land merchant. He whitewashed, cooked, dug graves, took care of stores, cleaned, built fires, waited tables, ran errands, all the time looking for someone he could trust with the plan he'd conceived for his freedom.

When he was twenty-five, he married fifteen-year-old Lavinia, known as Vina, whose wedding dress was a white frock covered with black patches. She had been enslaved in Edgecombe County, North Carolina, and now worked for Bernard McKiernan of Florence, Alabama, near the Gist plantation; he was one of the wealthier planters in Florence, where slaves produced cotton, corn, wheat, rye, oats and wool. Vina had been beaten by her mistress for leaving a silver ladle in the kitchen overnight. She repeatedly fought off sexual advances from McKiernan, who had brought his family to Alabama when the country was inhabited by Indians and opened a cotton plantation. Vina also tussled with another would-be lover, the overseer, Bill Simms, who supervised the slaves' work. Angered by her refusals, Simms beat her in the head with a bullwhip, causing an inflammation of the brain. She would bear eleven children and watch eight of them die. And like the other slave women, she would pick cotton while leaving a baby in her cabin with bread or a little mush on a rag on its finger.

As the years passed, Peter kept looking for an opportunity to purchase his freedom. It was a chancy enterprise. In 1834, Alabama had passed a law saying that a person who wanted to free a slave was supposed to announce his intentions in a newspaper and then apply to a local court for permission. A person freeing a slave also risked being hounded out of Alabama and branded an abolitionist.

In 1847, Peter found the man he believed would help him pull off his plan to buy himself. He had been hired out to work for Joseph Friedman in Tuscumbia. Friedman had a store and a younger brother named Isaac. Peter was drawn to Joseph Friedman after hearing him making some chance remark that suggested he sympathized with suffering people. Peter asked the Friedman brothers to help him buy himself, and they agreed, urging Peter to proceed slowly. Peter, then almost fifty, began pretending that he was broken down and ailing, his juice gone. Whenever his owner was around, he would slump, coughing and walking with a stoop. Finally, his owner agreed to sell him to Joseph Friedman for five hundred dollars. By 1848, Peter had saved up two hundred and ten dollars. Between January 26, 1849, and April 16, 1850, Peter gave Joseph Friedman five hundred dollars in five installments. On April 16, 1850, Friedman gave Peter a bill of sale and his freedom. Peter promised his wife and children that he would buy their freedom, too. Meanwhile, one Friedman brother would care for the Alabama store while the other one traveled to Ohio, bringing along Peter, who would receive his free papers at a Cincinnati courthouse.

Peter left Ohio with eighty dollars in his pocket and a worn carpetbag. He traveled by steamer up the Ohio River to Pittsburgh and then by stagecoach to Philadelphia, America's first capital city and home of the country's first bank, first hospital, first daily newspaper, first public library, first public grammar school, first U.S. flag and first antislavery society. He knew from old stories that he should look for his family in the Delaware Bay area. By chance he met a minister named Byas, who took him to the Philadelphia Anti-Slavery Office. There, the man then known as Peter Friedman told his story to a young black man. As the young man listened to Peter's incredible story, his face began to change. The details were so familiar, and the names were names he knew as well as his own. The young man also had a mother who had been named Sidney before she became Charity and a father named Levin, and he had grown up hearing stories about the two boys his mother had left behind, losing them to slavery. Moreover, the man calling himself Peter Friedman looked exactly like the young man's own mother.

"By this time I perceived that a wonderful development was about to be made," the young man wrote. "My feelings became unutterable, although I endeavored to surpress [*sic*] them with much effort, but the fact that this Peter was one of my long absent brothers stared me too full in the face to gainsay or dispute the evidence for one moment."

The young man was William Still, the youngest of the eighteen children Charity Levin bore after escaping from Maryland. After moving to Philadelphia in 1844, he had worked as a mail clerk and janitor for the Pennsylvania Society for the Abolition of Slavery, becoming chairman of the General Vigilance Committee in 1852. He had built a network of safe hiding places for fugitives, raised funds for them and carefully monitored the activity of slave catchers in the city. Under his direction, the committee aided nearly eight hundred fugitives by the start of the Civil War. However, the former Peter Gist/Peter Friedman found it difficult to believe that he was Peter Still and had stumbled upon a relative so easily. But little by little, as he met one family member after another, he had to accept the truth. His mother was still alive, and his five brothers and three sisters were comfortable. Charity and Levin had built a life for themselves in South Jersey, but they never forgot the two boys they'd left behind and never stopped sharing the tale with other family members.

Newspapers all over the world ran stories about Peter Still, calling him the "Man Who Bought Himself." Seth Concklin, a white abolitionist, came across a copy of the *Pennsylvania Freeman* newspaper containing Peter Still's story and read that Peter had a wife and children in slavery and would "as soon go out of the world as not to go back and do all he could for them." Concklin volunteered to travel on the Underground Railroad and bring Peter's wife, Vina, and their children out of Alabama. For most people, even Underground Railroad conductors, this would have been a bold act. But Concklin had always displayed a curious blend of caution and recklessness, stinginess and generosity, responsibility and daring.

After the death of his father, the New York–born Concklin supported his mother and sisters as a peddler, squeezing all he could from every penny. To help the family make ends meet, he once arranged for all of them to live in what was considered a haunted house, staying there rent-free for a year to prove the house wasn't swirling with spirits. He was a man who could walk fifty miles in a day and row a boat all night without resting. He was a man who squeezed pennies but would give his last dollar to a person with empty pockets. Once he became an abolitionist, he took that all the way, too.

Looking at history from a twenty-first-century perspective, it is easy to conclude that the abolitionists were right and the slaveholders wrong. Yet abolitionists made up only a small minority of nineteenth-century America, clinging to beliefs that most Americans either opposed or ignored. Some white abolitionists acted purely out of religious conviction, not caring for the actual company of blacks. Yet in both Syracuse and Rochester, Seth Concklin had shown a commitment to extreme actions, stopping two black men from being lynched by drawing the mob's anger on himself. In Springfield, Illinois, he aided fugitives escaping on the Underground Railroad, but seldom acted in concert with others. Liberating Peter Still's family was the perfect adventure for a man who had drifted in and out of a Shaker community that believed in Christian socialism, the gift of many tongues, prophecy and visions, communion with the dead, power over physical disease, everybody working for the common good and women having the same power and authority as men.

Peter Still would have preferred working and saving the money to buy his family's freedom just as he had worked and saved to buy his own. However, his brother William opposed paying slave owners for liberty. Peter finally agreed to Concklin's plan even though escaping the Deep South meant traveling thousands of danger-crammed miles. There were some safe houses even in the Deep South, such as stockyard owner Jacob Burkle's house on the outskirts of Memphis, only one-quarter mile from the Mississippi River. However, Concklin would have to provide his own havens. Peter gave him an apron of Vina's that he had brought with him and some traveling money. Vina would recognize the apron and know that Peter had sent Concklin. After memorizing directions to McKiernan's plantation, Concklin set out alone from Philadelphia early in January 1851. He had Vina's apron in his pocket. After making contact with Peter's family, he stitched together a plan that would take the family to Canada.

While buying a rowboat in Cincinnati, Concklin adopted the identity of a Southern slave owner, calling himself John H. Miller. Traveling in rowboats and on steamboats, he returned to Alabama. He met with the Stills while getting his shoes mended and made the arrangements for their escape. He took Vina, Peter Jr., Levin Jr. and Catharine away in a skiff and for seven nights they rowed, starting at the Tennessee River, passing Eastport, Mississippi, arriving at Paducah, following the Ohio River to the Illinois-Indiana border and then heading up the Wabash River. At one point a boatman ordered Concklin and his party to stop. When they didn't, someone fired guns at their boat. On Sunday morning, March 23, 1851, they landed at New Harmony, Indiana, and journeyed to several resting places. A black man named Charles Grier offered them his hospitality and then took them sixteen miles to David Stormont, who lived near Princeton, Indiana.

Southern sympathizers and slave hunters watched Stormont's log house, suspecting him of running an Underground Railroad station. When asked if he had helped runaways, he always replied that he clothed the naked and fed the hungry. Sometimes when he returned from church, men followed him. It was probably good that they kept their distance since Stormont took a gun as well as a Bible to church. Mrs. Stormont also kept a teakettle of boiling water handy, intending to blind anyone who tried to enter her house.

After leaving the Stormont house, the Still family was captured on Friday, March 28, by seven men on horseback. They were within thirty miles of Vincennes, the oldest still-existing lasting settlement in Indiana and the place from which William Henry Harrison, who was proslavery in the early 1800s, once governed the vast Indiana Territory.

An April 9, 1851, an account in the *Philadelphia Public Ledger* summarized the whole story in three sentences: "At Vincennes, In. on Saturday last a white man and four negroes were arrested. The negroes belong to B. McKiernan, of South Florence, Ala., and the man who was running them off calls himself John H. Miller. The prisoners were taken charge of by the Marshal of Evansville."

Concklin refused to leave the family, remaining in the wagon as slave catchers drove the fugitives twenty-five miles south to the jail in Vincennes. Concklin was free to go, but he remained nearby, visiting the fugitives every day and trying to reassure them. After McKiernan offered a six-hundred-dollar reward for the "thief" who had taken his slaves, Concklin was arrested, too. When McKiernan arrived, the five prisoners were taken from jail, Vina's sons and Concklin in chains, and placed on a coach to Evansville, Indiana. There they boarded a steamboat and started down the Ohio River for Alabama. Near Paducah, Kentucky, Seth Concklin disappeared from the steamboat, possibly while McKiernan was guarding him alone. His chained, mutilated body soon washed up on the shores of the Cumberland River. Some claimed he had killed himself, leaping into the river to avoid standing trial for slave stealing in a courtroom thick with Alabama hate. Others insisted he'd tried to escape from slave catchers and tumbled into the river's mouth, drowning in a tangle of panic and chains.

After hearing various explanations for Concklin's death—including accidental drowning and suicide—the Reverend R. N. Johnston, a Concklin acquaintance, decided he'd probably been hit in the head and thrown overboard. In his memoirs, Johnston wrote:

> I regarded the last opinion as the most plausible. On the side of his head was a very severe wound, probably a broken skull. The body was taken to a sand bank on the shore, not far distant, and buried in his clothes and irons as before death. All kinds of conjectures and reports were afloat. . . . All were fast asleep, and none could testify to the facts that would condemn the murder.

Meanwhile, McKiernan promptly sent William Still a letter offering to free Peter's family for five thousand dollars. The sum seemed so unimaginable nobody thought he could raise it. But he did. In November 1852, Peter began acquainting himself with the difficulties of fund-raising for freedom. It was a crowded field, full of people with stories, most of them true but some false. A Syracuse newspaper even warned people against "colored men" who were supposedly running a scam, soliciting funds for themselves instead of enslaved relatives. All the same, Peter Still began making the rounds of Northeast churches and abolitionists. He told his story. He passed out letters of introduction from leading abolitionists. He collected checks. He told his story again and again, talking to anyone who could listen, including Harriet Beecher Stowe, author of *Uncle Tom's Cabin*, and abolitionist William Lloyd Garrison. According to copies of his fund-raising receipts, he raised funds in Bath, Maine; in Portsmouth, New Hampshire; in Norwich, Connecticut; in Syracuse, New York; in Toronto; in Boston and many other places in between. Sometimes he collected as little as forty dollars, and sometimes he collected as much as $355 in one visit. It had to be a tiring and sometimes heart-wrenching time.

Finally, after two and a half years, he returned to Philadelphia with the money to negotiate for the release of his children. He was near collapse, but "with a force of affection, a perseverance, an earnestness of faith rarely seen," as the *National Era* put it, he finally arranged for the release of his family.

Early on Saturday morning, December 31, 1854, Peter Still stood at a wharf in Cincinnati, waiting for the arrival of the steamboat *The Northerner*. The boat docked and Peter's wife, Vina, stood in the doorway, clutching her black shawl with one hand and waving to him with the other. His children were there, too, ready for the carriage ride to the Friedman home and hot breakfast before an open fire. According to newspaper accounts, one son was twenty-seven and the other twenty-four. The articles don't mention the age of the Stills' daughter, Catharine. For the first time in her life, Vina enjoyed having someone serve her. Peter and Vina Still and their children headed east on January 3, 1855, reaching Philadelphia on January 10. Shortly after that, they came to Peter's mother's house in Burlington, New Jersey. By then Charity Still was in her seventies.

She had never thought she'd see her son again. Now here he was, standing proud.

Peter and Vina Still and their family lived briefly with relatives and then found work in a Burlington boardinghouse. This enabled them to buy a ten-acre vegetable farm in Burlington near Peter's mother. Young Levin Jr. became a blacksmith in Beverly, New Jersey, and Peter Jr. became a house servant and carriage driver in New Hope, Pennsylvania. Peter and Vina were among the eleven organizers of Burlington's Second Baptist Church, the oldest black Baptist church in the county. Kate Pickard, a teacher in the female seminary at Tuscumbia, Alabama, recounted their experiences in a book published in 1856 titled *The Kidnapped and the Ransomed, Being the Personal Recollections of Peter Still and His Wife, "Vina," after Forty Years of Slavery*. The *New York Daily Times* recommended it to "all those who really desire to fathom the heights and depths of that Iniquity which is threatening the destruction of our Republic." A *National Era* review of the book called it and other similar works proof that there was no truth to the "foul slander that the colored man cannot be elevated. . . ." Unfortunately,

Pickard's book was written while slavery still existed and the Still family remained in danger. To protect Sidney Still, who had changed her name to Charity, the book never talked about her flight to freedom and repeated the falsehood that Peter and Levin were free black children who had been kidnapped near Philadelphia and sold into slavery. Variations of that story still show up in modern history books.

Peter dedicated the book to Levin, the brother who didn't survive their years in exile and confusion, and to "all the brave-hearted men and women, who like him have fallen . . . and who now lie in nameless, unknown graves."

His dedication was a potent reminder that for every Charity, Levin and Peter Still who managed to snatch freedom, there were many more who failed. The Stills never succeeded in ransoming Peter's grandson, Peter, although a June 1855 letter noted that the once sickly baby had survived its illness and that he was "a perfect picture of [his grandfather, Peter]."

The Still story, a tale of extraordinary togetherness and achievement, continues. Today the family claims more than three thousand members, including athletes and inventors, artists and politicians. Though not all family members are professionals, they have racked up many achievements that would have made the Guinea prince proud.

Ephraim J. Still was a mayor of Lawnside, New Jersey, a one-square-mile black-owned and black-governed borough. At various times, it was known as Snow Hill and Free Haven, a refuge for newly freed blacks and runaways set up on land owned by a Quaker abolitionist and sold to blacks on long terms. It was about a mile from Guineatown, where the land was too sandy for farming; people would walk to Snow Hill or Free Haven to plant and farm. Nowadays, Lawnside, the name it gained in 1928, is a place where older people remember turning sweet potato vines over with little sticks so the sun could reach both sides and that of the forty-seven men who volunteered to fight in the Civil War, forty-seven came back.

One of Peter Still's brothers, Dr. James Still, wooed his first wife by learning a handful of songs and singing them whenever he went courting. He was a self-taught doctor who had only six months of schooling and was nineteen before he learned addition. Yet people, black and white, came from miles away to see the herb-using doctor in Medford, New Jersey, once he became famous for curing hip disease, cancer and other ailments. Many of his medicines were herbal cures using sassafras root, horehound, catnip, bloodroot, skunk cabbage, saffron, Virginia snakeroot and pleurisy root, most far gentler than the cure-or-kill remedies of his time. He had begun practicing to be a doctor while still a child, using slivers of pine bark for lancets and spittle for viruses. At the time, the family was so poor that James once snatched a piece of meat from a cat's mouth and ate it, determined not to let the cat steal his dinner. However, when he died he was the third largest landowner in Medford and had two sons who became doctors.

William Still, born in 1821 near Medford in Burlington County, became a famous Underground Railroad conductor in Philadelphia, sheltering thousands of fugitives in his home. His wife, Letitia, mended and cooked for the fugitives. His miraculous reunion with his brother, Peter, who died in 1868, inspired him to write a book called *The Underground Rail Road*, which contained stories and sketches of hundreds of fugitives who had passed through Still's home. He hoped it would help other people find their relatives. Still also became a successful businessman, investing in coal mining and opening a store handling new and used stoves. By 1867, his business was flourishing, enabling him to send his daughter Caroline to private schools and Oberlin College. At the time of his death on July 14, 1902, his estate was worth between $75,000 and $100,000, according to the *Afro-American* newspaper.

Dr. Caroline Still Wiley Anderson was among the first black Philadelphians to become a physician and one of the first female physicians in Pennsylvania. William and Letitia Still's daughter Frances became one of Philadelphia's first kindergarten teachers.

Their son William W. became a public accountant and lawyer, while another son, Robert, became a journalist and print shop owner.

Some twentieth-century Stills became stars, too. Art Still, a Camden High School graduate, became an all-pro defensive end for the Kansas City Chiefs. Valerie Still was a female basketball star who played in Europe and held an all-time career scoring record at the University of Kentucky. Cecil Still, author, herbalist and retired professor of biochemistry at Rutgers University, developed a natural pesticide; Winifred Still Davis became an opera soprano. Noted classical composer William Grant Still was a distant relative. Lewis Still was a flight instructor for the 99th Pursuit Squadron, one of the groups that made up the famed black World War II pilots known as the Tuskegee Airmen.

It was Dr. James Still who began the tradition of holding annual Still family reunions: he invited all of his brothers and sisters to his house. Such gatherings became all-important in the post–Civil War years when people began holding reunions and homecomings to preserve the history of families shredded, scattered and renamed during slavery. From 1861 through 1870, former slaves even placed information-wanted ads in the AME *Christian Recorder* newspaper. They sought their kin, but didn't describe them, knowing their appearance had changed. They talked about places, owners' names, incidents. The ads were supposed to be read in AME churches throughout the country. Some explicitly stated that their families had been torn because some members escaped before the Civil War.

James Still didn't call for his first reunion until 1870. "The Civil War was over in 1865, but the hostility was not over," says Clarence Still Jr. "In 1870, it was felt it was safe enough to have a reunion, call the family together."

Stills continue annually to share their stories and triumphs and celebrate the power of family traditions and names. They hold two or three reunions every year. Some of them say the experiences of their ancestors help them keep their lives in perspective, realizing their hardships don't compare with the hardships that earlier generations faced. Others say being a Still means maintaining close family bonds. "The primary effect our family history and my parents' teachings have had on me is to understand and appreciate that family is all-important," said Alfred C. Fisher, whose paternal grandmother was Susan Still (Fisher) of Sadlertown, New Jersey, and, later, Lawnside.

In 1855, William Gaines, an ex-slave from Virginia, bought his wife's freedom and moved with her to Marquette in Michigan's copper- and iron-rich Upper Peninsula. Photo courtesy of the Marquette County Historical Society.

7

FOOTPRINTS IN THE SNOW

It was just "nigger nonsense," young schoolteacher Henry Hobart huffed when he learned that four "darkies" planned to put on a show in the copper-mining town of Clifton, Michigan. "A person must keep silence in my position, but it is hard to do it sometimes," Hobart wrote in his journal in July 1863. "There is a nigger show at the hall this evening & William Pemberthy [one of Hobart's students] who is black as one and acts like one is delighted."

Hobart, who came from Vermont, liked teaching in the Lake Superior–bordering mining village of Clifton, but all sorts of things, large and small, chipped away at his joy and shattered his peace. His hate list included the Confederate army, drinkers, show-offs, "poor, snarling, sore-eyed . . . traitors," slavery, late mail, late newspapers, meatless meals, old molasses, filthy butter, breakfasts of dry wheat bread and water, cooks who served duck feet and duck heads and, of course, minstrel shows. It is not known how many Clifton residents plunked down their quarters to see the show that steamed up the scholarly teacher; yet many were probably only too happy to soak up a few hours of black prancing and dancing.

By the early 1860s, black entertainers, saloonkeepers, plasterers, cooks, servants, sailors, hatmakers, barbers, plasterers and miners—some, most likely, runaway slave couples—had carved out a small but definite place for themselves in Michigan's Upper Peninsula, a place where even the fog sometimes freezes.

History books paint vivid pictures of runaway slaves scurrying from slave catchers, tussling with dogs, hiding among sacks of potatoes, pretending to be pallbearers in phony funerals, busting out of jails, hiding in false-bottomed wagons or behind fake walls, sleeping in bushes and logs and walking for weeks and months to reach American and Canadian havens. Books and articles also describe the lives of runaway slaves who lived in swamps and hills, surviving on whatever they could catch, trade for or steal from plantations. In Michigan, stories about the Underground Railroad, the sometimes loose, sometimes spontaneous and sometimes organized network that aided fugitive slaves, highlight well-known stops on the road, including Vandalia, Schoolcraft, Battle Creek, Marshall, Niles, Adrian and Detroit.

Almost nobody talks about the blacks who became pioneers in the Northern Michigan wilderness of iron ore and copper mines, cascading rivers, deep valleys, gushing waterfalls, pine-capped mountains and brutal, nonstop winters. In fact, it is tough to find more than a few pages of census data about the black pioneers, some runaway slaves and some free people, who wrapped themselves in buffalo coats, tromped around on snowshoes and drove teams of blue- and brown-eyed huskies through Michigan's snow country.

Yet they were there, and some came with their families.

"There is strong evidence that fugitive slaves from the South migrated to the Upper Peninsula between 1850 and 1860, possibly feeling that the area's isolation and thinly populated land and snow-bound winters would protect them from slave catchers," according to Dr. Russell Magnaghi, director of Northern Michigan University's Center for Upper Peninsula Studies. Magnaghi believes that the blacks from the slave states "could have either been freedmen who had migrated northward or as was most probably the case, fugitive slaves who had made their way north via the Underground Railroad." Because roads were poor and trains had not yet penetrated the Upper Peninsula, blacks who traveled there before the Civil War most likely arrived on steamboats, the same lifeline that brought food to Upper Peninsula villages. At the same time, a small trading vessel manned by an all-black crew operated in the waters of Lake Michigan and might also have dropped off Underground Railroad passengers.

Whatever their starting point, these people faced long and dangerous trips to Upper Peninsula towns. It was 550 miles from Detroit to Houghton, 590 miles from Detroit to Gogebic County, 410 miles from Chicago to Mackinac County, 520 miles from Cleveland to Baraga County, 470 miles from Indianapolis to Chippewa County.

"For blacks in the 1850s and 1860s," wrote Magnaghi,

> the trip was long and dangerous by steamer from Detroit, then you had to spend the winter in a town as access was by snowshoe. Talk about cabin fever. The railroad would not come until the late 1860s; the boats ran from May to about October and then you were trapped in the communities; travel was by dog sled. Indians and mixed bloods would go to Green Bay to get the mail and when it arrived there was a holiday called so that everyone could pick up their mail and read it. . . . Once winter set in you were here for the duration. The Upper Peninsula was still heavily forested and the soft white pines had not yet been sawed and chopped away. Marquette would have been surrounded by trees. Animal life would have included bear and small animals. There is no indication that attacking bears were a problem. . . . The beaver was still around although people no longer made a great living trapping. The fur trade pretty much ended in the 1830s.

But how did black settlers who show up in the 1860 census of the Upper Peninsula hear about places as distant as Marquette and Ontonagon?

Did thirty-five-year-old John Anderson, of Alabama, know what awaited him in Houghton? If not freedom, what else might have motivated Charles Baker, fifty, a Houghton barber, to journey to the far North from Mississippi or Ellen Dickens, forty-five, to leave Kentucky to become a house servant in Ontonagon County? Why was Clayburn Harris, thirty-six, a carpenter and joiner from Canada, in Marquette, along with Lavenia Harris, thirty-six, and William J. Harris, a carpenter's apprentice?

Surrounded on three sides by Lake Superior, Lake Michigan and Lake Huron, the heavily wooded, lake-studded Upper Peninsula of Michigan remains, for the most part, wild country, an area where deer outnumber people in some counties and where hemlock trees never touched by axes stand guard in others. It is a place where people can step out of their doors and walk straight into nature's arms, stirred by the roar of waterfalls, the smell of pines, the sight of volcanic rocks or the majesty of Lake Superior, which, at 31,700 square miles, is the largest expanse of freshwater in the world. The area, however, is also a testing ground for the soul.

It has been in Michigan since the nineteenth century, part of a land swap that gave Toledo to Ohio and the Upper Peninsula to Michigan. The size of Delaware, Connecticut, Rhode Island and Massachusetts combined, it is a region of extremes. From the middle of May to mid-June, blackflies zip up your pant legs and burrow deep into the skin, hornets buzz and mosquitoes flit. It is better known, though, for winters that stretch on and on, and skies that seldom smile. Except for some isolated spots in northern New England, it receives among the largest annual snowfalls east of the Rocky Mountains. Houghton County, on average, piles up 204 inches annually and dips below zero on twenty-three days. In Marquette County, the average annual snowfall is 151 inches, and the number of days below zero is forty. In Iron County, it plunges below zero on an average of forty-one days. This does not compare to places like Antarctica or Siberia, areas that set the standards for what cold means and own the right to brag about it. Yet it is a place where the relationship between people and weather is crucial. A storm on Lake Superior with gale-speed winds and mile-high waves can sink the sturdiest ship. All the same, in the middle of February, while long-legged jack pines shiver in the wind, people drive snowmobiles to restaurants for Friday-night fish fries and roar into Marquette for dogsled races in which as many as thirty-seven teams compete on snow-packed paths.

There was a time, though, when the Upper Peninsula was more

than a hunting and fishing paradise or a place where people could be at home with nature in forests full of tall, straight white pines, trees with soft light wood used for construction and easy-to-cut fancy designs. There was a time when it was the site of a string of mining towns packed with immigrant workers speaking Gaelic, Yiddish, Finnish and scores of other languages. Those were the days when a lumber town called Seney was known as Helltown U.S.A. because so many bars lined its street, sandwiched between houses of prostitution at each end. This also was the time when the Upper Peninsula provided a little-known refuge for runaway slaves and pioneering African-Americans, including a family for whom part of Marquette is named.

Until the copper- and iron-mining boom of the mid-1800s brought more jobs and people to the Upper Peninsula, the number of black residents remained almost too small to count. In 1830 there were only five, and ten years later there were six. By 1850, though, fifty-two blacks lived throughout the region. There were thirty-seven in Mackinac County, eight at Sault Ste. Marie, six in Ontonagon County, which had a mile of sandy beach and great masses of copper, and one at Eagle Harbor, home of both eagles and the Eagle Harbor Mining Company. Sixty lived in the northern iron-rich frontier of Marquette, including a black sailor and his wife. Six were day laborers, and twelve men and women were cooks and servants.

All could tell stories about the strength they gained from working together.

Some came with freedom already in their pockets, drawn by the smell of opportunity in communities within walking distance of the mines. The first large deposits of ore were discovered in the Upper Peninsula in the 1840s. Copper, first used for ship sheathing and frying pans and later for electrical wiring and plumbing, was plentiful, in some cases brought to the surface by ancient volcanic eruptions. Around 1849, the family of Asa Jeffrey became among the few blacks to settle on the Ontonagon frontier at the extreme western end of the Upper Peninsula. Unable to find employment in lumbering and mining, male members of this family became barbers.

At night, the Jeffrey brothers worked as musicians and performers in the local hotel. Eventually, they opened the Jeffrey Brothers Saloon, a small one-room log cabin. According to census records, Asa Jeffrey came to the Upper Peninsula from Canada, and other sources say members of his family worked as barbers or owned barbershops in New York in the 1840s, the Upper Peninsula of Michigan in the 1850s and Minnesota, North Dakota and Iowa from the 1850s to the 1900s. By 1860, Asa Jeffrey had become a barber in the Lake Superior town of Houghton, a mining center built on a steep slope and surrounded by green hills. Later, members of the Jeffrey clan sold their claims and headed for Minnesota Territory, where they bought and sold land.

A rocky patch of land jutting into Marquette's harbor bears the name of another pioneering black family, the Gaines clan. Though they left Marquette long ago, members of this family are interwoven into Marquette's history. Virginia-born William Washington Gaines and his wife arrived in Marquette in 1855. Born a slave and freed by his natural father, Pitt Gaines, an aristocratic Virginia shipbuilder, William was sent on one of his father's ships to Houghton to work in the copper mines. He brought the woman he loved with him, an emancipated woman named Mary whom he had married after buying her freedom from Pitt Gaines. Falling ore injured him in the Houghton mines; it was only one of the hazards miners faced, including crushing cave-ins, choking dynamite smoke and ore dust and rats that stole their lunches. After William's injury, he and his wife moved to Marquette to work as coachman and groundskeeper for a white family. For years they lived on what became known as Gaines Rock, an odd outcropping of granite jutting into the Lake Superior shoreline and sitting between a brook and sandy beaches.

William Gaines's son, Charles, became a barber, porter and drayman and in 1914 unsuccessfully ran for a seat on the city commission. After Charles Gaines's death in 1917, his widow and her ten children left the city. The Marquette City Directory for 1912 shows the last entry for the family: Charles O. Gaines, Cassie E. and William E. all lived at 721 South Lake. In 1959, forty-two years after the Gaineses left Marquette, four of William Gaines's children returned for a visit. One owned a convalescent home and another owned several apartment buildings in Brooklyn.

All remembered how their grandfather, William, kept a sack of candy in one pocket and a handful of pennies in another, delighting any children he met. They also remembered Gaines Rock, which sheltered so many different kinds of people over the years, including hoboes and tramps in the Depression-socked 1930s and runaway teens in the 1960s. Most of all, they remembered how black self-help groups such as the Prince Hall Masons and the black, Prince Hall–affiliated Eastern Stars nurtured members of their family and helped them maintain "personal pride" despite the racism of the times.

Other early black pioneers came to the Upper Peninsula seeking a wilderness in which to hide. In 1860, Richard and Sarah Kenny and their two teenage children, Rebecca, seventeen, and William L. Davis, fifteen, were the only black family in the Lake Superior town of Munising. Richard Kenny is believed to have been a runaway slave, making him and his family part of the saga of family-loving freedom seekers who journeyed long distances to reach Michigan. They lived some twenty miles from the area's famed Pictured Rocks, those fifty- to two-hundred-foot-high sandstone/limestone walls that waves, wind and glaciers have shaped into caves and arches. Surrounded by bluffs stained by mineral-rich seepage, waterfalls, beaches, dunes and forests, the Kennys prospered. In 1860, they owned more land and had more cash than anyone around them: Richard owned fifteen hundred dollars in real estate and held a personal estate of one thousand dollars, while his wife also had fifteen hundred dollars in property and two hundred in her personal savings. Richard Kenny was originally from Virginia, and other members of the family had been born in Ohio. At some point, Sarah Kenny either divorced or buried her first husband, a Mr. Davis, and married Kenny, a plasterer. His stepson, William, was his apprentice.

While the Kennys prospered in Munising, John Anderson, a thirty-five-year-old black man from Alabama, was cooking in Houghton on a finger of land extending into Lake Superior. James Thompson cut hair at Barney's Exchange, a Marquette hotel, while his wife, Amira, made hats. James S. Brown, occupation unknown, had a personal estate of nine hundred dollars, one of the largest among all of the blacks. Blacks also worked as carpenters, joiners and varnishers. Daniel

Cooper, a black laborer from Georgia, worked in a lumber camp in Marquette County. Thomas Foster, a thirty-two-year-old black Kentuckian, ran a saloon in Marquette. Foster had a personal estate of five hundred dollars, a lot of money at a time when three hundred dollars bought an eight-room house. Living with him was his wife, Catharine, and their daughter, six-year-old Alice F. Foster. Robert Beasly, a twenty-five-year-old black man from Kentucky, waited tables on Mackinac Island, a four-square-mile island that has been at various times a sacred spot for Indians, the center of fur trading for the French, the place where Americans battled the British for control of the Great Lakes region, a playground for the wealthy and a refuge from the world of automobiles and hurry.

The average age of these black migrants was 24.5 years, and they included thirty-four males and twenty-six females. Of these African-American travelers, twenty-six came from Southern or slave states: two from Georgia, six from Virginia, eight from Kentucky, six from the District of Columbia and one each from Tennessee, North Carolina, South Carolina and Maryland.

During the Upper Peninsula's grueling winters, these early pioneers would have eaten whatever they'd stored during the summer in the cellar, a square hole under the center of the house. That would have included potatoes, turnips and other root vegetables, crocks of butter, lard, jars of fruit and wild honey. Some people would butcher a pig in the fall and then place pieces of the meat in crocks covered with lard, cutting through the lard to pull out pieces. People often ate whitefish and other types of fish. In the early 1850s, one woman in the western Upper Peninsula noted that she had prepared the abundant whitefish baked, fried, boiled, barbecued and in soup, and winter had just begun. Some might also have eaten siscowets, a fish peculiar to Lake Superior and delicate in flavor, though no recipes for it survive. Settlers in mining communities also bought tons of potatoes from the Ojibwa Indians.

To survive, though, black and white settlers mastered snowshoeing and dog-sledding. Evolution equips many animals, including wolves, foxes and snowshoe hares, for traveling over deep snow. Humans rely on snowshoes, which distribute weight so evenly that people can walk on snows eight or more inches deep without sinking more than a few inches. Traveling on sleds pulled by thick-coated wolflike dogs known as huskies, each one with a distinct voice and a different role to play, would have been another requirement for survival. Teams usually travel in silence; however, as dogs prepare to run, they often wail, the whole team eventually joining in a song of howls and gruff barks, yodels, whines, whoops, pants and whimpers. Some pioneers apparently became swept up in the adventure of traveling with a dog team through the hushed, white-washed wonder of snowed-in woods, a hypnotic journey into nature's heart. One of them was the black Canadian who organized the dog races held annually in Marquette.

But the history of blacks in northern Michigan and the Upper Peninsula began long before the days when the Upper Peninsula led the country in copper production. The first African slave identified in the records of the Church of Ste. Anne at Fort Michilimackinac, once located in Mackinaw City, was a little girl named Veronique, who was baptized on January 19, 1743. She was the daughter of Bon Coeur and Marguerite, slaves belonging to a French traveler forced to spend the winter in Michilimackinac, an old name for Mackinac County, on his way to the Illinois Country. Under the French, slaves did domestic chores or helped in the fur trade and could be freed at any time. Freed slaves usually remained in frontier communities. When the British took control of the territory, the number of African slaves in Canada and Upper Michigan increased. During the 1770s, John Askin, a merchant at the fort, had three African slaves, all used in the fur trade. Africans also rafted loads of lumber across the Straits of Mackinac, worked on construction projects and provided the music for parties and dances popular during the long winters. A few free blacks also visited and lived at Fort Mackinac, including Jean Baptiste Point de Sable, an educated trader who founded Chicago. A man known as Black Piter traded with the Native Americans in the Lower Peninsula. Around this same time, a small trading vessel manned by an all-black crew operated in the waters of Lake Michigan.

Jean and Marie Bonga were among thirteen slaves carried away by the British during an attack on Spanish forces in St. Louis. Brought to Fort Michilimackinac, they were held by Captain Daniel Robertson, who freed them. They married in the Church of Ste. Anne on June 26, 1794, and lived on Mackinac Island for years, purchasing a home, opening a tavern and raising a family. Eventually, they moved to Detroit, but a number of the Bonga children became fur traders in the North Country. In another version of the story, the British officer sold Bonga to a French fur trader with five Indian wives. Bonga became a favorite among the Mackinac Indians, who called him "Black Meat," or "Mu-Ko-Da-Weas," and declared himself free when the fur trader died. He then married the youngest of the trader's widows and left for what is now Superior, Wisconsin, and Duluth, Minnesota. About three miles north of the Bonga River, now called the St. Louis River, he built a trading post and home where his son, Pierre, was born about 1784 and other children later. Bonga, according to some historians, discovered Lake Itasca, the source of the Mississippi River, and "took a horseback ride to the Pacific in 1815."

Under the terms of the treaty that ended the American War of Independence, Michigan inhabitants could keep their slaves as private property, but couldn't introduce new slaves. Gradually those who remained were either freed or died. By 1810, Michigan had 120 free Africans and 24 slaves in a population of 4,762 people. In the area that included the entire Upper Peninsula and all the territory westward to the Missouri River, there lived 615 people, including fifteen Africans and one slave. Ten years later, there were 819 whites in the area that included the Upper Peninsula, but only five free blacks. In 1830, there were only five free blacks and in 1840 only six.

In the heyday of its mining years, the Upper Peninsula became a kind of cultural goulash, enriched by a population boom and the sights and smells and sounds of foreign-born miners. Many came from Cornwall, a famous mining area in the southwestern part of Great Britain. They also flocked to the Upper Peninsula from Ireland, Scotland, Wales, France, Canada, Sweden, Norway, Germany, Italy, Croatia, Poland, Hungary, Austria and, especially, Finland, bringing their folk beliefs and food, their thirst for land and their languages. In fact, the Upper Peninsula still has one of the largest populations of Finns in the country: some cluster in little enclaves like the iron-mining town of Palmer near Marquette, where people celebrate Little Christmas a week before December 25 and serve fruit and berry soup at feasts.

More blacks came as well, some free and some fugitives, who found freedom in Michigan wildernesses, where runaway slave laws weren't enforced. At one time, blacks enslaved in Canada ran to Michigan for freedom, too, knowing the laws against runaway slaves wouldn't touch them. In an 1897 survey of schools in Houghton's Calumet County, there were only 201 students with American-born parents out of 2,725. In one classroom, a black student "was the only American," according to author Arthur W. Thurner.

Blacks did not escape the stigma of inferiority created by slavery. In 1825 in Sault Ste. Marie, it became illegal for Indians and blacks and mixed bloods to vote. In Clifton, schoolmaster Hobart describes an incident in which a drunken Irish woman cursed out a black man whitewashing a house, believing he had muttered something insulting about her while he had actually simply sneezed. Hobart attributed the incident to drunkenness. Whatever difficulties they faced, though, the black settlers developed ways of coping, relying on each other for help.

On January 31, 1880, the *Weekly Mining Journal* ran an article about the birth of a black self-help group in Marquette. The article noted:

> The colored men of this city, about a month ago, organized an aid society, which embraces all of that race we have among us. At a meeting held Thursday evening, besides the dues, $5.80 was collected for the Kansas sufferers. The colored people of Marquette are generally good, well-behaved citizens, and this action of theirs shows that they have hearts full of sympathy for their suffering brethren.

The "Kansas sufferers" were the Exodusters, former slaves who moved in large numbers to Kansas between 1870 and 1879 at the urgings of Benjamin "Pap" Singleton, a former Tennessee slave who envisioned black colonies coexisting with white communities. Many mostly Southern black migrants moved to Kansas, often arriving without proper clothes or money for tools, teams of oxen or seed. Some spent their first winter in dugouts, unable to build homes until the spring.

But no amount of self-help or love could counteract all the harshness of frontier life in an area that could produce 100-degree summer days and winter lake-effect snows of six feet or more. Hobart writes page after page about students who died from scarlet fever and typhoid fever and about miners killed in accidents and about people being "caged up" throughout long winters.

Samuel Noll knew all about cages and how to break out of them: he had run, stumbled, sweated and clawed his way to a new life after his old one came apart. Born a slave in Virginia, Noll grew up on a plantation, married and fathered several children. Then, in 1858, his life shattered. He got into a fight with an overseer and injured him. Without knowing the overseer's condition but fearing it was serious, Sam fled into a swamp. Little by little, he worked his way north, first stopping in Detroit, then crossing the Detroit River to Windsor. He married again and after the Civil War moved to Marquette, where his wife cooked in a local restaurant and he assisted her. Starting in the 1880s, he became a guide for naturalist and photographer George Shiras III, who took the first flash photographs and trip-wire photographs of animals at night.

Eventually, many pioneering black families and their descendants—people such as Sarah and Richard Kenny, the Jeffrey clan and the Gaines family—moved away from the Upper Peninsula. By 1880, there were fewer than a dozen black families in Marquette County, including Sarah Kenny, then fifty-seven; a sixteen-year-old grandchild, Alex; and two other grandchildren—Adalade Davis, fifteen, and William Davis, nineteen—all born in Michigan. Joseph L. Smith, born in Amherstburg, Ontario, in 1851, settled in Marquette in 1877. A year later, he married Ida Bell French and opened a barbershop. He was known as a person with a genial personality and someone who could spin fascinating stories about local personalities and events. He promoted and managed sports events in Marquette, but is best known for organizing the dog races held there annually on George Washington's birthday. By the time he died in 1928, his wife and seven of his ten children were dead. His surviving children left the area. However, as many as thirty thousand people still come to the city's downtown every year for the two-hundred-forty-mile races.

A 1927 newspaper article noted that the winter of 1901 had devastated the Williams family, part of a Negro colony from Chicago beset by starvation and disillusionment after settling near Iron River. At county expense, the family was sent back to Chicago.

George C. Preston, a Jamaican, arrived in Marquette in 1865 and opened a barbershop. He also ran a restaurant and candy shop, and his two daughters, Charlotte and Bessie, were two of the earliest students at Northern Michigan University. Members of the Jeffrey family, once residents of Ontonagon and Houghton, worked as barbers in La Crosse, Wisconsin, in the 1870s. In 1879, James Polk arrived in the developing town of Norway and opened a barbershop. During and even after the slavery era, blacks dominated the catering, barbering and hairdressing professions, and many black barbers served white customers. A May 1891 issue of the *Menominee Range* indicated that a "colored bootblack" had returned to town after spending the previous summer in the mining community.

The three-hundred-room Grand Hotel on Mackinac Island, built in 1887, has employed large numbers of blacks over the years, including college students who come north in the summer. In 1897, there were 8,726 white miners working in Houghton County, but only one was black. Blacks, in some areas, continued to be viewed as exotic. The *Copper Country Evening News*, in 1897, noted that a minstrel show was coming to town with "some fifty genuine blacks." By the 1920s, Catholics, Jews, immigrants and blacks all had to endure Ku Klux Klan rallies and parades across the Upper Peninsula. The Grand Hotel even registered a gathering of Klansmen in the summer of 1924, but they reportedly had to pay double the usual rates, take their meals in their rooms and not loiter in the lobby.

In 1860, blacks in the Upper Peninsula made up only .89 percent, less than one percent of the total population of 18,085. In 1990, they were 1.3 percent, nearly as small a percentage of the population as they were in the nineteenth century. Like the area's white population, some left for other opportunities, other occupations, other loves, other chances to make their mark on the world.

Some early black pioneers, though, left deep and lasting footprints in the snow.

Mrs. Grace Jones, the granddaughter of Iowa Underground Railroad conductors, aboard one of the Piney Woods School's first traveling buses around 1926. Photo courtesy of the Piney Woods School archives, Piney Woods, Mississippi.

8

CHASED BY WOLVES

This is the story of a white woman who escaped with her own slaves, all of them spooked by the same set of troubles, all of them on the run. Yet it also is the story of a young black man who talked a lynch mob out of hanging him and who loved a brown-skinned woman he'd met only once. The two stories flow into each other the way lakes and rivers mingle their waters, making it hard to tell exactly where one stops and the other swirls and splashes to life. But the best place to begin is probably the day nearly two dozen people, some free and white, some black and enslaved, climbed into a covered wagon smelling of ginger cakes and bacon, coffee and secrets. When that wagon rolled out of Kentucky in the fall of 1853, wolves trailed it.

Well, actually, the story starts earlier than that.

It starts with the wolves.

They weren't the kind of wolves that spent a third of their lives on the move, chasing snowshoe hares, elk, sheep, beaver, deer, moose, cows and even flightless ducks and gorging on as much as eighteen pounds of meat at a meal. Yet, in some ways, the scheming, slave-snatching, lawsuit-filing, property-seizing Gordon brothers were scarier than wolves, ready to claw their own kin for cash. Joel and William Gordon's plots frightened their seventy-nine-year-old sister, Frances, so badly that she decided to run away with the slaves she was planning to free.

Her companions in an old schooner wagon rumbling out of Kentucky in 1853 were Charlotta Pyles, fifty-four, a copper-colored slave woman with glossy black braids; Charlotta's fair-skinned, free black husband, Henry, usually called Harry, sixty-seven; eleven of the Pyleses' enslaved children, five grandchildren and, eventually, a man named Claycomb, a white preacher from Ohio who came along to help shield the slaves from the suspicions of slave catchers. Catiline Walker, husband of Charlotta and Harry Pyles's daughter, Emily, and Joseph Kendricks, the spouse of daughter Julian Pyles, lived on different plantations and had to be left behind. But the same question probably plagued every member of this party, slave or free, male or female, black or white: What would Joel and William Gordon, men used to grabbing what they wanted, do next?

The stage had been set for this trouble when Harry Pyles, the blue-eyed mulatto son of a Kentucky slave owner, decided to "marry" Charlotta, an enslaved woman living on the plantation of Hugh and Sarah Gordon. The Gordons, who owned 422 acres in Washington County, Kentucky, lived in an area known for burley tobacco and bourbon, alfalfa, sorghum and hemp. Tennessee-born Charlotta Pyles was the daughter of a slave father and a Seminole mother, a tribe created by an amalgam of runaway slaves and refugees from other Florida tribes. Allowed to come and go as he pleased, Harry Pyles made harnesses, mended shoes, visited his family and, by 1840, lived on the Gordons' property. Like other free blacks with enslaved families, he lived with one foot in slavery and the other in freedom, knowing his wife could be sold at any moment and that he could not pass on his free status to his children.

It was Scottish-born Hugh Gordon and his never-married daughter, Frances, who changed what must have seemed, to most Kentuckians, like the natural order of things. While her father lay dying, Frances promised him that she would free any slaves he left her. Since none of her brothers and sisters made such promises, it is likely that it came from Frances's heart, inspired by the early, undiluted antislavery teachings of itinerant Methodist preachers. When Hugh Gordon died in 1834 he left two wills, the first one splitting his estate equally among his twelve children. However, his second will gave Frances Gordon something extra—the enslaved woman named Charlotta Pyles. The Gordon heirs all signed papers saying they agreed to this arrangement, which gave Frances the family plantation for life as well as Charlotta and some of her children. However, in 1853, the Reverend Joel Gordon, a Baptist minister, and his brother, William, the administrators of their father's estate, decided to break the deal. Actually, they grabbed a hammer and smashed it.

They kidnapped Charlotta's son, tall, fair-skinned Benjamin Pyles, and sold him in Mississippi to William P. Moore, who took him to Missouri to raise hemp. Suddenly, Benjamin Pyles was Benjamin Moore of Lafayette County, Missouri. Suddenly, both the Pyles family and Frances Gordon were hip deep in quicksand. "This cowardly act of her own relatives caused Miss Gordon to take immediate action toward removing her slaves to the North and giving them their freedom," wrote Grace Morris Allen Jones, Charlotta and Harry's granddaughter.

Frances Gordon hurriedly began organizing a move to Minnesota Territory so she could keep her promise to release the Pyleses, all of whom she now owned. However, when word of her plans spread to her family, her brothers swooped down again. The Reverend Joel Gordon filed a lawsuit in September 1853, charging that Frances Gordon, then nearly eighty, could no longer handle her affairs. He portrayed her as a woman turning soft around the edges as she melted into old age. If he had won, Joel could have seized legal control of his sister's assets, including her slaves. However, in court, Frances proved she was not the dull knife her brother had described—she cut straight to the point. She didn't waste time attacking slavery in a state where slaves were bought and sold. She merely pointed out that slave owners had the right to do whatever they pleased with their slaves, including moving them to another state, and that the Washington County Court had no jurisdiction in the matter. Swayed by her dead-on logic, the jury decided Frances Gordon was, indeed, both sane and sharp.

That should have ended the sparring and jabbing between Frances and her brothers. Instead, the brothers scheduled a rematch in the same ring. Joined by Joel Gordon and other relatives, William Gordon filed a second lawsuit on October 22, 1853, disputing Frances's ownership of her slaves, claiming she had no right to leave the state with them and, once again, calling her incompetent. This time, the sheriff of Washington County hauled the Pyles family off to the Springfield, Kentucky, jail, "in the night and in the rain," according to the sheriff's bill for the arrest. The bill came to $51.35, including $2.25 for hiring three horses, $5 for guards, $1.10 for road toll fees and $40 for seizing the Pyleses. Frances Gordon accompanied the family to Springfield and stayed with them until her lawyers got them released two days later. Springfield jails were not always safe havens. In January 1870, a group of men in disguise would whisk two farm laborers from the Springfield jail and hang them on a tree one mile east of town, leaving their bodies suspended until morning. However, the Pyleses survived their jailing, and Frances Gordon began plotting each step of her escape with her slaves. She even wrote to an old friend, a white Ohio minister named Claycomb, asking him to accompany her. He agreed. Meanwhile, Charlotta Pyles, who was famous for her cooking, began baking gingerbread, cakes, meats and other food for the trip.

By March 1854, the court had thrown out the Gordon brothers' second lawsuit against their sister, but by then Frances Gordon and the Pyleses were just memories in Kentucky. In the fall of 1853, they took off for Minnesota in an old time-weathered schooner wagon drawn by six thoroughbred Kentucky horses. Household goods crowded the wagon bed, and the women and children filled the remaining space. It is likely that they, like other pioneer travelers, took along cast-iron pots, frying pans and a Dutch oven that could bake almost anything while resting on hot coals. When Frances Gordon discovered she had forgotten her register book, most likely a property tax list showing an inventory of her slaves, she returned for it. However, the officers of the court were so angry over her decision to free her slaves that they refused to surrender it. So she went on without it.

The group traveled overland to Louisville and there boarded a side-wheel steamboat on the Ohio River to Cincinnati, possibly to pick up Claycomb; they then backtracked downriver to the Mississippi and north to St. Louis. In St. Louis, they met a white man named Nat Stone, who offered to guide the group to Minnesota for one hundred dollars.

Fearful of any setbacks or lost time, Miss Gordon agreed to his price, and the party set out again in a covered wagon. When Stone demanded another fifty dollars to keep from turning Charlotta and her children over to Missouri slave traders, Frances Gordon paid that, too. "In those days when the pro-slavery interests were at fever heat . . . it was a very dangerous experience for colored people, especially free negroes, to move about from place to place," Charlotta Pyles's granddaughter, Grace Jones, would later write.

After St. Louis, they traveled overland, with Barney Pyles, Charlotta and Harry's oldest son, doing most of the driving. When the Pyleses crossed the muddy Missouri River on a ferry to Howard County, they were just a few miles from their kidnapped son, Benjamin, who now farmed hemp in Waverly, Missouri, the place where abolitionist John Brown supposedly buried one of his children on his trek to Kansas. On the Gordon plantation, Benjamin also had hacked hemp, a raw material used to make rope and rough cloth—it was a job that typically required cutting, hauling and pounding open eighty to one hundred pounds of hemp stalks per day. The Pyleses had no idea they were near their missing son. They were well aware, though, that trouble had followed them from Kentucky. They had left the Gordon brothers behind, but real wolves now sometimes tracked them.

"It was a tiresome and difficult journey," wrote Grace Jones. "Often it was necessary to throw out some meat and to use powder to keep bears and wolves away from the wagon at night."

Men also stopped the wagon again and again as it creaked and rumbled through Missouri, suspecting it might contain runaway slaves with rewards on their heads. However, the presence of two white men and a white woman protected the black passengers. By the time the group reached the spot where the Des Moines Rapids and the Mississippi River came together in a whoosh of water and power, the skies had turned a threatening gray, and the wind had ice on its breath. In the mid-nineteenth century, steamboats could not go beyond this point. Passengers had to continue by land or take another boat upriver. Since Frances Gordon's canvas-covered schooner wagon was no match for a torrent of snow and ice, she and the Pyleses stopped there, too.

They had reached Iowa, a place where corn grew high enough to look a man in the eye and laugh. Though a free state, Iowa was hardly a black haven. Out of a population of 192,214 in 1850, it had only 265 "free colored" residents, 31 of them in Lee County, where the Pyleses settled. When it came to black issues, though, Iowa often sent out scrambled signals. In 1851, the Iowa legislature had passed a law excluding black migrants, but it was enforced only once, in Keokuk in 1857. Iowa senators George Jones and August Dodge had voted for all five parts of the Compromise of 1850, which included the rigorous Fugitive Slave Act, which made it easier to round up and return fugitive slaves. The Iowa legislature enacted a law letting blacks testify in court, but it wouldn't let blacks vote. However, geography made it impossible for Iowa to duck the slavery question: slaves escaping from Kentucky, Missouri and Tennessee passed through the state on their way to free Canada.

The Pyles family and Frances Gordon made a home for themselves in Keokuk at the southernmost tip of Iowa—a place named for a Sac chief named Keokuk who married seven women, loved horses and liquor, and didn't resist the arrival of the whites. Harry Pyles, a carpenter, stonemason and leatherworker, built a substantial brick house for his family and for Frances Gordon on Johnson Street. The street became the principal thoroughfare of the raw muddy village and, later, the site of industry and business as well as residences. Frances Gordon remained with the Pyleses for the rest of her life, now and then visiting relatives in Illinois, most likely in the Warren County village of Cameron, where her sister, Sarah Gordon Whitman Johnston, lived. However, Frances's true family had become the Pyleses. Both she and Charlotta Pyles belonged to the First Baptist Church of Keokuk and, according to one Gordon descendant, "Frances came to love Charlotta's family more than her own siblings, Charlotta as a daughter and Charlotta's children as her grandchildren." Actually, Gordon had all but adopted young Mary Ellen Pyles while she was still enslaved, taking the gray-eyed girl to church with her, keeping her in the Big House and shielding her from punishments. On April 2, 1857, Charlotta and Henry Pyles took another step to strengthen their family, legally marrying in their church.

However, another wolf now stalked the family, and its name was lean times.

Barney Pyles had found work driving a freight wagon overland from Keokuk to Des Moines. Mary Ellen Pyles, then seventeen, worked for a Quaker family in Salem for room and board and the chance to gain an education. Her sister, Mary Agnes, was able to attend school, too. Yet by their second year in Iowa, the Pyles family, which included eleven children and five grandchildren, staggered under a stiff financial load. Charlotta Pyles came up with a plan to ease that burden, but it was as rough as the family's journey to Iowa.

She would raise the money to purchase the freedom of her two left-behind sons-in-law so they could move to Iowa and help their families. She had letters written to their owners and discovered that the men could be bought for $1,500 each. To raise that amount of money, Charlotta Pyles, an unschooled former slave who knew nothing about the wider world, decided to go east and make antislavery speeches. While making her travel plans, she heard from her kidnapped son, Benjamin, in Missouri, who somehow had learned about her plan to free her sons-in-law. He suggested that she buy his freedom and that of only one son-in-law.

In William Styron's novel *Sophie's Choice*, the Nazis force a female concentration camp prisoner to decide which of her children will live and which one will die. The act of choosing between her baby daughter, who clutches a one-eyed teddy bear, and her young son, who can read both German and Polish, leaves Sophie permanently scarred and gushing guilt. Charlotta's choice must have been almost as agonizing. There really was no right choice: whatever she did would wound someone. She loved her kidnapped son, but he was a single man without children. Her sons-in-law had wives, children and responsibilities: they needed to be with their families, and their families needed them. But would Benjamin understand if she refused to free him? Or would he feel doubly betrayed? Charlotta finally chose her sons-in-law. She sent Benjamin a letter, probably through Underground Railroad agents, urging him to ask God for the strength to run away on his own. She never heard from or saw him again. In 1870, he still lived in Waverly, Missouri, and had married a woman named Adeline and fathered four children.

Meanwhile, Charlotta, armed with letters of recommendation from prominent citizens in Iowa, traveled to Philadelphia, New York and New England. Wearing a black bonnet over her shiny black braids, she raised money for her sons-in-law, speaking in churches, halls and homes about the evils of slavery. "It was a difficult task for a poor, ignorant woman who had never had a day's schooling in her life, to travel thousands of miles in a strange country and stand up night after night and day after day before crowds of men and women, pleading for those back in slavery," Grace Jones noted. During her travels, Charlotta met Frederick Douglass, the runaway slave who had become a great writer and orator, Lucretia Mott and Susan B. Anthony, suffragettes and abolitionists, and many other leaders in the struggle for human rights. It is possible that Charlotta Pyles's association with Douglass continued. On April 12, 1866, Douglass lectured at the Chatham Square Church in Keokuk, and in February 1869 he also visited Keokuk on his way to Des Moines.

And Charlotta must have picked up some of Douglass's ability to sway audiences as well. In six months, she raised three thousand dollars.

Frances Gordon accompanied Charlotta Pyles to Kentucky to purchase her sons-in-law. However, Charlotta, her husband and Gordon soon made another difficult decision, this one laced with danger. In 1854, the Civil War that broke out in Kansas Territory, southwest of Iowa, had pushed more Iowans to take sides on the slavery question. The conflict between forces who wanted Kansas to become free territory and those who wanted it to embrace slavery became so violent that Kansas became known as "Bleeding Kansas." Meanwhile, by the middle 1850s, abolitionists had become strong enough to establish a working Underground Railroad in Iowa. The Pyleses decided to make their home a stop on the road.

The main line of the Underground Railroad entered Iowa at the southwestern corner near Tabor, where the Reverend John Todd, a Congregationalist minister, hid slaves in his barn. It passed through

Lewis, Des Moines, Grinnell, Iowa City, West Liberty, Tipton, DeWitt, Low Moor and Clinton, the home office of the U.S. marshal and a place where slave catchers often lay in wait. Slave-freeing John Brown of Kansas, with his long broom of a nearly white beard and straight-ahead eyes, sometimes stayed at the home of George B. Hitchcock, a sympathetic Iowa Congregational preacher. Hitchcock's house had two basements, one of them secret. While Brown traveled to Canada in the winter of 1858–1859, he stashed his arms in U.S. congressman Josiah B. Grinnell's "liberty room," and his company of runaway slaves slept there. William Maxson, who shipped blacks as potatoes in railroad box cars, got a scare one day when one of the sacks of potatoes sneezed, but the load went on its way all the same. Reverend Todd once dressed a runaway slave woman to look like his wife, swaddling her in a veil, cloak and gloves, and drove her over fifty miles in his buggy in daylight. Deacon Theron Trowbridge of the Congregational Church in Denmark, Iowa, strapped on his gun after a slave girl arrived at his house wailing that she had been forced to abandon her baby at a Missouri farm about fifty miles southwest of Fort Madison, Iowa.

He rode off on his horse, returning two nights later with the woman's baby. In May 1857, the *Fort Madison Plain Dealer* ran an editorial lamenting the fact that the town of Denmark "has the name of being the rendezvous of men who occasionally engage in negro-stealing, at the same time professing the religion of the gospel."

Sometime between the middle 1850s and 1860, the Pyleses and Frances Gordon joined this slave-assisting network, too. They don't show up in the 1860 census, a year when their house is described as vacant. It is possible they avoided census takers during their most active years on the slave-aiding network. However, in Iowa, which still contained many proslavery elements, they ran a real risk in welcoming fugitives. Yet Charlotta, in particular, became a legendary figure.

"Many a slave, coming from Kentucky, Tennessee and Missouri," wrote Grace Jones, "found at the gateway into Iowa an enthusiastic member of their own race in the person of Grandma Pyles. She received them into her own home and, with the aid of many white friends she had made on her trip, helped them to make their escape to Canada."

But the most remarkable thing about the Pyleses and Frances Gordon is that they never really died. Oh sure, Charlotta, Harry and Frances eventually passed away: Harry Pyles, eighty-seven, died in 1870 of "old age," according to his medical records; Charlotta Pyles, seventy-six, died in 1880 from heart disease; and Frances Gordon passed away in the 1870s. But they haunted their families and haunted Iowa, too. Nobody in the Pyles family could forget their stories or shake off their influence. Tales about their adventures and achievements became the rhythm to which their descendants rowed through life. Charlotta Smith, one of Charlotta and Harry Pyles's daughters, went to war with the Keokuk school system. In 1874, Smith's son, Geroid, was one of two black boys denied admission to the Keokuk schools, which were open and free to whites between ages five and twenty-one. After Charlotta Smith took the case to court, the Iowa Supreme Court ruled that black children could not be excluded from the public schools or compelled to attend a separate school.

However, it was Grace Morris Allen, granddaughter of Charlotta and Harry Pyles, who would carry her family's courage all the way to Mississippi and help a young man who loved her on sight create a miracle amid pine-scented woods. Grace was the daughter of Mary Ellen Pyles, who'd obtained an education by working for a Quaker family, and James Addison Morris, a steward on a line of steamboats operating between St. Louis and St. Paul. Grace had taller, wider dreams than her mother or grandparents. She taught school, opened a short-lived industrial school for blacks in Burlington, Iowa, and spent several years rallying support for a black school at Cave Spring, Kentucky.

It was during a 1905 Baptist Missionary Society meeting in Iowa City that Grace, by then a young widow, met Laurence Jones, a junior at the University of Iowa. Jones would later write that he had never been so moved by anyone as he was by his first glimpse of Grace, a brown-skinned wisp of a woman who was, in some ways, his mirror image. She was the smartest and most upbeat black woman he'd ever met and had come to the meeting to raise funds for an industrial school in the South. She also was slightly shorter than Jones, who stood about five feet five inches. Laurence had nothing to offer Grace when they met; he was still a student while she was already a widow. Yet over the years, they would exchange letters and meet "occasionally," according to author Leslie Purcell.

After graduating, Missouri-born and Iowa-educated Laurence Jones surprised everyone by turning down a job at Alabama's well-established Tuskegee Institute to teach in a small school in Hinds County, Mississippi, determined to help the poorest of the poor. He found his mission, though, in the pine-covered hills of Rankin County, Mississippi, where 80 percent of the people could neither read nor write. Unable to add or subtract, they had no way of knowing if they received their full wages or if stores charged them correctly. In lean winters, they often lived on cornmeal and dried peas, never having learned to preserve wild berries or summer vegetables. Laurence wanted to start a school where people would learn to use their heads, their hearts and their hands, but he seemed destined for failure. The black farmers didn't trust the educated stranger, figuring he was working some kind of scam and would run off with any money he managed to raise. Whites, most of whom weren't that educated either, saw no need for black education.

Then, one day in 1909, Laurence sat on a pine log under the shade of a one-hundred-year-old cedar tree, going through his mail. A sixteen-year-old boy showed up and stood staring at Laurence's newspaper. Jones handed the paper to the boy, who held it upside down, unable to read a word. So Jones began teaching the young man the basics of reading. The next day, three youngsters sought out Jones, and he taught them, too. He might have been inspired by his maternal grandfather, Prior Foster, an Underground Railroad operator in Coshocton County, Ohio, who with his brothers, Joseph and Levi, founded Woodstock Manual Labor Institute in 1846 in Woodstock Township, Lenawee County, Michigan. Foster's school lasted ten years. Laurence Jones, known to his students and neighbors as the Little Professor of Piney Woods, would be a lot luckier, in part because of the gift he'd one day receive from long-dead Charlotta and Harry Pyles.

As more and more people, young and old, began showing up for lessons in the woods, Jones's dream took shape: Ed Taylor, a black man most people considered mean, donated an old abandoned cabin being used as a sheep shed, forty acres and fifty dollars. It became Jones's first schoolhouse. A white sawmill owner donated ten thousand feet of lumber for a new schoolhouse, which Jones and his students built. A University of Iowa alumnus donated eight hundred acres. A millionaire industrialist shipped down a small herd of cattle to provide milk for the children. Another businessman sent fruit and pecan trees. This became the nucleus of the Piney Woods Country Life School, slightly more than twenty miles south of Jackson and set among pine and hickory, sweet gum, sassafras and magnolia trees.

However, starting a black school in Mississippi in 1917 was, in some ways, more dangerous than escaping to freedom in a covered wagon with bounty hunters and wolves on your trail. Between the years 1882 and 1951, 4,730 people were lynched in the United States, 3,437 of them black and 1,293 white, according to figures from the Tuskegee Institute. Some died for trivial offenses such as "disputing with a white man" or "peeping in a window." In 1916, fifty-two black men and one black woman were lynched, including Jeff Brown in Cedar Bluff, Mississippi, whose "crime" was accidentally brushing against a white girl as he ran for a train. In 1917, the wolves came after Laurence Jones, armed with cocked rifles and rope. Two white youths raised up a mob by claiming they'd overheard Laurence Jones urging blacks at a religious revival to riot. Jones actually had told the group that life was "a battleground" and that they must stay "on the firing line." The youths assumed that he was gathering an army to attack whites. A mob of fifty men soon surrounded Jones. With a noose around his neck, he talked about how he'd raised money to buy supplies for his school. He mentioned the names of prominent white men who'd helped him and explained how the white boys had misunderstood his remark. He even tossed in a pinch of humor, making the grim-lipped crowd smile. A lynch mob with nothing but murder on its mind wound up collecting fifty dollars for the school.

But the "Little Professor" had never forgotten Grace Allen, granddaughter of Charlotta and Harry Pyles. In one of Grace's letters, she mentioned that she would be spending the summer in Des Moines. Laurence met her there, and she was all that he remembered and more. The school she'd founded for black children in Burlington, Iowa, had been so successful that white families had sent their children there. And she seemed to find the short, brown-skinned and handsome "Little Professor" equally fascinating, despite the long hair and bushy mustache he'd grown to make himself look older. On June 29, 1912, twenty-eight-year-old Laurence Jones married the thirty-six-year-old woman who had learned the value of schooling from her mother and aunt, the need to make bold leaps from her grandparents and the power of commitment and compassion from tales about Frances Gordon. Laurence believed Grace would help him put meat and bones on the skeleton of a dream. He was right.

She taught all the English classes in the upper grades. She also taught sewing, domestic science, weaving and textiles and basketry courses to girls in homemade gray uniforms, showing students how to weave rugs they could sell and how to make baskets out of pine needles. She wrote several essays about her grandparents' escape from slavery with Frances Gordon, preserving history that might have been lost otherwise. As part of Grace Jones's work with the Mississippi State Federation of Colored Women's Clubs, she taught mothers about child care, sanitation and nutrition. She managed and traveled with the Cotton Blossom singers, a group that raised funds for the school. She was the mother of three children, Turner Harris, Laurence Clifton Jr. and Helen, a girl the Joneses had adopted when she was six months old. Under Grace's leadership, the number of local clubs in the Mississippi Federation grew from seventeen to seventy-three. Grace Jones was fifty-six when she died of pneumonia in 1928. Mourners wrote letters to the *Pine Torch*, the school's newspaper, recalling her gentle ways, her charm, her creativity and her skill at fund-raising. She was buried under the cedar tree where her husband began his school in 1909.

Piney Woods didn't die, though. In 1937, Laurence Jones founded a school band he called the International Sweethearts of Rhythm to raise funds and create good public relations for the school. His adopted daughter, Helen, became a trombonist with the band at the age of eleven. The Sweethearts were the school's primary musical messengers and fund-raisers during the 1938–1939 school year, appearing at dances, resorts and conventions. In 1940, band members, including Helen, ran off to Washington, D.C., in a school bus, lured by a promoter's promise that they could see the world and make a good living. In 1944, *Downbeat* magazine named the group America's top girl orchestra. They were also the first integrated girl orchestra, but the white girls in the band wore dark makeup in the South, passing for black to avoid getting jailed for race mixing. This, after all, was an era when it was illegal for blacks and whites even to play checkers or dominoes together in Birmingham, Alabama, and when black and white members of fraternal orders in North Carolina and Virginia couldn't call each other brother.

But the Piney Woods saga didn't end with the International Sweethearts of Rhythm, either. Helen Jones, the adopted child of Laurence and Grace Jones, later married William Alfred Woods, the first African-American to earn an accounting degree from Creighton University in Nebraska. In 1947, the Woodses had their first child, Cathy. Cathy Woods, now better known as Cathy L. Hughes, became founder and owner of Radio One, the first radio chain to target the African-American market. Cathy Hughes, great-great-granddaughter of Charlotta and Harry Pyles, is now a board member of the Piney Woods School.

The family's most lasting legacy is the Piney Woods boarding school, a place founded by Laurence Jones, nurtured by Grace Jones, inspired by Prior Foster and aided by Mary Ellen Pyles, who moved to Piney Woods in her later years to help out at the school.

Started with three students, the Piney Woods School now has two hundred and sixty students from twenty-nine different states and four or five foreign countries, including Mexico and Ethiopia.

Started with a pine log and then a shed, it now has three girls' dormitories and two dorms for boys, five man-made lakes and two thousand acres, five hundred of those acres an educational farm with pink and black pigs, donkeys, sheep, cows and the rest timberland roamed by skunk, armadillos and deer.

Started by a man with only a few dollars to his name, Piney Woods now has housing for visitors, a post office and a $6.5 million annual budget.

Once a place where students could pay their tuition with eggs, hogs, butter or molasses, it has become a school where the majority of students receive some kind of scholarship, all work ten hours a week and more than 90 percent of those who stick it out go on to college. All students receive four years of English and literature, social studies, math and science with emphasis on writing and thinking. They attend two-hour classes, pray every morning, attend church services on Sunday, study for at least two hours every evening and wear uniforms. Some show up at the black boarding school with uncontrollable tempers and other problems, but they return home ready to make up their beds and clean up their rooms without being told. Students' grades are checked weekly, and anyone with any grade below a C is barred from participating in any extracurricular activities.

This was supposed to be a story about a wagonload of people who ran away from Kentucky together, some white, some black, but all chased by wolves. Yet it is also a story about a man and a woman, both grandchildren of Underground Railroad conductors, who ran from ignorance and made the pine trees of Mississippi sway with purpose and song.

Slaves who reached the Detroit River could cross it to free Canada. Photo by Timothy L. Hughes.

9

THE WOMAN ON JOHN LITTLE'S BACK

He carried his wife to freedom on his scarred and beaten back—that's really all you need to know about John Little. Among slaves, backs were storybooks, telling a person's whole saga, recording where he had been and suggesting where he might go. The back of a Mississippi slave named Gordon shows up in nearly every book about slavery: his knotted and furrowed back looks like a geography lesson, a cluster of islands here, a mountain range of pain there. Yet between them, a North Carolina–born slave named John Little and his Virginia-born wife, Eliza, might have had as many scars as Gordon, but they also had something else: an incredible memory of an incredible day.

John Little became a runaway after his master refused to give him a Sunday pass to visit his ailing mother. He went to see his mother anyway and returned to take his punishment, five hundred stinging, cutting lashes across his back. After that, a slave breaker beat him steadily for three months, trying to snap his spirit, twist his will, but nothing worked. When he was sent to Norfolk to be shipped to New Orleans, Little ran back to North Carolina to his mother. Taken to Tennessee, he married a woman with soft hands, a woman who couldn't stand too much sun, a woman as gentle as he was strong. But he was jailed again and about to be resold; that's when he broke out of jail. When his wife told him the overseer planned to whack him three hundred times with a wooden paddle, he prepared to run away again, waiting in the woods until his ailing wife healed.

Once the Littles began walking, they journeyed nine miles before an exhausted Eliza Little collapsed on the floor of a barn. John Little kept trying to rouse her, but couldn't. Benjamin Drew, a nineteenth-century researcher, describes what John Little did next:

> I seized and shook her—"wife! wife! master is coming!"—but I could not awaken her. I gathered her up, put her across my shoulder manfully, jumped the fence, and ran with my burden about a quarter of a mile. My heart beat like a drum, from the thought that they were pursuing us. But my strength at last gave out, and I laid her down under a fence, but she did not awaken.

Over the years, Eliza, who married John at sixteen, had been battered almost as much as her husband. She had three scars on her hands and arm and one on her forehead, inflicted by a mistress who had thrown pieces of a china plate at her, even though Eliza wasn't the person who'd broken the plate. She had been beaten with a piece of wood, leaving her with a scar over her right eye. Maybe that was a part of what made her so special to her husband. Like the people who stare in amazement at famous pictures of the slave Gordon's back, John could look at his wife and taste her tears.

"I bled like a butcher," Eliza told Drew.

> One piece [of glass] cut into the sinew of the thumb and made a great knot permanently. The wound had to be sewed up. This long scar over my right eye was from a blow with a stick of wood. One day she [her mistress] knocked me lifeless with a pair of tongs. . . . I belonged to them until I got married at the age of sixteen. . . . I was employed in hoeing

> cotton, a new employment: my hands were badly blistered. "Oh, you must be a great lady," said the overseer, "can't handle the hoe without blistering your hands!" I told him I could not help it. My hands got hard, but I could not stand the sun.

During Eliza and John Little's journey to freedom, Eliza's shoes gave out, and she wore out her husband's old shoes, too. Barefoot, they stumbled on. When they crossed the Ohio Bottoms leading to the river, John Little once again proved that he was more than a man with a strong back. He told Benjamin Drew:

> The water was black and deep. I bound our package on my wife's back, placed her on a log as a man rides on horseback, and I swam, pushing the log, holding it steady to keep her up. Had the log turned right or left, she would have slipped off, and the packs would have sunk her. It would have been death, sure—but worse than death was behind us, and to avoid that we risked our lives.
>
> From Jackson to the Ohio River was called one hundred and forty miles. . . . We crossed into Black Hawk territory. There I was so lost and bewildered that I had at last to go up to a house to inquire the way. I found there a man with true abolition principles, who told us the route. He said a man and his wife had been carried back to slavery from that neighborhood. He did not take us across the river, but we found a way over. Then we walked on—my wife was completely worn out: it was three months from the time we left home before we slept in a house. We were in the woods, ignorant of the roads, and losing our way. . . . Many such roundabout cruises we made, wearing ourselves out without advancing: this was what kept us so long in the wilderness and in suffering. I had suffered so much from white men, that I had no confidence in them, and determined to push myself through without their help. Yet I had to ask at last, and met with a friend instead of an enemy. At Chicago money was made up to help me on, and I took passage for

> Detroit, and then crossed to Windsor, in Canada. That was the first time I set my foot on free soil.

After stopping off in Windsor, the Littles finally journeyed into the Canadian wilderness. They had nothing but two axes, one suit of clothes, an iron pot, a Dutch oven, a few plates and forks, some pork and flour. Around 1842, they marched into the snowy wilderness known as the Queen's Bush, a vast tract of land in the Huron area. Settlers moved there on their own, one family at a time. There were no roads, no markets, no mills to grind flour. The Littles built a home amid wolves and bears and raised wheat and potatoes. Eliza Little chopped wood right beside John, the man who had carried her on his back and paddled her across a river, impelled by love.

10

ANGELINE'S BLUES

Angeline Palmer's story has the bittersweet beat of those cotton field songs and street corner shouts that became the blues. She grew up amid snow-crusted hills and whispering streams, not fields watered by sweat and bleeding feet. She came from Massachusetts, where black people eventually considered themselves free, not Mississippi, where they always knew for sure they weren't. Yet even at the age of eleven, Angeline Palmer knew all about sorrow struggling to turn itself into joy. The three young men who loved her saw to that.

She was a black girl living near Amherst, Massachusetts, among the lower foothills of the Green Mountains. She was a motherless child, and a fatherless one, too: that started her blues. Her mother, Sylvia, had died about 1831 from smallpox, one of several deadly diseases, including cholera, yellow fever, scarlet fever, typhus and typhoid, that regularly roared through nineteenth-century towns. In 1830, Angeline's father, Solomon, was one of eight black men with families in Amherst; however, by 1834, he had become an official "transient," a temporary resident, a man expected to drift off in the first cold wind. His name soon disappeared from Amherst's public records, but it's possible he was asked to leave because he might need public assistance. Such things had happened before. An elected official had escorted a white woman named Meg to the town line and urged her to go. Others had been booted out of town, too. The bottom line was this: Angeline Palmer was on her own. So that she could earn her keep, town officials had made her an indentured servant for Mason and Susan Shaw of Belchertown, Massachusetts, ten miles southeast of Amherst. After the Shaws moved to Georgia and later to New Jersey, Angeline lived with the couple's son-in-law and daughter. However, in the spring of 1840, the Shaws decided to deepen eleven-year-old Angeline's sorrows. They plotted to take the child down to Georgia, let a slave trader sell her into slavery and pocket their profits. Whenever she returned to Massachusetts, Mrs. Shaw would tell people the girl had run away.

By the time Amherst was settled in 1728, slavery already existed in Massachusetts. It was small-scale slavery, a few people here and a few there, usually working beside their owners. When the 1780 Massachusetts Constitution established the principle that all men were free and equal, it seemed to end slavery. However, it took several legal cases to dismantle and bury all the bones of the institution, including a lawsuit by an uneducated black woman named Elizabeth Freeman, who left her owner's house after his wife struck her with a heated kitchen shovel. Attorney Theodore Sedgwick Sr. took her fight for freedom to court and made it a test of the legality of slavery under Massachusetts's new constitution. The jury agreed that slavery was illegal and forced Freeman's former owner to pay her thirty shillings. Though this ruling did not emancipate all enslaved blacks in Massachusetts, the verdict—coupled with other legal victories for blacks—eventually flushed slavery out of the state's legal system. It remained in the hearts of people like the Shaws, though.

Their plan to sell Angeline Palmer into slavery leaked out in May 1840. Susan Shaw, who had returned to Massachusetts for a visit, read aloud a letter from her husband detailing their plot. One of her servants overheard it and passed on the information. She put it on the drum, moved it on the grapevine. Word reached Angeline's half-brother, Lewis B. Frazier, a twenty-year-old unmarried laborer who visited the girl when he could. He couldn't support Angeline, but that didn't mean he didn't love her. Frazier shared the grim news with two black male friends, Henry Jackson, a twenty-three-year-old single stable hand, and William Jennings, a twenty-seven-year-old unmarried laborer. They brought what they'd heard to the Amherst Board of Selectmen, but nobody took the story seriously. The Shaws were respected people and had taken another black servant to the South and returned with her. Why should anyone believe they planned to turn a free black eleven-year-old orphan into a slave?

Actually, people often tricked, dragged or kidnapped free blacks, especially children, into slavery. In December 1851, two slave catchers came up to the back door of a rural farmhouse in Chester County, Pennsylvania. When sixteen-year-old Rachel Parker answered the door, one of the men grabbed her by the arm and pulled the free black Philadelphia-born girl outside. Both she and her previously kidnapped sister, Elizabeth, wound up in Baltimore and, in Elizabeth's case, in New Orleans before they were eventually freed and brought home. Meanwhile, Rachel Parker's employer, Joseph Miller, who had charged one of the girl's abductors with kidnapping, disappeared from the platform of a train. His body was later found hanging from a tree about nine miles from Baltimore.

But Lewis Frazier and his two friends were determined no one would kidnap, jail, rough up or drag Angeline into slavery. Instead of waiting to rescue the child from slavery, they would rescue her before she became enslaved. There are no well-documented stories about Underground Railroad activity in Amherst, no tales of people hiding slaves among sacks of potatoes or lumps of coal or arising in the middle of the night to transport a load of fugitives to the next stop on the road to freedom. However, Lewis Frazier and his friends were about to become Angeline Palmer's rescue team, forming their own Underground Railroad on the spot. On May 25, 1840, two days before her planned journey to the South, Angeline took a stagecoach to Amherst to visit her grandmother, Margaret Sash Pharoah, whom she called Aunt Peggy. No doubt she also sought out her brother to tell him about her travel plans and learned that he planned to snatch her off the stage when she returned home to the Shaws in Belchertown. And no doubt she shared her brother's plan with her grandmother. That was a mistake. Angeline's grandmother didn't like the smell of the plan and quickly took it to her employer, Hezekiah Strong. Strong hurried to Deputy Sheriff Henry Frink's livery stable in Amherst and hired him to take Angeline and the Shaws' other female servant back home from her grandmother's place by a different route, taking the long way to Belchertown. As a result of this switch in plans on May 26, Angeline was not inside the coach when Frazier and his friend William Jennings waved for it to stop.

Meanwhile, Sheriff Frink's black employee, Henry Jackson, had overheard enough to alarm him. Jackson, who was part of Frazier's rescue team, left his job, found Frazier and Jennings and took charge of the rescue. With a horse and buggy borrowed from a white butcher, the trio galloped to Belchertown by a roundabout route and stopped at the Shaw place. Now it was time for those blues guitars to wail. Now it was time for loud, foot-stomping music and shouts. Mrs. Shaw and several women were inside the Shaw home. Frazier raced up to his sister's room, alarming the women. One threw the bolt on the outside of Angeline's room, trapping Frazier and Angeline inside. Jackson and Jennings then ran into the house and rushed to the third floor, plowing through Mrs. Shaw and her friends. The two men unbolted the door and led out Frazier and Angeline. As the men left the house, they shoved aside Mrs. Shaw, who fell on a landing. Her three rescuers then rode off with the girl, heading back to Amherst. On the way, they passed Sheriff Frink, who ordered them to stop. It was panic time again. What did the sheriff know and how had he learned it so soon? However, Sheriff Frink knew nothing. He merely lectured the young men on the dangers of speeding and let them ride on.

The young men left Angeline at the home of Sarah and Spencer Church, a white couple in North Amherst. Although the Churches had eight children of their own, they agreed to care for Angeline. However, Angeline's rescuers knew that the Church home was not a safe long-term hideout—the girl needed a more distant refuge. On the advice of a black woman named Huldah Green Kiles, who also lived in North Amherst, the three men quickly moved Angeline to the remote town of Colrain on the Vermont state line. The Scotch-Irish had settled this area, many coming from the Province of Ulster and the towns of Londonderry and Colrain. They had been clear-headed, frugal people: they introduced flax spinning to New England and saved their shoes by sometimes walking barefoot to church, not donning shoes and stockings until they were nearly there. In Colrain, Angeline stayed with Huldah Kiles's brother, Charles Green, and began to breathe freely at last. While Jackson and Kiles took Angeline to Colrain, Angeline's brother, Lewis Frazier, had remained in Amherst to confuse the authorities. After that, Jackson and Jennings briefly left the area.

On May 27 in Amherst, Mrs. Shaw filed formal complaints against Frazier, Jackson, Jennings and Deputy Sheriff Frink, whom she believed was somehow involved in Angeline's disappearance. All four men were charged with abduction and unlawfully imprisoning Angeline Palmer and assault upon Mrs. Shaw during the kidnapping. Frazier posted bond, Frink agreed to appear in court when called and Jackson and Jennings soon surrendered. When their jury trial finally began in March 1841, tall, straight, spare Edward Dickinson, a man cool enough to handle any emergency and the father of future poet Emily Dickinson, defended the four men. The three black defendants were found guilty of all charges, but the judge offered to free them if they would reveal Angeline's location. They refused. Each served three months in the Hampshire County Jail, in neighboring Northampton, the county seat. However, the jailer allowed them to leave during the day and return at nightfall. Many visitors showed up at the jail with clothes and food. When the three young men returned to Amherst, they walked like heroes: people, black and white, congratulated them for rescuing Angeline.

Ten years after proving how much he loved his half-sister, Lewis B. Frazier died of what was called a "hip complaint"; he was buried at West Cemetery in Amherst. Soon the Civil War rode into town and created more black heroes. Between 1863 and 1865, twenty-two black men from Amherst served in the war, including two of Angeline Palmer's rescuers. In 1863, William Jennings, then fifty, and his son, William H.H. Jennings, both enlisted in the famed 54th Massachusetts Volunteer Infantry Regiment to fight for the Union army. The elder Jennings was disabled in an accident while in the 54th Regiment, but at age fifty-one he enlisted in the 5th Massachusetts Cavalry and served in Virginia. Henry Jackson, mastermind of the Palmer rescue, became another kind of hero. He was a stable hand when he helped rescue Angeline, but in later years he became a respected teamster, hauling goods to Springfield and Millers Falls and often serving as a bank courier, carrying large sums. He even introduced the town to a new industry: he brought loads of palm leaves to Amherst and distributed them to families who turned them into hats and other goods. Jackson owned parcels of land, too, and shares of First National Bank of Amherst. After the death of his first wife, Celia, from consumption, he married Olive Prutt, widow of Angeline Palmer's brother, Lewis Frazier.

Angeline Palmer continued to live in Colrain, a part of hilly, water-rich Franklin County, a place where, in the presidential election of 1860, the majority of residents voted for Abraham Lincoln. On May 13, 1851, she married Sanford C. Jackson, a man who, perhaps, loved too much—or at least too often. After Angeline's unrecorded death, sometime between 1851 and 1859, Sanford Jackson married Emily Jane Mason, twenty-seven, in 1859, in South Wilbraham, and a year later, he married Nancy A. Newport, fifteen, in Worcester. Fortunately for him, the two wives didn't know about each other. In 1863, Jackson, thirty-two, enlisted in the 54th Massachusetts Volunteer Infantry Regiment just as his friend William Jennings had done. He was wounded in action at Fort Wagner at Charleston, South Carolina, where the 54th led the attack. The regiment of mostly free Northern blacks lost 259 of 650 officers and men, but, in death, it achieved an enduring victory. The doomed, desperate assault on Fort Wagner became powerful proof that blacks could fight as bravely, as resolutely, as any other soldiers under attack. On September 14, 1863, Private Sanford Jackson died of gunshot wounds at the

Union Army General Hospital at Beaufort, South Carolina. After the war, both of his wives applied for his pension, triggering an investigation. There is no record of what action, if any, the government took. Nor is there any record of which of his three wives Sanford Jackson loved the most or whether any of them ever gave him a taste of Angeline's blues.

In 1859, Lucy E. Millard, a young white woman born in New York, married runaway slave Isaac Berry in Canada. Photo courtesy of Marie Loretta Berry Cross.

Book II

CROSSING THE COLOR LINE

★

11

SUSPICIOUS LYNCHINGS, PASSING FOR WHITE, PASSING FOR BLACK AND MIXED MARRIAGES IN DEADLY TIMES: A CHRONOLOGY

Among the most daring travelers on the Underground Railroad were the interracial couples who sometimes risked mutilation or death to marry. This historical timeline sets the stage for their stories.

1619: A Dutch ship carries the first blacks to Jamestown, Virginia, where they become indentured servants, working for a fixed period of service. The population of Virginia is then about two thousand. Eventually, black slaves will replace the indentured servant system, providing a free pool of laborers who will find it more difficult to run off and hide and whose dark skin and non-European culture allow them to be viewed as heathens doomed to a lifetime of servitude because of the sin of Noah's swarthy son, Ham.

1630: Virginia authorities sentence a white man named Hugh Davis to a public whipping "before an assembly of negroes & others for abusing himself to the dishonor of God and shame of Christianity by defiling his body in lying with a negro. . . ."

1640: Robert Sweet, another white Virginian, is convicted of dishonoring himself with a Negro, and the woman is whipped.

John Punch, a black indentured servant, is made a servant for life as a punishment for running away, but the two whites with him receive only four additional years of servitude.

1662: Virginia rules that "children got by an Englishman upon a Negro woman shall be bond or free according to the condition of the mother, and if any Christian shall commit fornication with a Negro man or woman, he shall pay double the fines of a former act."

1664: Maryland turns Negro servants into lifelong slaves, gaining a free labor supply to help tame a new land. The Africans are considered better suited to agricultural labor than the Native Americans, less likely to perish from tropical diseases than either Native Americans or whites and less able to run away successfully in an unfamiliar land where their color makes them conspicuous. At the same time it enslaves blacks, Maryland also enacts the first colonial law against racial intermarriage, beginning a trend that will create more social distance between whites and blacks, and promote the idea that blacks are an inferior race cursed by God and meant to be servants.

1681: Maryland's law is amended after the Irish Nell case in which a white woman claims she's been forced to marry a slave so a planter can get her labor free. The revised law exempts the woman from involuntary servitude if she is entrapped by a master. Nell Butler had married "Negro Charles," the slave of Major William Boarman of St. Mary's County, in August 1681. A Catholic priest conducted the ceremony, and Lord Baltimore is said to have been present on the day of the marriage and to have warned Nell of the consequences. About a month later, Maryland passes a law that releases white servant women and their mixed-race children from slavery if the marriage was permitted or encouraged by the master.

1691–1725: The Virginia Assembly rules that any whites who marry Negroes, Indians or mulattos "shall within three months be banished from this dominion forever. . . . And it is further enacted, that if any English woman being free shall have a bastard child by a Negro she shall pay fifteen pounds to the church wardens and in default of such payment, she shall be taken into possession by the church wardens and disposed of for five years and the amount she brings shall be paid one-third to their majesties for the support of the government, one-third to the support of the parish where the offense is committed and the other third to the informer. The child shall be bound out by the church wardens until he is thirty years of age."

1702: After a white woman named Ann Wall violates Virginia's ban on intermarriage, she is made a temporary slave for five years, and her two mulatto children are sold into involuntary servitude for thirty-one years. The court rules that when Ann Wall's term of service expires, she will be banished to Barbados if she returns to her home in Elizabeth City, Virginia.

1705: Virginia rules that any free white man or woman who intermarries with a Negro will be confined to prison for six months without bail and pay ten pounds to the parish. Ministers marrying such persons will be fined ten thousand pounds of tobacco. Other states follow suit.

Intermarriage is banned in 1705 in Massachusetts; in 1715 in North Carolina; in 1717 in South Carolina; in 1721 in Delaware and in 1725 in Pennsylvania. Punishments for violating these laws vary. Free blacks who break these racial barriers can be enslaved and those already enslaved can be sold away from their colony. White men and women who marry slaves can be fined, jailed or also enslaved.

The laws create a class system that makes many poor whites feel superior to slaves and prevents them from uniting with slaves to challenge the wealthy. The law is aimed specifically at white women and designed to protect the economic interests of slaveholders who do not want white women to produce mulatto children with a claim to freedom.

Virginia state law makes all imported blacks lifelong slaves unless they are Christians.

1738: Runaway slaves form the first free black community in North America, Gracia Real de Santo Teresa de Mose, better known as Fort Mose, in Florida. Soon the Indians follow, remnants of the most resistant tribes, including the Creek, who have been fighting the Europeans. Together they become known as Seminoles. They harbor runaway slaves, who live in their own villages and give corn to the tribe as a tax. Intermarriage becomes common.

1785: A New York statute starts the process of freeing blacks, but they cannot vote or hold public office and marriage with whites is forbidden. This gradual emancipation bill frees children born to slave women after 1785.

Esteban Rodriguez Miro becomes governor of Spanish Louisiana, and in his inaugural speech orders free black women to wear plain head wraps and bandannas instead of silks, feathers and fancy curls. People call the new restrictions the Tignon (or turban) Law. It is designed to break up the practice of light-skinned, fancily dressed free unmarried black women living as mistresses of white men in little houses near the ramparts.

1807: George Thompson is born around this time in Madagascar, an island in the Indian Ocean off the coast of Africa. In the early 1800s, he is enslaved in Boone County, Kentucky. But he eventually escapes, traveling to freedom on the Underground Railroad until he reaches Pennsylvania. He continues on to Canada, finding a job in Trois Rivieres as a coachman for an Englishman named Ford. Ford's daughter falls in love with Thompson and the pair elope, living for a while on the Indian Reserve on Walpole Island. Thompson runs a blacksmith shop. By 1850, they own farmland in Malden Township, Ontario. In 1862, Thompson makes a plow in his smithy shop, using forged steel in some parts of it. It is a forerunner of the modern plow.

1810: The third U.S. census reveals that America has 7.2 million people, 60,000 of them immigrants and 1.2 million of them slaves.

1827: After the emancipation of New York slaves, free blacks flood the city's infamous Five Points neighborhood (Anthony, Orange and Cross streets), joining the unskilled Irish. In the Old Brewery building, blacks with white wives jam the cellar compartments. Their children mostly stay indoors, fearing they will be snatched by kidnappers and thrown aboard boats headed for the South.

1830: In Virginia, a slave named Peggy and her black mate, Patrick, kill their master and burn his house. Peggy claims that when she refused her master's sexual advances, she was chained to a lock and kept in a meat house. At her trial, she claims she refused the man's advances because he was her father.

1851: In the January 1, 1851, issue of the *Voice of the Fugitive*, Henry Bibb talks about two letter writers in the *Amherstburg Courier* on December 7, one anonymous, one named Edwin Sarwill. The letter writers complain that blacks are inferior and ignorant and that if they are allowed to settle in Canada they will marry the whites and degrade both races.

Bibb's response: "We think it would be paying their daughters a very poor compliment to suppose such a thing if the colored people were half as worthless as these writers have represented them."

1853: William Atwood is born a slave on a plantation in Wilcox County, Alabama, the son of his master, Henry Stiles Atwood, and a woman who is part African and part English. When Henry Atwood dies in 1853, his will frees his son, William, William's mother and twenty-one other slaves, sending all of them north to Ripley, Ohio. There, both mother and son attend school. As a result, William later becomes a wealthy lumberman in the timberlands of East Saginaw, Michigan.

1855: Celia, a Missouri slave, is hanged on December 21, 1855, after clubbing to death her widowed owner, Robert Newsom, whom she claimed had forced her to have sexual relations over a period of years. She had borne him two children, both of whom became his property. Although the second article of Section 29 of the Missouri statutes of 1845 forbids anyone "to take any woman unlawfully against her will and by force, menace or duress, compel her to be defiled," Judge William Hall refuses to instruct the jury that the enslaved woman is covered by the term "any woman."

1858: Henry Newby, a white Virginia planter born in 1783 and growing up in Culpeper County, Virginia, frees his common-law wife, Elsey Newby, born an enslaved African-American in Fauquier County, Virginia, about 1799. He also frees their children. In the 1850s, he owns 248 acres and at least seventeen slaves. On September 17, 1858, he sells his Culpeper land, then files a deed freeing four slaves, Evaline Newby, then twenty-six, and her three children. The decision of most Newby family members to move with Henry Newby to the free state of Ohio liberates over a dozen people. By 1860, Newby's household has disappeared from Culpeper, and the white seventy-seven-year-old farmer lives in Bridgeport, Ohio, across the Ohio River from Wheeling. In his will Newby acknowledges Elsey as the mother of his children named and leaves most of his property to her.

A police officer boards the steamboat *Portsmouth* in Louisville in search of a thirty-five-year-old slave belonging to Mrs. Susan Pugh of Stewart County, Tennessee. The slave is believed to have run away with a poor white woman named Lucinda Legett. According to historian Blaine Hudson, authorities find Mrs. Legett, a dog, three children and a pine box on the steamer. It takes them a little longer to find the slave, who is hiding inside the pine box.

1859: Dion Boucicault, an Irish playwright and actor, writes *The Octoroon*, a play about the love of a white man for a black girl.

1860: Hoping to find a refuge from white men who threatened to torch the homes of blacks in Missouri and slaveowners who bring slaves into the free state of California, Sylvia and Louis Stark leave the United States. They and their two children move from California to mountainous Salt Spring Island off the coast of Vancouver, British Columbia. It is a place where mussels hug the rocks, clams hide in the sand, wild strawberries and blackberries flourish and the sea churns with oysters, salmon, cod and crabs. The central area is settled mainly by blacks, mostly from California, and by Portuguese.

However, Salt Spring Island—the name is later officially shortened to Saltspring—is neither a peaceful settlement nor an all-black one. White Americans, Englishmen, Germans and Polynesians also preempt land on the rugged island. To survive, settlers have to knead bread with guns beside them, trap cougars so large they call them panthers, watch out for black bears and gray wolves and deal with the sniping at and shooting of some black settlers, allegedly by Native Canadians. Conflicts flare up between island residents, but in a land this hard and flinty, residents cannot afford major strife. Intermarriage, in fact, becomes common.

1861: At least nine biracial couples live in Buxton, a black settlement near Chatham in Ontario, Canada. They include a white male and black female, seven black males and white females and one Native American male and mulatto female.

1867: Bill Wyrnosdick, a Crenshaw, Alabama, black man, pays a two-hundred-dollar fine and goes to jail for thirty days for living with a white female employee.

1870: The radical Mississippi legislature repeals the 1865 ban on racial intermarriage.

1880–1940: The myth that black men, if not restrained, will roam the country raping white women fuels the wholesale lynching of black males during this period. According to Tuskegee Institute figures, between the years 1882 and 1951, 4,730 people were lynched in the United States, 3,437 Negro and 1,293 white. The accusations against black persons lynched, according to the Tuskegee Institute records for the years 1882 to 1951, included felonious assault, rape, attempted rape, robbery and theft, insulting white persons and miscellaneous offenses. In some cases, there were no explanations for the lynchings.

However, in the South, where white women have been enshrined as symbols of virtue and chastity by men still mourning the loss of the Civil War and the erosion of their power, rape can mean many things. A black man can be considered guilty of assault with intent to rape by showing up in a woman's backyard, sitting next to her on a trolley or looking at her in the "wrong" way.

1893: Henry Smith is lynched in Paris, Texas, after he is accused of brutally murdering the four-year-old daughter of a local policeman. The only evidence against the mentally retarded man who does odd jobs is that he was once arrested by the policeman. Rumors circulate that he assaulted the child and then killed her. A local Methodist bishop claims he tore the girl apart with "gorilla ferocity." However, an autopsy finds no evidence of rape. The girl had been choked. Some ten thousand people show up to watch Smith tortured with branding irons and set on fire.

1908: A white woman named Mabel Hallam accuses George Richardson, a black man, of raping her. Later, the Springfield, Illinois, woman admits to a grand jury that she lied to cover up an affair with a white man. By then, two blacks have been lynched during a two-day rampage. The victims include William Donnegan, eighty-four, a black man who owns half a block of real estate and has a white wife. A mob drags him from his porch and hangs him.

1915: *The Birth of a Nation*, the film that sparked the revival of the Ku Klux Klan, premieres in the Atlanta Theater. It is based on Thomas Dixon's novel and play *The Clansman*. Among other things, it depicts a lust-mad black man pursuing a white woman until she leaps to her death. The Klan then kills him. A light-skinned black woman also has an affair with a white abolitionist senator. In Chicago, minors cannot see the film, and twenty-five thousand people gather at the Massachusetts state capitol demanding it be banned. However, the film creates a sensation in many places, including Atlanta, where people pay two dollars to see it even though the regular price of a movie is only fifteen cents. In the film, white actress Mary Alden darkens her face with cork to play a light-skinned black woman.

1921: A mob armed with rifles, shotguns, kerosene and even machine guns burns Tulsa's thriving black community, Greenwood, to the ground. Between seventy-five and three hundred people are killed in what was known as Black Wall Street (Greenwood Avenue) after an apparently unfounded complaint that a black man had attempted to assault a white woman in an elevator.

1923: A mob attacks a small black town of about two hundred in Rosewood, Florida, after an unidentified black man supposedly sexually assaults a white woman. Homes are burned, and the inhabitants are chased into the wilderness.

1924: Eugene O'Neill's play *All God's Chillun Got Wings*, which deals with race mixing, raises such a storm that the *New York World* demands that the Board of Aldermen in New York suppress it. Political leaders are urged to do something about the play because it depicts "an act which is illegal in more than half the country . . . to be represented in a manner indicating approval."

1925: The Negro-Caucasian Club is organized at the University of Michigan and lasts five years, possibly the first interracial student association on any American campus. The original membership includes twenty-six students and faculty, black and white, who want "to encourage a spirit of friendliness and fair-mindedness between the races, and to study and discuss, impartially, the problems arising in relations between them." In the mid-1920s, there are about sixty black students at Michigan, of whom fewer than ten are women, in a student body of about ten thousand.

1931: A fight breaks out between young white men and black men riding a freight train in Jackson County, Alabama. The white men demand that the black riders leave the car, but the blacks put all of them except one off the train. The bloodied white men notify the sheriff, who searches the train. They turn up the nine black riders, ranging in age from thirteen to twenty, a white youth and two young women, Ruby Bates and Victoria Price. As the black men are about to be transported to the Scottsboro, Alabama, jail, Bates claims the blacks raped her and Price. In the subsequent trials, the jury finds each man, with the exception of the thirteen-year-old, guilty, and they are sentenced to death. Supporters get them a stay of execution and appeal the case to the U.S. Supreme Court.

In November 1932, the Court orders the case retried on the grounds the state failed to provide the men with adequate counsel. During the new trials, which begin in March 1933, Ruby Bates retracts her story, but the jury discounts it and two defendants are again convicted. Two years later, the U.S. Supreme Court reverses the convictions on the grounds that blacks have been improperly excluded from the jury. The next round of trials begins in 1935 and by 1937 all charges have been dropped against four men; the rape charges against one man are dropped but he receives twenty-five years for assaulting a deputy sheriff. One man receives seventy-five years for rape, another ninety-nine years and the third a life sentence. However, the defendants are paroled, one by one, and in 1950, Andrew Wright, the last Scottsboro boy still in prison, goes free. In 1976, George Wallace pardons Clarence Norris.

1933: On June 15, a white woman named Effa Brooks and a black man named Abraham Manley marry in New York City, but their marriage certificate describes Effa as "colored." Her father is listed as Benjamin Brooks, her mother's first husband, who was black. However, Effa later changes her story, claiming she was nearly grown before her mother told her she had a white father, a wealthy financier. For most of her life, the olive-skinned woman chooses to live as black and represents herself as such to the black community. She and her husband run the Newark Eagles, a baseball team in the Negro National League.

1937: The management of a Detroit theater makes singer Billie Holiday smear dark greasepaint on her high-yellow face while she performs with Count Basie. Apparently, the management worried that, in a certain light, Billie might look like a white woman jamming with black musicians.

1955: The bloated and battered body of Emmett Till, a fourteen-year-old black Chicago youth visiting relatives in the South, is found in Mississippi's Tallahatchie River, murdered after supposedly whistling at or flirting with a white woman in Money, Mississippi. His mother has the body shipped home to Chicago so mourners can view the boy's swollen lump of a face and unrecognizable body. According to author Maryanne Vollers, the two local men acquitted of the crime, Roy Bryant and J. W. "Big" Milam, later sell a story describing Till's murder to *Look* magazine.

1958: A poll finds that 96 percent of whites disapprove of marriages between blacks and whites.

Two Virginians, Richard Loving, a twenty-four-year-old white man, and Mildred Jeter, an eighteen-year-old who is black and Native American, decide to marry but can't do it in their home state: mixed marriages are banned in Virginia. Loving and Jeter grew up near each other in the town of Central Point in rural Caroline County. It is a community where people with the surnames Loving and Jeter have lived for centuries and where racial mixing is common. Tolerance has not always been the rule, though. In 1736, a slave named Andrew was hanged for the alleged rape of a white indentured servant, although the evidence suggested she consented to the act. Both parties were first convicted of adultery, but the court changed the sentence for Andrew after some people complained. Andrew was hanged, but there is no record of the Caroline County Court punishing other black men for such an offense.

Mildred Jeter, a tall, soft-spoken woman, and Richard Loving, a brickmason who loves racing cars on country tracks, marry in Washington, D.C., which has no laws against intermarriage. They move back to Virginia, where Loving builds a white cinder-block house. Six weeks after their marriage, Sheriff R. Garnett Brooks and two deputies enter the Lovings' house through an unlocked door. They shine flashlights into the couple's eyes and wave a warrant charging them with violating Virginia's law against marriage between whites and blacks. The law defines a white person as someone without a trace of any blood but Caucasian, something that is impossible to prove.

Found guilty of a felony, the Lovings are sentenced to one year in jail, but are told their sentence will be suspended if they stay out of Virginia for twenty-five years.

In his ruling, Judge Leon M. Bazile justifies Virginia's ban on interracial marriage by declaring that "Almighty God created the races white, black, yellow, malay and red, and he placed them on separate continents. And but for the interference with his arrangement there would be no cause for such marriages. The fact that he separated the races shows that he did not intend for the races to mix."

The Lovings leave Virginia for Washington, D.C., but dislike city life. They soon return to Caroline County in the northeastern part of the state, a place with sharp contrasts in weather and plenty of loblolly pines, gum and cypress trees, rain and history. They have three children and live as fugitives for nine years. Friends and family shelter them.

At the time, their kind of marriage is almost as rare as lettuce in a butcher shop. In 1960, there are only 51,000 black/white married couples in the entire United States. The Lovings are determined to be among them. They file a class action suit, which is denied, and then take their case to the Supreme Court of Appeals of Virginia. It, too, upholds Virginia law. However, the American Civil Liberties Union takes the case to the U.S. Supreme Court, which strikes down the Virginia law as a violation of the Equal Protection Clause of the Fourteenth Amendment. The justices describe it as a law with no purpose other than discrimination. This ruling not only ends Virginia's ban on interracial marriage, but wipes out similar laws still on the books in fifteen other states.

1959: John Howard Griffin, a white novelist from Texas, shaves off his straight hair, darkens his skin with oral medication, a sunlamp and a topical stainer, and tours the South as a black man. In his 1961 book *Black Like Me* Griffin talks about bus drivers who refuse to let him off at his stop, his inability to cash traveler's checks, being advised not to look at movie posters of white women, his failure to find a nonmenial job and, most bizarrely, numerous white men who offer him rides so they can quiz him about his sex life. Griffin claims one man even asked to see his penis.

2003: The family of the late senator Strom Thurmond of South Carolina acknowledges in December that Essie Mae Washington-Williams, a retired teacher, is the daughter of Senator Thurmond, known for his strong segregationist stands, and a black teenager who worked for his family as a maid in 1925. Under the laws of the time, he could have been prosecuted for "fornication," defined as extramarital sex, and fined at least one hundred dollars.

2004: According to an Associated Press story, in a Gallup poll commissioned by the AARP and the Leadership Conference on Civil Rights nearly 90 percent of whites, 73 percent of blacks and 76 percent of Hispanics say race relations have improved somewhat. The same poll finds 73 percent of Americans approving of interracial marriage.

2004: The Justice Department announces that it is reopening an investigation into the unsolved 1955 Emmett Till murder because two documentaries about the case suggest other people might have been involved besides the two original and now dead suspects.

12

HOUND DOGS HATE RED PEPPER

Isaac Berry's story—about running away from slavery to meet a white girl who had offered him sips of cool water and chunks of red-hot preaching—sounds like a tall tale whispered around campfires.

Yet it has been passed from one generation of the Berry family to the next, as timeworn and true as an old man's Bible.

Berry, a fiddle-playing, ox-driving, horseshoe-making slave, began walking from Missouri to Michigan in the spring of 1858. He met his first major challenge when he stopped to shave by a stream in the Illinois woods. Two white men tramping through the woods confronted him.

"Looks like we got ourselves a runaway," one said. "See if he's got some money."

As they drew near, Isaac pulled out a Bowie knife as long as a slave's scream.

"I got weapons, and I'm goin' to defend myself," he said, according to the memoirs of his daughter, the late Kate Pointer. "It gonna be your life against mine."

"We just hoboes," one of the men said.

They began backing away and finally turned and ran. Things might have gone differently, though, if they had understood that Isaac was not only running away to avoid being sold off like a hog as his brother, Harve, had been. He also was keeping a promise to Lucy Esther Millard, a white preacher's daughter who had stirred up feelings that could leave a brown-skinned man bleeding on bluegrass. She had been his neighbor in Palmyra, Missouri, and she had vowed to find him once he fled to Canada.

For what Isaac was planning he could have been whipped until the sun got tired of shining on fat fields and thin slaves. He could have been dragged by dogs, castrated or buried up to his neck in Missouri mud, sugar sprinkled on his head to draw flies. Until well into the twentieth century, real or imaginary relationships between black men and white women—a suspicion of rape, the whisper of love—became grounds for lynching and mutilating black men. But Lucy was in Isaac's plans now and, no doubt, in his head—feet propped up, eyes shiny with backdoor secrets, brown hair yoked into a bun but reflecting the light. There was no way he could make her memory get up and go home.

It was Juliann Berry Pratt, Isaac's owner, who had warned him that it was time to go. Her husband, Jim Pratt, she told Isaac, was going to sell him down the river, a threat that could make even the hardiest slaves shiver. The river was the Mississippi, and it led to the Deep South, often to Louisiana. It might mean spending eighteen hours a day plucking cotton bolls from prongs with tips that could slash like knives while carrying a bag of cotton on your shoulders. Or it might mean chopping sugar cane, which had to be slashed at just the right slant so it could grow again and cut without pausing in the steaming heat. The life expectancy of sugar cane workers brought south from border states like Missouri ranged from seven to nine years.

Why did Juliann urge Isaac to run? According to family legend, she was Isaac's half-sister, both of them the children of Uriah George Berry of Livingston County, Kentucky. In the 1850 Kentucky census, Uriah Berry is listed as a merchant with property worth eight thousand dollars, which made him the most prosperous man in his area. Uriah Berry died in the mid-1850s, and under the terms of his will, neither Isaac nor his pale-skinned sister, Nancy, were to be whipped or sold. Such arrangements were common in families where mulatto slaves cooked meals, groomed horses, scrubbed floors, emptied chamber pots and fanned away flies while the darker-skinned slaves often plowed and picked crops. Yet customs meant nothing to Jim Pratt, an Irish-born riverboat gambler whom Juliann had met while selling her family's molasses near Frankfort, Kentucky.

A compulsive gambler, Pratt always needed money and raised it any way he could. He already had sold Isaac's brother, Harve, to pay a debt and sold the horse Isaac had raised from a colt. As the man of the house, he controlled all the money and made the decisions. After warning Isaac of what her husband planned to do, Juliann, according to family stories, handed Isaac a gold coin and told him to take her horse, ride it as far as he could and then turn the horse loose. That meant leaving Palmyra, Missouri, Isaac's home, as well as leaving his mother, Mary Clara; his two remaining brothers, John and Elijah; and his sisters, Nancy and Mary, family members who might be sold and scattered, too, one day.

Isaac was a slave, but his life had been different from the lives of slaves who were beaten with hot elm switches for failing to pick one last sprig of cotton or for looking their masters' wives in the eye. Yet, according to historian Richard M. Dorson, who interviewed Isaac's daughter, Kate Pointer, "[Isaac] was afraid. He had always been afraid." He could wander ten miles from his home near Palmyra, but not one hundred or one thousand. He could plow a field, play a fiddle, shoe a horse or carve a canoe, but when his name later appeared on a WANTED poster, he couldn't read it. He had his own revolver and could hunt deer and wild turkeys, selling the meat to a woman who ran a hotel in St. Louis. This was how he saved enough money to buy food after he ran away. The woman would give him a dollar and a half for the deer's saddle, and he would take the rest of the meat home to his family, who mostly lived on ham bones and hog heads. And when he took up his fiddle and began to play that old half-sad, half-snappy music, he could lap up joy and even taste hope. Yet in some way those little glimmers of good times, those shots of liberty, were more a curse than a blessing. And he could have been hanged or shot if people knew that Lucy had sworn nothing would separate her from his smile.

A few days after Juliann gave him a gold piece, Isaac told the Pratts he was going to play his fiddle at a dance.

Isaac had taught himself to coax a sound from his instrument that no fiddler in the area could match. He regularly made money playing at weekend dances: his favorite songs were "The Devil's Dream" and "Old Aunt Kate Ain't Got No Shoes." Slave narratives describe Saturday-night dances where people high-stepped and stomped away the drudgery of working from 4:00 A.M. until sundown. Dancers did the promenade and jig, some dancing with glasses of water on their heads to see who could keep moving the longest without spilling water. They danced the pigeon wing, swinging their partners around and around in the moonlight under old oaks. Some danced awhile, slept and then leapt to life again, keeping time with beef rib bones while fiddlers and banjo pickers played.

But for Isaac these dances were more than a chance to lap up joy by watching people doing reels, waltzes, polkas, quadrilles and buck dances. He had made important friends at these gatherings, free blacks such as Albert Campbell, who lived in Quincy, Illinois, just across the Mississippi. Campbell promised to help Isaac escape. He said he would have a lantern on the Illinois side of the river and turn it up and down three times when he was ready to pick up Isaac in his boat.

On a Saturday in April 1858, Isaac packed for his journey, stuffing only a few pieces of the past in his knapsack. He took his revolver and bowie knife to fight off slave catchers, his fiddle and razor to pump up his spirits and cayenne pepper for the tracking dogs. To muffle their scent and confuse the hounds on their trail, runaway slaves sometimes rubbed raw onion on their backs, waded in water, tied pine brush to their legs or put red pepper in their shoes or around the bases of trees in which they hid. "That was one of the secrets of the Underground Railroad," according to Marguerite Berry Jackson, Isaac's late granddaughter. "Cayenne pepper."

On his way to the banks of the Mississippi, Isaac had to pass through tall grass prairie, the sea of grass that was a real sea millions of years ago. Jim Pratt had made extra money renting out Isaac to new German-speaking settlers struggling to make homes on the flat prairie. The German immigrants would rent Isaac for a year to bust up their sod. The ground had hardened almost to stone and grass speckled with red, purple and cream-colored wild hyacinth grew high enough to reach out and shake your hand. With a heavy hammer, ax and plow, Isaac broke up the hard-faced earth, disappearing inside swirls of dust and sunshine. "One of the places where he was rented must have been close to the Millards," Jackson notes.

That was how Isaac met the Millard sisters, Lucy and Clarissa, who brought water to him in the fields. The Mormon Church has no records documenting that Lucy and Clarissa's father, Solomon Nelson Millard, became a member of The Church of Jesus Christ of Latter-day Saints during the turbulent, war-torn nineteenth century. However, the Berry family's oral history and Lucy's marriage records suggest he did.

Most religious services for slaves featured white preachers telling slaves to obey their masters and mistresses and not steal their chickens. There was no mention of souls or salvation. However, when Lucy came to the Pratt farm to visit Juliann—her only friend—Juliann suggested Lucy read the Bible to Isaac. That was how he learned the ways of God—a mixture of hail and fire raining on Egypt, walls tumbling to the roar of trumpets, lightning running along the ground. He also learned about another Palmyra, in the western part of Lucy's native New York. In the early 1800s, this Palmyra was a stomping ground for all kinds of preachers trying to win converts to their churches. The stretch of New York where it sat was called the Burned-Over District because religious fires swept through it so many times, scorching every soul in their path. People there claimed they could talk to the dead and hear taps from beyond the grave—possibly because nineteenth-century people were sometimes mistakenly buried alive. Meanwhile, a farm boy founded The Church of Jesus Christ of Latter-day Saints.

While Lucy read the Bible to Isaac, the two of them fell under each other's spell. There is no way to tell how Isaac managed to rise above his fears and dream of loving a white woman who had crisscrossed the country with her kinfolks, watched an elephant drown and learned that it was possible to keep turning the pages of your life, creating one adventure after the next. Nor is there any way of knowing whether Lucy Esther Millard, a young woman who believed in grabbing life by the throat, realized how much she would have to give up to spend her life with a slave. Since her family had previously lived in Michigan, she would have known that the Detroit River was the gateway to free Canada and a new life. So as she and Isaac talked, they apparently made plans to meet in the Detroit/Windsor, Canada, area.

On the day that Isaac ran off from his master, he stopped at the Mississippi River, smacked his horse and sent it home to Juliann. Then there was nothing to do but wait for Campbell's signal indicating he was coming with his boat—three blinks and then another blink.

But even after flashing his light, Albert Campbell never sailed across the Mississippi to rescue Isaac. It was early spring, and the river had swollen, its foam-flecked waves rising up to splash at the sky. It was not a flood, but it must have stirred up images of twisted trees and drowned houses and barns. Isaac stayed on the river's west bank until the sun rose that Sunday morning.

He couldn't fight the Mississippi's angry waves and whirlpools, so he stayed in the brush along the river for another day, watching and waiting.

His savior was a white family on a flatboat.

He watched a white man, woman and two small children dock on the Missouri side of the Mississippi and gather firewood to cook their breakfast. Finally, he approached them and offered them his five-dollar gold piece to ferry him to the Illinois side. He said he had a job in Quincy and needed to get to it. They took him across.

He came ashore at Quincy, Illinois, which begins at the Mississippi, leaps over steep bluffs, levels out on the uplands and trails off into woods and farmlands. When slavery-fighting men set up a church there, they called it the Lord's Barn. One night, a mob gathered in front of the barn to wipe out the slavery fighters. However, somebody warned them the mob was coming, and they hid clubs, hatchets and muskets under the pulpit. The deacons led the assault when the congregation rushed out to greet the mob.

But there were no slavery fighters to help Isaac that morning.

He saw a hollow log by the river and decided to climb inside and wait for dark. But he soon changed his mind about hiding in a place with only one way in and one way out, shimmying up a pine tree instead. He nodded off in the tree and awakened to see a rifle-carrying bounty hunter riding up to the log. When he thumped the log to see if it sounded hollow, a rabbit ran out. The bounty hunter galloped away.

Isaac was in a part of Illinois usually heavy in springtime with the husky, wood-rich aroma of sassafras, pine and dog fennel. He would have waited for nightfall before knocking on Albert Campbell's door. According to family stories, Campbell gave him a crudely drawn map that traced the way to Chicago and from there either to central Indiana or southern Michigan, where he was supposed to find the Purdues, another free colored family. Both possible stops were named Coloma. (An old log building served as the official Underground Railroad station in the tiny Quaker village of Coloma, Indiana.) Most likely, Albert's wife stuffed Isaac's knapsack with food that would keep on the road—slices of cold cornmeal mush, macaroni pie, hardtack bread made from nothing but flour and water and toasted on a stick or "fat cornbread" made from cornmeal, salt, soda, hot water and crisp pork rinds.

Then Isaac resumed his journey. He later told family members that he followed the path of the railroad. Soon hunger followed him. One day, he darted into a barn and milked a cow into his big, floppy slouch hat, swallowing all the milk in one great gulp. A few days later, he came to a stream, where he washed himself and shaved. That was when he met bounty hunters and ran them off.

Isaac kept on walking, traveling by night, hiding in trees during the day and following the routes of old railroad tracks. He later estimated he walked about twenty miles a day, unless he had to detour around swampland. If he caught rabbits, squirrels or other game, he cooked them around noon so the smoke and fire wouldn't stand out in the glare of sunshine.

He had been shown how to look up at the night sky and find the Big W, the middle star pointing to the North Star that guided runaways. He also knew that moss grew only on the north side of trees in the north. Yet following a star or watching for moss is harder than it sounds on foggy or nearly moonless nights. In densely wooded areas, Isaac probably notched trees or bent bushes in the direction he was traveling so he could tell if he began going in circles.

The land he crossed would have been the home of wild asparagus and corn, strawberries and rhubarb, snap beans and peas, apples and beets, dewberries, raspberries, mulberries, huckleberries and black haws, pokeweed and peaches. Also, wild currants, grapes, muscadines and chokeberries, cattail bulbs and roots, wild fern roots and greens. But it was April, the corn and soybeans had just been planted, the berries wouldn't ripen until June, and the apples wouldn't be ready for harvest until fall. So hunger haunted Isaac, and thirst kept him company.

If he found spring water, he would have drunk it. If his thirst became desperate, he might have notched maple and birch trees, let the sap flow into his hands and gulped it down. Cattail stalks also contained a little sac filled with water. And he might have known that carrying a clean pebble or hickory nut in his mouth would reduce the sensation of thirst.

One day, he noticed two wagons rumbling westward. The people in the wagons were throwing out scraps of food for the dogs following them. After the wagons and dogs passed, Isaac climbed down from his tree. He fell on his knees, scrambling for food that dogs had already sniffed, licked or stepped on. "It was survival," says his granddaughter Jackson.

Soon he had reached Chicago, a flat muddy town where people

warmed themselves before grate fires. Though Isaac didn't know it, local newspapers published long lists of advertisements for slaves, often described as branded on the hand or having fresh whipping welts on their backs. And there was a five-hundred-dollar reward for him, dead or alive.

He stopped in the city, pulling down his slouch hat to hide as much of his light brown face as possible. He was hungry from head to toe, but didn't want anyone to smell his desperation. So he waited for darkness and then bought a cigar, which he smoked like a man with no reason to hurry and nothing but tobacco on his mind. Afterward, he bought a loaf of bread and some cheese from a little country store.

He was still walking at night and sleeping during the day. The cayenne pepper in his shoes not only threw off tracking dogs: it blistered his feet, already swollen from walking. So he stumbled on, his fiddle in his bag and Lucy's good-bye wedged inside his head.

In the Midwest, spring is a wind-tossed blend of fallen limbs, scattered rocks, long-buried autumn leaves and resurrected grass. It is a season that has trouble making up its mind: some days start off smelling like summer, then surrender to winter's grip, gray skies and even snow swallowing newborn sunshine. Isaac, himself a mixture of fears and hopes, managed to reach the Purdues. The free black couple gave him his first real meal since leaving Quincy, Illinois. He rested with them for a week, learning for the first time that he was not safe even in free states because federal laws and judges could return him to his master.

When Isaac left the Purdues, he headed for Detroit, the last stop on the Underground Railroad for thousands of fugitives who crossed the Detroit River to Canada. Though less than 1 percent of Michigan's population likely belonged to the antislavery movement, they were a bold band. On July 1, 1859, the *Detroit Free Press* reported that a group of blacks ran aboard a ship returning from Superior City when it docked in Detroit. A Kentucky lady named Mrs. Moore was returning from her summer vacation and accompanied by two mulatto slaves. The Detroit blacks whisked the woman's slaves off the ship. But despite such spontaneous uprisings, the majority of the state's antislavery fighters did no more than hide hungry, harried people in their attics and barns, basements and false-bottomed wagons or hurry them to their next stop.

Erastus Hussey, a Quaker, ran the Battle Creek station. When his daughter, Susan, was sixteen, she woke up one night and discovered thirty black men and women standing near the door. She was home alone, but she invited them in, boiled cauldrons of coffee and managed to supply them with food contributed by neighbors. She then gave them a note to a man in Marshall and sent them on their way. In Ypsilanti, Michigan, one Underground Railroad station was the home of Leonard Chase, and it stood on the summit of the Cross Street hill. Mrs. Eurolas Morton sometimes baked bread at night and carried it to the Chase home to feed runaways, creeping through backyards so she wouldn't be seen.

Isaac Berry's first stop after leaving the Purdues was Saline in the southeastern part of the state, an area swirling with bounty hunters, antislavery activists and, more than likely, spies and counterspies. By the time he got there, he could barely put one foot in front of the other. Stumbling down a road, he met a free black man carrying a dinner pail. The man, who often helped runaways, couldn't stop staring at Isaac, who looked ready to collapse at his feet.

"The man asked him are you a fugitive slave," according to Marguerite Jackson. "Grandpa told him 'none of your business.' But the man told him to go [to his house] and 'tell my wife I said feed you and put you to bed.'"

He followed the man's directions to his house, and the man's wife gave Isaac something to eat. That night, the house swelled with people who had come to see, hear and touch a runaway slave who had already worn out two pairs of shoes, including sturdy, club-shaped brogans built to fit either foot. Isaac had cobbled together a second pair of shoes by ripping out the sleeves of his coat and putting cardboard soles inside the sleeves. He then made a knot at one end of the sleeves, tying the cardboard to his feet.

People in Saline took up a collection and bought Isaac some carpet slippers, black or gray felt shoes in which the dead were sometimes buried. Two people then took him to Detroit in a wagon with a false bottom. They left him at Finney's barn, at the northeast corner of Griswold and State streets, a hiding place for escaping slaves waiting to cross the Detroit River to Canada. Finney, who came to Detroit from western New York in 1834, owned a hotel and livery stable. Legend has it that many fugitives huddled in fear in Finney's stable while the men who pursued them dined in Finney's hotel.

According to Jackson, Isaac was taken to Windsor late at night. There he looked up Albert Campbell's aunt, Celia Flenoy, who found him a job. He also returned to playing his fiddle on weekends.

Other relatives say that after Isaac reached Detroit, he wandered along the shore of the Detroit River trying to figure out exactly where escaping slaves swam or sailed across to Canada. Then he noticed a white man walking toward him.

"You're not a runaway are you?" the man said.

"What business it of your'n?" The Detroit River was just a ribbon of water, no more than a mile wide where Isaac stood. He could look across it and see freedom glinting in the sun. And there were no snow houses on its banks and no crows to peck him or pull out his eyes, as the slave owners claimed in stories meant to frighten slaves.

"You're gonna get caught out here," the white man insisted. "You'd better stick with me."

He followed the man to Grosse Pointe, a wooded and swampy area on Lake St. Clair, just east of the Detroit River. They had to travel along a plank toll road, a four-hour horse-and-buggy trip through the mud. On the way, they would have passed roadhouses selling frog leg dinners and drinks. The man hid Isaac in a shed, bringing him food and water. Locked in the shed for three days, Isaac likely became convinced he'd stepped into a trap.

But the white man did not betray him.

A mist shrouded Lake St. Clair one morning, allowing the white man to ferry Isaac to Canada without being seen. He dropped him off and told him to head south. That was how he wound up tracking down Albert Campbell's aunt, Celia Flenoy, and landing a job farming for John Martindale in the village of Puce on the Puce River, near Windsor, Ontario. It was a place thick with maple, elm and spruce trees and memories of black men and women who'd knelt down to kiss free soil when they first arrived. Isaac and two other black men lived on Martindale's land. Isaac also worked for a whiskey distiller named John Bryant who forced him to take part of his pay in pails of liquor. Bryant also made Isaac hide nondistilled whiskey for him in straw sacks.

Isaac still had no idea what had become of Lucy and whether or not she could keep her end of their dangerous bargain. Yet somewhere between the gaping mouth of the Mississippi and the narrow gash of the Detroit River—between Palmyra, Missouri, the source of Isaac's fear, and Palmyra, New York, the source of Lucy's Mormon faith—Isaac Berry had tasted something with the tang of true freedom. It was like new honey on hot bread, and he gulped it down.

Lucy Millard's ears stuck out as though they longed to escape her face and go their separate ways, and her lips were a blade-thin slash of serious business. As a child, she'd cried because she didn't have her sister's curly hair. She also wept when one of her uncles gave the two sisters wine-colored velvet bonnets but only Clarissa's bonnet had a feather. However, as an adult Lucy wore her straight coppery hair in buns so tight her scalp looked ready to bleed. All the same, she had a huge hunger for all of life's sights and smells and her every move set off sparks.

People who knew Lucy in her later years paint a vivid picture of her puffing on her corncob pipe stuffed with corn cake tobacco or putting on her old gray bonnet and shawl and taking her children and grandchildren into the woods to search for healing herbs and teas. They also remember her stitching quilts in her favorite Flying Geese pattern, her fingers as nimble as snakes; chugging the homemade wine she loved and could make from just about anything, including pin cherries, mulberries and black cherries; and using a needle and thread to reinforce the magazine that came with the weekly newspaper *Grit*: that way, she could help preserve its recipes, serialized fiction stories, Bible stories for children, sewing patterns, thrift tips and other features.

Mostly, though, they remember how she never backed away from a fight.

"She got caught in a storm one day, wandered home and was put to bed," said her great-grandson Raymond Pointer. "They had a doctor out there who gave her three months to live. Two days later, she was out on the lake."

Lucy once pretended to be a witch to silence her noisy next-door neighbor. She dressed all in black, put on a peaked hat and walked around and around the man's house with a pail of ashes, sprinkling them on the ground.

"She circled the house three times and sprinkled ashes and said, 'Dust thou art and to dust thou shalt return,'" said Pointer. "The guy moved. People were superstitious in those days."

She was a woman used to expressing her feelings, so the day came when Lucy could no longer keep her love for Isaac Berry squeezed inside a locked box.

"She went to her father and told him she wanted to marry, and he said can't you find somebody else besides that . . ." said Marguerite Jackson.

Then Isaac ran off in the spring, and that fall Lucy was sent away to a finishing school in Springfield, Illinois. She boarded a train in Hannibal, Missouri, ten miles from Palmyra. She had pretended she was going to obey her father's orders, stay in school and learn how to smooth away her rough edges so she would have the shine to attract a rich suitor.

However, when her train reached Springfield, Illinois, she got off, strode into the depot and bought a ticket to Detroit, just as she had told Isaac she would. She paid for that second ticket with the money she was supposed to use for her finishing school tuition. Then she boarded an eastbound train with a whistle that was like the wail of a lost child. As she passed one seat, she saw a WANTED poster offering a reward for the return of Isaac Berry, according to Katy

Pointer. For all she knew, he could have been caught and dragged to the far South or even lynched. All the same, she stayed on the train.

She traveled from Springfield to Chicago and on to Michigan. She was used to traveling and tracking down dreams. According to family history, Lucy Millard's father, Solomon Nelson Millard, was part of that army of true believers who moved westward, struggling to plant seeds of their new Mormon faith in stony ground and resisting hearts. Lucy's marriage records identified both her and Isaac as church members. She was about twelve when her family left New York to head west in search of their green kingdom of God.

She and her family had come by the Erie Canal up to Buffalo on a flatboat with all their belongings. Lucy later told her grandchildren that she remembered seeing a circus near Niagara Falls and watching an elephant fall into the water, get sucked into a whirlpool and ride over the rushing falls. She never forgot that elephant and whatever lessons it taught her about life's sharp and sometimes violent turns.

The Millards first stopped in Ohio and then in Plymouth, Michigan, where Lucy's mother, Diana Taylor, wasted away from tuberculosis and her two daughters, Lucy and Clarissa, longed for companionship. Lucy and her family arrived in Michigan around 1850, just as people from Europe and the eastern United States flooded the state—previously believed to be nothing but swamps, bogs and Indians—all hungry for the state's $1.25-an-acre land. But cheap land was not enough to make Lucy's father shackle himself to one spot. He had a mission. It lay in the West, where Mormons had experienced conflicts and all-out wars, sometimes because they represented the balance of power among political groups, sometimes because their plural marriages offended members of other faiths and sometimes because their leaders refused to accept non-Mormon governance. Lucy's father and his brother tried to set up a Mormon settlement in Plymouth, Michigan, but failed. So Solomon Nelson Millard buried his wife and moved to northeast Missouri near Palmyra, south of an earlier thriving Mormon center in Nauvoo, Illinois, on the Mississippi River. That's where Lucy Millard and Isaac Berry became neighbors.

Although Lucy's father owned no slaves and taught his daughters to treat slaves kindly, he belonged to a religion that, at the time, preached that blacks were a cursed race that could not become priests. Even blacks who went to heaven would be servants there, according to nineteenth-century Mormon theology. Yet Lucy's father encouraged his daughters to take water to Isaac in the fields, where he busted the hard ground for immigrants. He also allowed Lucy to read the Bible to Isaac Berry, "a handsome man," according to the late Marguerite Jackson. By then Lucy was close to twenty, an age when most nineteenth-century women either had husbands and children or had dedicated themselves to teaching school or tending relatives. Still, she must have thought twice about giving up everything she knew to keep her promise to find a runaway slave in Detroit.

"You had to have a strong love to do something like that," said Isaac's granddaughter Marie Berry Cross.

When her journey from Springfield ended, Lucy Millard got off the train in Detroit, then a city of forty-five thousand people. Next door to the passenger depot of the Michigan Central Railroad, a billboard directed passengers to the terminals of the Grand Trunk Railroad of Canada. Shopkeepers sold clothes; carpets; plant, flower and fruit seeds; paints and varnishes; dry goods and stoves; jewelry; life insurance and liquor. Wandering around town, Lucy could have seen people riding in horse-drawn carriages and people visiting the city in ox-drawn carts. Lucy found accommodations in a rooming house, took a job in a shirt-making factory and began searching for Isaac in Detroit and then across the river in Windsor. She knew he'd be somewhere sweating out music and inhaling good times.

One Saturday night, she was walking along a Windsor street, heard a fiddler playing and recognized the sound of Isaac's instrument. She stopped a couple entering the tavern and begged them for a favor. She asked them to tell the fiddler that "Lucy is here," says Pointer.

We can only guess what a tangle of emotions their reunion triggered—astonishment, disbelief, joy, pride in their escapes and optimism about their future. They had found each other, and their magic was still strong.

In April 1859, Isaac Berry and Lucy Esther Millard were married in the tiny town of Little River, Canada. He was twenty-seven and she was twenty-one. Oddly enough, two marriage records show up for the couple, both of them correctly identifying Isaac Berry but spelling Lucy's name in different ways, "Lusea Millon" and "Lucy Miller." On both certificates she's identified as a member of The Church of Jesus Christ of Latter-day Saints. However, she is no longer called white. On one certificate she's called an African and on the other a mulatto, as if in marrying Isaac she somehow stopped being the New York–born and census-counted daughter of white parents and became black by association. Marie Berry Cross, their granddaughter, says that is exactly what happened. Lucy had one of her wedding certificates framed and put it over the head of her bed. It showed two swans fastened to a boat, and the caption read "sea of matrimony."

They made their home in Puce, a village near Windsor. They stayed in Canada for nineteen years and had six of their eight children there. Yet Canada was not quite the Promised Land. "When they were all over in Canada, the school where they all went divided them [by color]," according to Marguerite Jackson. "The Berry kids sat with the white kids and the [children of ex-slave Absalom Johnson] sat on the other side. Then Grandpa Berry went down there, and the teacher moved [the Berrys] over on the black side."

"Granny said one winter all they had to eat was potatoes in Canada," added Marie Cross. "Grandpa became a fisherman, and he would catch the big sturgeon."

Lake sturgeon can weigh as much as three hundred pounds, grow six to seven feet long, whip water into foam before your eyes and give a fisherman the fight of his life. Early Detroit settlers considered them such a nuisance that they fed the fish to their pigs and burned them as fuel in steamboat boilers. However, Isaac caught sturgeon in wire traps and ate or sold enough to survive.

In 1877, the Berry family traveled from Canada to central Michigan in a covered wagon, bound for Webers' Lumber Camp, which was selling cut-over land for $1.25 an acre. Stephen and Caroline Kahler Todd journeyed with them. Like Isaac Berry, Stephen Todd originally came from Kentucky. He had escaped from slavery four times, settling in Indiana. On September 22, 1864, Todd enlisted in the armed forces as a substitute for Andrew J. Huff of Washington Township, Marion County, Indiana. He served in the Indiana 28th Regiment of U.S. black volunteers. After meeting Caroline Kahler, the daughter of German-born parents, Stephen ran away to Canada with Caroline. They were nearly captured while crossing the St. Clair River in a raft from Port Huron, Michigan, to Sarnia, Ontario. On August 29, 1874, they married in Windsor, Ontario, according to Stephen Todd's pension records. Isaac Berry and his son, William, witnessed their wedding.

For Isaac and Lucy Berry life in a sparsely populated Michigan wilderness gave them the freedom they always had sought. The family built a log cabin on their eighty acres in a part of Mecosta County now known as School Section Lake Park. It faced a still lake and an eleven-acre island. Isaac planted trees on his land—maple, white cedar and apple trees, grafting together different species of apples that still bloom on his old homestead. He set aside two acres for a log schoolhouse in which Lucy became the first teacher. Isaac also carved and rented out canoes and built two bathhouses, one for men and one for women, so people could change into their swimming clothes. In the winter, he spread sand on the ice and let it settle beneath the melting ice, building a beach, layer by layer, just as he was building a life. And thanks to Lucy, Isaac finally learned to squeeze sense from words written on paper.

However, both Isaac and Lucy Berry paid a high price for falling in love with each other and with central Michigan's birch, pine, beech, maple, hemlock and basswood trees, white-tailed deer, timber wolves, bobcats and lynxes.

Lucy received just one letter from her sister, Clarissa, and nothing from other family members. "Granny was cut from the family line," said Marie Cross. "When she got on that train, it was the end. She never seen her family again."

Isaac also left pieces of his heart in Missouri. He never saw his mother, brothers or sisters again and never shook off his feeling of unease, his sense that someone was following him with a branding iron, ready to claim him as escaped property. Even though he lived in Canada for nearly twenty years and then moved to Michigan after the Civil War, he continued to look over his shoulder in fear of being taken back into slavery or killed, according to relatives. Lucy always answered the door and acted as the go-between when strangers came asking for him. Isaac kept close guard over the details of his life, leaving it to Lucy to talk about his adventures. And he and Lucy named their children for people they had loved. Mary Clarissa was named for Isaac's mother and Lucy's sister; Louis Harve for Isaac's brother, Harve; Malinda Diana for Lucy's mother, Diana, and their son, Benjamin Nelson, for Lucy's father, Solomon Nelson.

The past showed up in other painful disguises, too. While Isaac was still living in Canada, a neighbor urged him to return to Detroit to play at a dance. But Lucy suspected a trap and urged Isaac not to go. After thinking it over, he agreed and spent a couple of nights with a neighbor. The man who'd urged him to go to Detroit later admitted he'd been motivated by the five-hundred-dollar bounty Jim Pratt had put on Isaac's head.

One time Pratt himself came to their home and pounded on Isaac's door, according to Pointer Sr. However, the Berrys refused to open the door, and Pratt never tried to force his way in. Census records from 1860 show Pratt living in Hannibal, Missouri, some ten miles from Palmyra, and list his occupation as laborer, so it is possible he lost the farm after selling off his slaves and Isaac's running off.

According to their headstones, Isaac Berry died in 1914 and Lucy Berry in 1928. They are buried side by side in Mt. Hope Cemetery in Mecosta County, Michigan. Engraved on Lucy's headstone is a flaming torch, the perfect emblem for a woman who never lost her fire.

This couple's story comes to life at annual August reunions attended by descendants of the original fifty-eight pioneer families—some free blacks and others runaways—who settled in central

Michigan starting in the 1860s. The pioneers married each other, eventually becoming one family.

They hold their reunions in School Section Lake Park, a tree-shrouded park and picnic grounds that contains a monument and plaque honoring the area's original "Negro Settlers." That park was Isaac and Lucy Berry's original home. The families who eat and share memories there at reunions have a lot to talk about while their children skip stones across the face of the lake.

They talk about old Tom Guy, who sometimes paid people with chunks of smoked shoulder and ham to clear his fields, and Grand Norman, who stashed his money in tin cans and buried them around his sixteen-acre homestead.

They remember whiskey distiller John Bryant, who moved to the area, raised hogs and called himself John Bracey.

They talk about Simon and Polina Sleet, who ran away from separate plantations in Kentucky and their children from a third. Simon died at age 104 in Boyne City, Michigan.

They talk about Arthur Cross, who preached for thirty-eight continuous years, baptizing 179 people and delivering more than twenty-five hundred sermons. He also performed more than one hundred marriages.

They remember Mary C. Berry Pointer and Mary Johnson Luke, who served as midwives to the community of Little River.

They remember Merze Tate, a descendant of black pioneers in Isabella County, who became the first black American to receive a bachelor of arts degree in literature from Oxford University. She published five volumes on international affairs.

They remember a time when African-Americans found ways to turn suffering into art, crises into opportunities, desire into religious fire and tears into joy.

And they remember Isaac and Lucy Berry, one black, one white, one walking, one riding, and their search for a green hideaway, their own personal Palmyra, where love could glow and grow under free skies.

The Joseph Davis family of northern Lower Michigan around 1900 included Joseph and his third wife, Rose (at right with a child on her lap), surrounded by their children and Pearl (top), Rose Davis's daughter from her first marriage. Joseph Davis's parents, William and Mildred Davis, moved from Pennsylvania to northern Michigan after neighbors allegedly poisoned William's white father for letting a black woman run his household. Photo courtesy of Calvin Murphy Jr.

13

THE SCHOOLTEACHER HAD TO DUCK DEAD CATS

Their story isn't the sort of saga you're likely to see in any made-for-television movies about slave escapes. Who'd believe a story about a mixed couple who pretend they're not really married, a slave who dies to save other runaways and a dying white man who leaves his wife and children to his slave?

Oh, it's easy enough to imagine Jane King Walls, the well-bred and well-traveled daughter of a white nineteenth-century landowner, baking an apple pie in her wood-burning stove. It's just as easy to picture her playing the old upright piano in her little Canadian log cabin with pebble and dirt floors, a spinning wheel and high-backed chairs.

It is not at all easy to imagine Jane's dying white North Carolina husband, Daniel Walls, asking his best friend and slave, John, to take care of his family. It is almost impossible to picture black John and white Jane falling in love in the 1840s, fleeing together on the Underground Railroad and winding up in a Canadian village.

Yet the cabin John Freeman Walls built in 1846—furnished with an old upright piano and blue-and-white gingham curtains and tablecloths—still stands in Puce, Ontario.

This drama began in 1813 in Troublesome Creek, North Carolina, when two baby boys, one white, one black, were born on the same day. John's mother, a slave from Guinea, lived, but Daniel's mother died in childbirth, according to research gathered by Bryan Walls, a descendant of John and Jane Walls. The two boys grew up best friends, always playing together. It was common practice to give a white child a slave of his or her own age to play with—or, in some cases, abuse, beat and practice on to become a petty tyrant. However, Daniel and John became actual friends. But Daniel's father, Eli Walls, whipped John severely when he spotted the two boys playing master and slave one day, with black John pretending to be his white son's master. John's father, Hannabal, wanted to kill his master for whipping his son over a game. Instead, Hannabal ran away. During the long chase, his heart apparently gave out—he fell dead. John Walls knew then that he, too, would chase freedom one day, but he couldn't have suspected he'd chase it with his master's widow.

As Daniel Walls lay dying from an unknown illness, he freed John and left Jane and his four children in the care of his friend, urging John to look after them. Soon Jane Walls, an educated, deeply religious and slavery-hating woman, and John Walls, a slave who had been taught to read, found themselves in love. They knew it wouldn't be safe to stay in North Carolina, so they left Troublesome Creek and headed north.

During their flight to freedom, John killed two wolves with an ax, according to Bryan Walls's book *The Road That Led to Somewhere.* When a slave catcher overtook them, Jane pretended to be John's owner and whipped him to prove it. Finally, they reached a Quaker safe house in Indianapolis, where they married. Around most people, though, John pretended he was the husband of a fugitive slave woman traveling with him and Jane. While the couple still lived in Indiana, Jane, accompanied by a group of former slaves, returned to North Carolina and led nine slaves to freedom. When slave catchers came after the group, three male slaves lured the bounty hunters away from the women, one slave losing his life. Jane returned to North Carolina once more to say good-bye to her father. Then she and John and a former slave named Corliss traveled on the Underground Railroad from Indiana to Ohio and on to Canada. Eventually, they settled in Puce, Ontario, in Maidstone Township, on rich land some distance from the Detroit River so easily crossed by slave hunters. They encountered prejudice and rejection in Canada, but there were no whips, no overseers, no violence. In fact, John and Jane Walls's home became a place of refuge for other fugitives. The area's first church services were held in their home until a building was erected for the First Puce Baptist Church.

John died in 1909 at ninety-six and Jane a year later at eighty-eight. Both are buried in the cemetery behind their old log cabin, the original homestead John built in 1846. Today that cabin is part of an Underground Railroad museum operated by the Wallses' descendants. People who visit the John Freeman Walls Historic Site and Underground Railroad Museum in Puce get a chance to reenact the journey of a runaway slave on a trail running through nearby woods. The experience includes the sound of dogs yelping and men shouting.

All the same, it is nearly impossible to picture the long and difficult road that brought John and Jane Walls to Essex County, Ontario, at a time when loving each other was just about the most dangerous thing they could do.

What kind of people crossed the color line during the slavery era and immediately afterward, a time when the Southern code required white women to remain beyond the reach of black men and black women to experience white lust but never love?

Were those who risked their lives to violate these taboos trying to make a statement against slavery, enthralled by forbidden fruit, naturally rebellious or simply unwilling to deny the urgings of their hearts?

What did Molly Welsh and her slave husband, Bannaka, have in common with Richard Loving and Mildred Jeter, the white man and black woman whose desire to live as man and wife in Virginia finally wiped out slavery-inspired U.S. laws banning mixed marriages?

Why did a fugitive slave named John Hall dare to take an Englishwoman as his fifth wife after burying four black wives? Why did Prudence Crandall's decision to open a Connecticut finishing school for black girls stir up fears that her school would encourage intermarriage?

What was a black female cook named Mary Jane thinking when she tried to elope with a white gentleman aboard a steamboat in 1856, protected by nothing except a veil? And why were there no laws shielding black women from owners who raped them and produced new slaves, but tons of laws designed to keep white women from having mulatto children who would eventually be free? The answer to that last question is obvious: planters lost money when white women produced free children but made money when they impregnated their own slaves. But what drove people like John and Jane Walls to risk so much for an uncertain future?

Molly Welsh knew the penalty for breaking Maryland's laws against marrying across the color line, but how many women could resist a tall, dark and handsome prince who carried his dignity with him like a cape? Certainly not Molly Welsh. She had been in trouble before and knew its texture and smell.

She had been nearly hanged in England for spilling milk while working as a dairy maid on a cattle farm, possibly in Wessex County. After the cow she was milking knocked over its pail, she was arrested on charges of stealing milk, a felony that carried the death penalty. However, Molly Welsh could read and that made her eligible for a pardon as well as shipment to America to help build the new colony. Instead of a noose, she faced life in America as an indentured servant required to work a certain number of years to pay off the cost of her journey.

She arrived in the province of Maryland around 1683 and was purchased by a tobacco planter with an estate on the Patapsco River. She worked seven years to pay for the voyage and earn the money for land. She won her freedom around 1690 and set up her own farm, first working alone and then purchasing two slaves from a ship anchored in the bay. One was Bannaka, or Bannke, a dignified and thoughtful man who had been captured by slave traders. He belonged to the Wolof tribe, a tall people known for their good looks and grace and for giving America the banjo and such words as *yam*, *banana*, *jive* and *dig*. Bannaka was believed to be the son of a tribal chieftain in Senegal on the western coast of Africa. Unlike her other slave, Bannaka was not a good worker, preferring to spend his time thinking and tinkering with inventions. Around 1696, Molly freed and married him anyway. By that time, it had become illegal in Maryland for a minister to marry a Negro and a white woman so it may have been a common-law marriage. As of 1684, any such woman who married a black man or had his child lost her freedom and became a servant.

Molly Welsh may have reasoned that no one would pay attention to what she did at her farm in the wilderness. She withdrew from her white neighbors and changed her name to that of her husband. They had four daughters—Mary, Katherine, Esther and Jemima. Mary married a native African named Robert and their firstborn son, Benjamin, became a thinker just like his African grandfather. In fact, Benjamin Banneker—the name had been Anglicized by then—became America's first black scientist. He was around twenty-two when he made a wooden clock. A self-educated mathematician and astronomer, he watched the night sky with a crude telescope or traveled it with his imagination. He also created almanacs and assisted in surveying the federal territory that was to become the District of Columbia.

Benjamin Banneker never married, but his sister Jemima married Samuel Delaney Lett around 1758 in Baltimore County, Maryland. Samuel was a white man who had a black stepfather. The Letts had eight children. Glenn Barnett II of Columbus, Ohio, has compiled a list of Jemima's descendants over the centuries, most of them living in Ohio and Michigan. Their last names include Lett, Stevens, Cummins, Cummings, Norman, Pointer, Harper, Morgan, Lucas, Harris, McGinnis, Chapman, Johnson, Payne, Sleet, Weaver, Caliman, Male, Sawyer, Cook, Green, Berry and others.

Prudence Crandall also crossed the color line when she knew that it was dangerous, but her "crime" was less obvious than Jane Walls's and Molly Welsh's offenses. In 1833, Crandall owned just about the largest and best-looking house in Canterbury, Connecticut, but that didn't stop people from pelting it with dead cats and chicken heads, rocks and rotten eggs, insults and threats. People also dumped manure in Crandall's well, refused to sell her food or medicine, held meetings where her representatives couldn't speak and even tossed her in jail.

In the eyes of her neighbors in the prosperous village of Canterbury, which had a jewelry store and small factories, the white Quaker-bred schoolmarm had betrayed them by admitting a black girl to what was supposed to be an elite school for their white daughters. An editorial in the *Norwich Republican* made the nature of Crandall's transgression even plainer. She was, the newspaper charged, trying to turn black girls into ladies and make them more desirable to white bachelors. In other words, she stood accused of promoting what had become the crime of all crimes, intermarriage.

Prudence Crandall was twenty-seven when residents of Canterbury invited her to move there from Rhode Island in 1831 and start a boarding school for their daughters. Her face was a curious blend of hard and soft, strong and yielding qualities—soft, curved lips, strong chin, wide, lustrous eyes and heavy eyebrows. The steely part of her nature won out. Her school opened in November 1831 and became an immediate success. However, after Crandall began reading the *Liberator*, William Lloyd Garrison's uncompromising antislavery newspaper, she decided she should help educate blacks.

In January 1833, a black girl named Sarah Harris, daughter of an industrious black farmer, entered Crandall's boarding school. Harris wanted enough education to become a teacher herself. Slavery was still alive in Connecticut in 1833, though the 1784 gradual emancipation act provided that black and mulatto children born after March 1 of that year would become free at age twenty-five. In 1797, another bill reduced the age of freedom to twenty-one. However, Connecticut did not completely abolish slavery until 1848.

The moment Sarah Harris enrolled in Prudence Crandall's school, the citizens of Canterbury showed their true colors. Some parents took their daughters home, no doubt believing Crandall would soon back down. Instead, she recruited other black students and, in February 1833, dismissed her remaining white students to open a school for "young ladies and little misses of color." The school reopened in April with fifteen black students from Philadelphia, New York, Providence, Boston and Connecticut. That's when the stew really hit the stove.

Under pressure from Canterbury's leaders, the state legislature passed Connecticut's so-called Black Law, on May 24, 1833, just six weeks after Crandall's school reopened. The law banned private schools for nonresident blacks. Crandall was arrested, tried and convicted of breaking this new law; however, the Connecticut Supreme Court threw out her conviction on a technicality. Crandall wanted to press on, but in September 1834 her school was set on fire. The fire was extinguished quickly, but the town's rage still flamed. Men armed with crowbars and clubs smashed the school's windows and threatened students. Crandall, who had married a preacher named Calvin Philleo, finally closed her school and shelved her dreams. After her husband's death in 1874, she moved to Kansas, where she had a brother named Hezekiah. In 1886, the Connecticut state legislature granted her a small pension. She was then eighty-two. In 1995, Connecticut, which once had gone so far as to forbid anyone from wearing garments that didn't match their place in society, finally recognized Prudence Crandall's courage. She became Connecticut's official State Heroine.

In 1843, John "Daddy" Hall and his fifth wife broke the color barrier, too. They arrived at Sydenham Village near Canada's Owen Sound, where Hall became the first black settler. While Hall built a shack and cleared the land, his English wife traveled back and forth from their former home in Rocky Saugeen near Durham, where she milked the cows: she had a baby bound to her back. In areas as remote as Sydenham Village color might have mattered a lot less than having the grit to survive in a rugged frontier.

Hall, born around 1807 near Amherstburg, had been kidnapped when he was about ten by slave raiders. They took him and eleven other members of his family to a Kentucky plantation. Eventually, an adult Hall and his first wife, an enslaved woman, ran away to Toronto. After his first wife died, Hall married three more times. In Sydenham Village, he became a legendary figure, reportedly living to be 118. People claimed he had grown a third set of teeth and sprouted hair after he turned one hundred. They also said he had regained his sight after a spell of blindness. By the time he died in 1925, he had served as the town crier and bell ringer and a walking newspaper, leaving his mark on the land and on the women he loved.

On February 21, 1856, an article entitled "Elopement Extraordinary" appeared in the Louisville press, raising suspicions about another kind of interracial affair, an apparent love affair between a white man and a black woman. The article claimed a twenty-two-year-old black female cook named Mary Jane had been captured in New Albany, Indiana, with a white Easterner named Elisha Hillyer. According to historian Blaine Hudson's account, the woman supposedly rendezvoused with the man in Louisville and then the pair rode a ferry across the Ohio River. However, the ferryman noticed the woman's color when her lover lifted her veil to kiss her.

There was more than romance at work, though, when Charles Storum or Storeman, who was half African and half American Indian, married a French-Canadian woman named Mary Ann Fowler sometime in the 1800s. In 1751, Storum had been born in Fishkill, New York, a village which, at the time of the Revolutionary War, contained only about a dozen houses, a tavern, two churches and a school. After his marriage, he and Fowler had four sons—Charles Jr., William, Samuel and John—three of whom grew up to be Underground Railroad conductors.

Charles Storum worked on whale ships so he could receive papers showing he was free. Catching thrashing whales capable of crushing a man or a boat was dirty and dangerous work, and in the seventeenth and eighteenth centuries many blacks did it. In fact, Lewis Temple, a black resident of New Bedford, Massachusetts, used his skills as a blacksmith to design an improved harpoon that kept whales from slipping loose from hooks.

While Charles Storum sailed the seas catching whales, his wife remained in the Windsor, Connecticut, area and cared for their children. They obviously knew their heritage and learned to cherish freedom. Two Storum sons moved to New York state—Charles Jr. settling in Watertown, William near Jamestown—and Samuel moved to Warren, Pennsylvania. John eventually moved to Lapeer County, Michigan. The three sons on the East Coast formed their own slave-helping network, moving fugitives from the home of one brother to the next. William and Sarah Storum had an even closer connection to the antislavery movement. In 1840, their daughter, Caroline, married a runaway slave named Jermain Loguen, and they settled in Syracuse, New York. At the time, Syracuse had about two hundred blacks in a community of seven thousand. Loguen became an African Methodist Episcopal Zion Church minister and principal agent of the Syracuse Underground Railroad station. He actually ran notices in the local press about Underground Railroad activities, urging people to hire fugitives. He also joined Frederick Douglass on the lecture circuit. And his daughter, Helen, married Douglass's son, Lewis, continuing the family pattern of activism.

There was a pattern to the legend of William Davis, too. In the 1850s, a Scots-Irishman living near the Pennsylvania-Virginia border fell in love with his black mistress, scandalizing other whites. The scandal wasn't the interracial sex; it was the fact that this white bachelor farmer allegedly allowed his black mistress to run his household. Soon the Scots-Irishman became ill and began wasting away. Believing that he had been poisoned, he called the woman and their three children to his bedside and urged them to leave his farm and flee as far north as possible to avoid getting poisoned, too.

This, according to descendants, was the beginning of their family saga. It's the story of a black family who became pioneers in the Michigan wilderness, a place teeming with land far from the reach of slave owners, bounty hunters and kidnappers who didn't distinguish between free and enslaved blacks.

The William Davis who wound up in northern Michigan was one of the Scots-Irishman's three mulatto children. In Philadelphia, he married Mildred Brand, a midwife who smoked a clay pipe after every meal and had hair long enough to sit on. After they had two children, they left Pennsylvania in a covered wagon and journeyed to Medina County, Ohio. They lived there for three years and had two more children. Around 1862, the family finally arrived in what later became Benzie County, Michigan, in the northwest corner of the Lower Peninsula. This, they decided, was their safe haven, their home. Davis homesteaded one hundred and sixty acres, and so did his oldest son, Joseph B., then about twenty-three. William and Mildred raised their own six children and sixteen others, including a newborn baby found in a gunny sack by the side of the road.

Remembering how it felt to be outcasts and on the run, they sheltered any child, black, white or Indian, who needed a home. Twice a year, their son, Joseph, walked to Traverse City, thirty-five miles away, for supplies, spending a whole week trudging down Indian trails. On his way to his destination, he would spend the night with families he knew, repaying them by dropping off supplies on his return. The round-trip for sugar, flour and other supplies took about a week. At age twenty-five, Joseph married a seventeen-year-old girl who was one of the children the Davises had taken in. In 1864, the couple had a son named Horace Burr Davis, the first baby to be born in Joyfield Township after the place got an official name.

On May 15, 1941, a light-skinned black man named Calvin Clark Davis passed for white to join the 5th U.S. Army Air Force, 90th Bombardment Group, 400th Squadron. He was the son of Horace Burr Davis and a white woman named Hattie. At the time, blacks were considered incapable of handling complicated machinery and maneuvers and barred from the Air Force. Around the same time, the famed black pilots known as Tuskegee Airmen began their training: like other black fighting units, the Airmen were considered experiments to see how blacks would perform in aerial combat.

There always have been people who passed for something or somebody they weren't. Most of the time, they were light-skinned blacks, like Davis, who passed for white, sometimes to escape slavery, sometimes to gain economic or social advantages and sometimes to live or die for their country. Other light-skinned blacks, like William Webb, spied on slave catchers. NAACP official Walter White, a light-skinned blue-eyed black man, infiltrated groups such as the Ku Klux Klan to collect information about lynchings. He published his research in the 1929 book *Rope and Faggot.*

Calvin Clark Davis graduated from army radio school, and after running a radio station at Rapid City, South Dakota, he was picked for combat duty in a heavy bombardment group. He arrived in New Guinea on June 30, 1943. Three weeks later, he was a radio gunner on a B-24 Liberator. He completed fifty missions, or three hundred hours of flying, in a few months. Wounded on both his first and last missions, he earned two Purple Hearts. He was among a bomber crew that received the Distinguished Flying Cross for heroism during an attack on a Japanese-held airfield in Wewak, New Guinea, on August 29, 1943, and for heroism in a flight over Rabaul, New Guinea, on October 25, 1943.

Though he experienced the same fears as any combat soldier, Davis told his hometown newspaper that he felt most at home in war-torn skies, his senses whipped to a boil by the struggle to stay alive. After flying enough missions as a gunner aboard a B-24 to escape further combat, he volunteered to continue flying with the 8th Air Force in Ipswich, England. He wound up in Europe as a radio operator and gunner with the 8th U.S. Army Air Force, the 390th Bombardment Group, 570th Squadron. Friendly but reserved, he was older than most of the crew. When they went out on weekend passes, he never joined them, socializing on his own. He flew on sixteen missions. His last one came at the end of November 1944, the year Nat "King" Cole released a song called "Straighten Up and Fly Right" and Allied soldiers walked into a storm of gunfire off the French province of Normandy.

Bill Pace, the ball-turret gunner on Davis's plane, had troubling dreams on the night of November 29, 1944, dreams that made him take his parachute into the turret of the Asterisk, a B-17 bomber. On November 30, the crew's target was the oil refineries of Merseburg, Germany. The B-17 dropped its bombs, and the Germans began firing antiaircraft guns at the formation, taking down more than fifty bombers. The antiaircraft hit the radar ship, and its pilot lost control of his plane, landing on top of the B-17 containing Davis. The plane broke in half. Six of the bomber's nine crewmen, including Calvin Clark Davis, were killed. The remains of Technical Sergeant Calvin C. Davis rest in Ardennes American Cemetery, Neupre, Belgium, plot D, row 10, grave 29. It is surrounded by white crosses and dark memories, especially for soldiers who fought bigotry at home and abroad.

In 2002, one of Davis's cousins, Calvin Murphy of Bear Lake, Michigan, revealed that Davis had passed for white to fight in World War II and urged Congress to find out if he'd received all the medals he'd earned. In a February 18, 2002, ceremony at Davis's old school, Bear Lake High School, the airman posthumously received the Distinguished Flying Cross with two bronze oak leaf clusters, the Air Medal with one bronze oak leaf cluster, the Purple Heart with one bronze oak leaf cluster, the World War II Victory Medal, the European-African-Middle Eastern Campaign Medal, the Good Conduct Medal and the American Defense Service Medal.

"The story of Calvin Clark Davis deserves to be heard," said Congressman John Conyers. "If ever there was a soldier worthy of recognition, it is Mr. Davis. He should be honored not only for his heroic efforts as a soldier, but for his willingness to serve a country that did not necessarily want his service."

"There were many great sacrifices made by our troops in World War

II, but I have never heard of someone going to the length Calvin Davis did to serve his country," said Congressman Pete Hoekstra. ". . . Mr. Davis' dedication to his country, in spite of the prejudice of his time, is a testament to his personal strength and the strength of the American character."

Book III

FREE AT LAST

★

After lives of toil and triumph, Samuel and Rebecca Ballton rest in the Huntington Rural Cemetery in the village of Huntington, New York. Photo courtesy of Greenlawn-Centerport Historical Association.

14

GUNS AND PICKLES

He could have been shot to shreds at any moment, his mission a failure, his name as forgotten as a song played just once at a whooping, stomping, all-night slave dance. Yet in the spring of 1862, nothing could stop Samuel Ballton from roaming through death-drenched Virginia alone. During perhaps the most dangerous time in American history, this runaway slave and Union army cook returned to Confederate territory, a perfect target for rifle muskets that could hit targets six hundred yards away.

One simple, irresistible desire drove him.

He wanted to see his wife.

All across America, Union and Confederate soldiers with Bibles in their pockets blew up railroad bridges; rode horses until the animals fell dead; slogged through downpours and droughts; died from cholera, lung disease, measles, typhoid, mumps, syphilis, tuberculosis and infected wounds; and killed one another in unmatched numbers. Still, Ballton never doubted he could make his way back to Ann Rebecca Ballton in Westmoreland County, Virginia, even if it meant sneaking past Confederate lines. He was, after all, a man who had escaped from slavery with food under his shirt and who had escaped capture and dodged death while cooking for the Yankees.

But even luck can take a vacation. Without so much as a whispered good-bye or wave, it suddenly abandoned Ballton on a spring day in 1862.

He stumbled upon a Confederate camp and, suddenly, rebels with guns surrounded him. In dealing with blacks who strayed or ran off from their plantations or farms, rebel soldiers did not follow the conventions or rules of war. Blacks could not expect to be held in prison camps or treated for their ailments and injuries. They could expect to die at the hands of men who considered them traitors to their way of life and an insult to Southern white fighting men.

Yet Ballton didn't die the day the rebels caught him. He could never explain how he'd figured out what would save him: the right words just fell from his lips and landed at his captors' feet. The Yankees had dragged him off, he told them, but he had escaped. Now, bless God, he was just trying to get back home to his good old master.

"Many, many 'good niggers' were bestowed on him when he told that story," according to a story about Ballton that later appeared in a Brooklyn newspaper. Then he passed through their lines, heading home to a brown-skinned wife with smiling eyes.

The year of his escape, Samuel Ballton was twenty-three years old, but he had been put to work at the age of seven. He could neither read nor write nor count, but he had scooped up bits of knowledge from everything that swirled around him. He stood only five-six or five-seven; yet he had always had a large idea of himself. On January 1, 1838, he had been born a slave in Westmoreland County, north of the capital of Richmond and sandwiched between the Rappahannock and Potomac rivers. Maybe it was those ever-flowing rivers that had stretched his imagination and made him dream of sailing off and moving on, his energy as constant, as ceaseless as the sway and splash of waters. Yet there was no way he could have guessed that one day he would live within sight of a sea that embraced the Atlantic Ocean. He certainly could not have guessed that he would develop and sell houses or that he would learn to write well enough to compose snappish letters to newspaper editors.

Still, even while living in that shadow land called slavery—a place where some black people were treated like pets and others might be beaten to death for looking a white person in the eye—he'd shown flashes of inner fire. His master was a man named Vincent Marmaduke, who had inherited slaves, cows and beds from his grandfather. Samuel Ballton had listened carefully to the Marmadukes as they read newspapers aloud and talked about Yankees and freedom and a brewing war. In his later years, Ballton never claimed that his owners had starved or beaten him, corrupted by their own power. However, he fell in love with the idea of freedom as soon as he heard about it. It was like a molasses-soaked biscuit that a field-worker hid inside a rag and stole bites from throughout the day. It was an idea that he bought at once without even bothering to find out what it might cost or how long it would last.

When the war started, Ballton and all the other able-bodied slaves on the Marmaduke plantation had been hired out to work as section hands on the Virginia Central Railroad in the Blue Ridge Mountains, which would have been coming alive just then with redbuds and songbirds. Romantic stories later came to surround men like these, the so-called gandy dancers, who sang as they worked: they moved like circling dancers as they dragged or lined up the thirty-nine-foot rails or nailed spikes to the thick wooden planks supporting the tracks. However, in the Civil War, railroad repair gangs became vital parts of the war machine; they repaired track and bridges destroyed by the enemy so troops, ammunition and other supplies could keep rumbling to their destinations.

Suddenly, Samuel Ballton, who had never been more than twenty miles from the Marmaduke plantation, found himself two hundred miles away. In April 1862, General William Rosecrans, a ruddy-faced man known to his men as Old Rosy, cut in behind the headquarters where Ballton was laboring. The slaves were transferred to Frederick Hall station, fifty miles from Richmond. The idea of escaping, already a seed, ripened in the spring air, and Sam Ballton wasn't the only one who felt it growing. Already, other slaves had run to Yankee boats in the Potomac and Rappahannock rivers. In the first year of the war, most fugitive slaves ran alone, not sure what kind of reception they'd receive from Northern troops and not yet having the means to support their families. Ballton's chance came during the Whitsunday holiday, celebrated the seventh Sunday after Easter; it was a festival commemorating the descent of the Holy Spirit on the day of Pentecost. During the celebration, which ran from Saturday until Tuesday, Ballton and five fellow slaves felt their own spirits rise and decided to make their break for freedom.

They stuck a little flour and bacon under their shirts and took off. They traveled seventeen miles that Saturday, running into the roadmaster of the railroad. The encounter rattled the slaves, but the roadmaster suspected nothing. Sunday night, they continued toward the North and freedom, each day staying in the woods out of sight. On Monday night, they got lost and felt sure they would be missed and recaptured. However, heavy rains pounded them, giving them added pools of time: no one would expect them to slosh or wade their way through such a storm. Wednesday morning, about four miles from the Spotsylvania Court House, they ran into Yankee pickets, a group of soldiers placed in front of a line to warn of the enemy's advance. The pickets took them in.

That was how Sam Ballton became a cook for the Yankees in the 6th Wisconsin Regiment in Fredericksburg in the northeastern corner of Virginia, an inspection and shipping point for tobacco, agricultural exports and slaves. However, he couldn't stop worrying about Ann Rebecca Richardson, whom he had married in April 1861 in a ceremony conducted by John Bates, the overseer for Rebecca's owner, John Kricher. In some cases, the families of fugitives were jailed, resold or forced to do the work of those they'd left behind.

After fooling the rebels, Sam spent three days with Rebecca, but didn't take her with him, wanting to save more money before moving her to Fredericksburg. However, he took three other slaves with him. They stole four mules at a nearby farm and managed to reach Fredericksburg safely. After piling up more earnings, Ballton returned to Ann Rebecca, this time ready to carry her over the threshold of freedom. Later, he would tell a reporter for the *Brooklyn Eagle* that it was the proudest day of his life.

"Rebecca, I'm going to take you to freedom," he told her.

Besides Rebecca, he also guided her mother and another pair of slaves to Fredericksburg. He was their personal conductor on his own impromptu road to liberty, and he knew every twist, rise and dip of the way.

The group left on a Sunday, creeping away in the shadows. Their journey of more than fifty miles lasted fourteen hours. It wore out everyone in the group, stripping them down to tingly nerves, sore feet and sweat, but Samuel and Rebecca later claimed they felt not even a whiff of fatigue. Ballton settled his wife in Alexandria, north of Fredericksburg. The river port, which sat directly across the Potomac from Washington, D.C., had been occupied by the North in May 1861 and turned into a Federal supply base and hospital depot.

Like many other African-American men, Ballton had wanted to fight in the war from the start, sensing in it the potential for unleashing freedom. Yet, while the South early on used blacks as military laborers, forced conscripts and, in some cases, voluntary fighters, the North was slow to unveil its secret weapon. Slavery was the match that had set the country on fire in 1861, but it was not the cause that inflamed Northern white men riding off to battle. All their speeches and slogans called it a war to save the Union, and that was how they saw it. However, as the Union army advanced into the heartland of the Confederacy, enslaved people like Samuel Ballton, who had dreamed of running to the North, realized they no longer had to travel thousands of miles to find havens. They could travel hundreds—or, perhaps, only five or six.

In the beginning of the war, Northern troops usually sent fugitive slaves back to their masters. However, by the summer of 1862, Union troops began to get smarter. They didn't see themselves as avenging angels come to liberate slaves, but they began to see the common sense in bringing slaves to their lines and putting them to work. Soon, runaway slaves began fleeing in groups, black men, women and children showing up by the hundreds at refugee camps, all of them "contrabands of war." Samuel Ballton himself was a contraband for the 6th Wisconsin before joining the 5th Massachusetts

Cavalry. In most camps, conditions were dreary, but the camp at Corinth, Mississippi, actually became a village with compounds, streets, numbers, schools, a commissary, hospital and a cooperative farm that produced cotton and produce that the army bought.

In January 1863, with the Union army stumbling and losing steam, President Lincoln finally rolled out his big guns and loaded them. He issued the Emancipation Proclamation, freeing the slaves in rebelling states. This, in turn, opened the door to using officially organized black troops who would serve under white commanding officers. Oh, the sneers, laughter and skepticism this set off.

"He [the Negro] has not the mental vigor and energy, he cannot stand up against adversity," wrote Colonel Charles Francis Adams Jr., commander of the cavalry unit that Samuel Ballton would join. "A sick nigger, for instance, at once gives up and lies down to die, the personification of humanity reduced to a wet rag. . . ." Adams added in a November 2, 1864, letter to his father.

Colonel Adams Jr. began a September 18, 1864, letter to his brother, Henry, by joking that the Negroes ate and slept too much, had oversized feet, "sugar loaf craniums" and spirits that would snap under the slightest pressure. The great-grandson of President John Adams and the grandson of President John Quincy Adams, Colonel Adams believed Negro infantry would be as effective as any if well led. However, he was doubtful that individual blacks, their initiative whittled away by slavery, could function as scouts and advance guards in cavalry units where "single men in every exposed position have only themselves and their own nerve, intelligence and quickness to rely on. . . ."

Other skeptics doubted that black soldiers would have the presence of mind to load rifle muskets, get into prime positions, half-cock their rifle muskets and fire while artillery boomed around them and men lost arms and legs or fell into meshes of trip wires. They felt, like Adams, that blacks would either wilt or wander off.

They didn't expect hordes of prospective black soldiers to show up at recruiting stations with the scars from whippings on their backs and dog bites on their legs. They hadn't counted on people like Alfred White, a black man from Michigan, who enlisted just five days before the birth of his son and fought at Honey Hill, South Carolina. They didn't realize that Joshua Dunbar, the forty-year-old father of poet Paul Laurence Dunbar, would enlist in the 55th Massachusetts Infantry Regiment and the 5th Massachusetts Cavalry.

They didn't anticipate that Lucy Higgs Nichols, a fugitive slave, would dash into the camp of the 23rd Regiment of Indiana Volunteers near Bolivar, Tennessee, in 1862, stay with that regiment for the whole war and become a legend. The *Arcata Union* newspaper claimed that "She was a slave & escaped with her husband & little girl from a cruel master. They joined the regiment at Bolivar, Tennessee & when her husband was killed she took up his rifle & marched in his stead." The *Sandusky Star* told a similar tale, claiming the soldiers had protected her when her master tried to reclaim her and that she had participated in twenty-eight battles, burying a daughter at Vicksburg. Her government pension file, however, only documents that she served as the regiment's unofficial nurse, cook and laundress and later became an honorary member of the Grand Army of the Republic. In 1899, a special act of Congress granted her a pension of twelve dollars a month.

Nor could any of the doubters have imagined that in 1864 a runaway slave and civilian scout named Alfred Wood would crawl through a clump of dead Confederate soldiers, slip on one of their uniforms, steal a rebel horse and journey to the Union army at Vicksburg to get help for the besieged 3rd U.S. Colored Cavalry. Or that Octave Johnson, a runaway who had lived for more than a year in a swamp four miles from his former Louisiana plantation, would enlist in the 99th U.S. Colored Troops on August 27, 1863. Or that an exceptional North Carolina slave named George Moses Horton, who earned money composing letters and poems for college students, would escape to Union lines after failing to earn enough to move to Liberia. Or that during the two-day battle at New Market Heights in Virginia, fourteen black soldiers would win Congressional Medals of Honor for fighting with blown-apart hands and leading their units to victory after their white officers had been killed or wounded. Or that thousands of fugitive slaves safely in Canada would ride the Underground Railroad in reverse, returning to America to fight for the Union. Or that an unknown, unremarkable former slave like Samuel Ballton would become a cavalry man.

In March 1864, Ballton enlisted in Company H of the 5th Massachusetts Regiment, Colored Cavalry, in Boston, the only cavalry regiment from Massachusetts composed entirely of black men. Despite his spunk and sass, Ballton performed no acts of personal heroism to match the exploits of Alfred Wood, the scout and spy who escaped on a horse with his wife, Margaret, riding behind him, and who, in the summer of 1864, took home a fourteen-year-old boy he found wandering through the streets of Vicksburg. Nor did he achieve the wartime celebrity of Lucy Nichols, whose Indiana unit made her an honorary member of the Grand Army of the Republic. Yet the war gripped Ballton in its jaws, and he felt its teeth.

He served in Virginia, the site of 519 battles between Union and Confederate troops, battles where the woods groaned with the sound of repeating rifles, sawed-off shotguns, mortar bombs, red-hot shot designed to set fires and artillery battles that could be heard more than ten miles away. He fought in Washington, Arlington Heights, Fortress Monroe, Baylor's Farm. He was at Petersburg, the scene of more fighting than any Virginia community except Richmond, and the site of a nine-month siege in 1864–1865 that remains the longest such operation on American soil. He was in City Point, which became a legend after the Confederacy blew up a huge Union supply depot there, killing 58 and wounding 126 and nearly killing General Ulysses S. Grant. He also was one of the men who guarded Confederate troops in Point Lookout, Maryland, a place that Colonel Adams described as "on a low, sandy, malarious, fever-smitten, wind-blown, God-forsaken tongue of land dividing Chesapeake Bay from the Potomac River."

By the war's end, some two hundred thousand African-American troops had fought for the Union, and black soldiers had participated in 449 separate fights with Confederates. The supreme irony came when Union forces marched into Richmond after the surrender of the South on April 2, 1865. Samuel Ballton's group, the 5th Massachusetts Cavalry, entered the city first after the rebels evacuated it. They were followed by troops of the all-black 25th Army Corps under Major General Godfrey Weitzel.

"I was in the column in advance in Richmond on a Monday morning from Deep Bottom to Richmond on the 3rd of April 1865," Ballton pointed out in a letter he wrote to the Department of the Interior seeking a raise in his pension.

Ballton's final assignment was on the Rio Grande in Texas, guarding the frontier. Sleeping on the Texas earth, he, like so many other troops, black and white, contracted the malaria, chronic diarrhea and rheumatoid arthritis that would plague him in later years. His conditions would not have been relieved by primitive Civil War medical practices, which often regarded daily whiskey and porter as cures for everything from typhoid to mumps. His military career ended with his discharge on August 1. After mustering out from Clarksville, Texas, on October 31, 1865, Ballton rode the troopship back to Boston Harbor. In the latter part of November, the men were paid off and discharged. Samuel Ballton now could call himself a freeman, though not yet a satisfied or whole one.

He finally rejoined Rebecca in Alexandria. He could start to forget the thump and roll of drums and the almost sulfuric smell of gunpowder mingling with the stench of dead horses. There would be no more soldiers shot while chewing fatback or dipping hardtack bread into a brownish brew that passed for coffee, no more desperate reunions under cover of darkness, no more battlefield baptisms. Samuel Ballton had survived the first war to use trench warfare and dog tags, made from handkerchiefs or pieces of paper, the first war bent on destroying not only men, but territory, property, towns, cities and families, the first war in which iron-clad naval vessels were used and the first war to use repeating arms that fired several rounds without reloading. Now the life he had run away to find could begin.

The post–Civil War period was a time of rising black hopes. Samuel and Rebecca headed north, living for a while in Brooklyn, where Ballton joined the William Lloyd Garrison chapter of the Veterans of the Grand Army of the Republic. But the former slave and former soldier was not through trying to discover who he might have been if he hadn't started his life as a slave. In 1873, Ballton, then thirty-five, took his beloved Rebecca to a hamlet on the heavily forested north shore of Long Island, New York. It was a region of streams, large projecting rocks and stones, hills high enough to be seen at great distances by approaching seamen and the Long Island Sound, a sea separating the island from Connecticut's mainland and connecting with the Atlantic Ocean at each end of the island. In this, their final Promised Land, a small man named Samuel Ballton discovered that, with a boost from his wife, he could become a giant.

The roughly two-square-mile hamlet of Greenlawn sits inside the town of Huntington in Suffolk County, Long Island. It was part of the "First Purchase" of land from the Matinecock Indians, recorded in 1653. Slavery had begun around the same time in Suffolk County, with most slaves coming from Africa and the West Indies, but by 1798, the fifty-three slave owners in Huntington Township had freed their slaves. Located on fertile upland plains, the area then known as East Fields and later as Oldfields was pastureland for white settlers' livestock. The 1783 census shows twelve families living there. In the early 1800s, other farm families, mostly from Huntington, settled at Oldfields, farming large stretches of land. However, in 1868, the extension of the Long Island Rail Road through the sparsely settled farmlands changed the character of the town, unleashing a tide of tall ambitions and wide hopes. Suddenly, farmers would have a way to sell surplus cash crops, including pickles and cabbages, to New York City markets and to purchase soap, cloth, flour and factory-made items. Suddenly, young and old would get lessons in geography simply from reading the place names printed on the sides of freight trains.

Greenlawn's earliest homes and businesses clustered around the railroad depot: the Greenlawn Hotel went up across the street, a butcher shop opened, a post office began operating in the general store. At the freight-loading platform, farmers could leave crates of live chickens or vegetables and cans of milk for railroad workers to transport to dealers in the city. The depot became Greenlawn-Centerport and then Greenlawn. However, no settlers believed more in the potential of the little hamlet with one grocery store, one butcher shop and one hotel than two ex-slaves, Samuel and Rebecca Ballton.

At first, Samuel farmed with Charles Duryea Smith, one of Greenlawn's wealthiest men. Then he sharecropped for Alexander Gardiner on his six-hundred-acre estate west of the hamlet, no doubt inspired by Gardiner's success. Gardiner had built a cider mill, a sawmill that turned out oak and chestnut lumber, mostly for local shipbuilders, a brickyard, an ice house and a gristmill. He was best known, though, as one of the area's first farmers to recognize the potential of pickles as a cash crop. He planted fields of pickles, a name then given to cucumbers less than four inches long even before they were processed and flavored with jalapeño, dill and other flavors. The pickle works that Gardiner built on his property adjacent to the railroad processed not only pickles from his farm, but pickles grown on many neighboring farms. As a result, over the years, he became known as Greenlawn's Pickle Pioneer.

In many ways, though, Ballton matched him, stroke for stroke and crop for crop.

In those days, people pickled cucumbers and other vegetables in brine or vinegar, eating them in winter when fresh vegetables weren't available. But pickle farming was stoop work, bent-over work, continual work. A pickle farmer would pluck a handful of seeds from the cloth bag of cucumber seeds he carried over his shoulders, make a little hole at an already marked and fertilized spot, drop in about six seeds, kick in the dirt, stamp on it and move on to the next mark. Because weeds grew faster than the plants, a farmer had to keep cultivating all the time. The stables and streets of New York City supplied the manure to fertilize the growing plants. A farmer would take a whole load of manure home in his wagon, spread it in his fields and return for another load. Sometimes it took three or four days just to unload a freight car.

Samuel Ballton became a master at both growing and picking pickles. In the summer of 1899, he was said to have raised 1,500,000 pickles. That's when people began slapping him on the back and calling him the Pickle King. However, he wasn't content. Sharecropping wasn't slavery, but it was just a few houses down the road from it, the same kind of no-end, no-exit toil. Though he had never spent a day of his life in school, Ballton had picked up what a *Brooklyn Eagle* article called "a much larger share of horse sense and business acumen than usually falls to the man not trained to business." Translation: he began buying pickles for the Boston Pickle Agency, gathering up produce from other people and getting a dime for every thousand he delivered.

He still had bigger dreams in his pocket, though—dreams of houses that would be monuments to his hustle and drive and Civil War struggles. After getting personal loans from wealthy farmers and using the money to buy property, he began building homes for people such as blacksmith William Hudson Jr. and the Howarth family, the first owners of the general store, and the touring vaudeville team of Charles Gardner and Marie Stoddard. In some cases, his white friends had to buy the land for him and then sign it over to him. He promoted himself, too. The *1896 Lain & Healy's Brooklyn & Long Island Business Directory* contained an ad for "Samuel Ballton, real estate agent, Greenlawn, L.I., Houses and lots for sale in different parts of Long Island." He used former slaves and carpenters from the South to build the homes. When he built a house at 67 Boulevard, he put a room upstairs for the bathroom even though there was no running water at the time. Between 1905 and 1910, he erected a building on Taylor Avenue near the railroad tracks for use as a store. However, when the depot was built farther west, he converted the building into a four-room home.

Meanwhile, Rebecca Ballton was also growing, feeding on her husband's visions. The only surviving picture of Rebecca shows a sturdy-legged brown woman, her skin as smooth as apples, her almond eyes squinting slightly in the sun. The picture doesn't show her shrewdness, but, like Samuel, she could smell an opportunity while it was still taking shape. During the war, Samuel had walked her to freedom. In peacetime, she helped escort him to prosperity. No matter how grand Samuel's ambitions became, Rebecca did whatever she could to keep them afloat. Unlike Samuel, she never learned to read or write, but she cooked well enough to earn extra money selling Sunday dinners. She and her youngest daughter, Jessie, also laundered clothes to help feed the family's eight surviving children. Rebecca was the kind of homemaker who would spend half the night on family chores after working all day in the homes of wealthy white families in nearby Northport. Like other women of the period, she sewed, knitted, quilted, canned fruits and vegetables and preserved meat as well, especially when her husband annually butchered a pig. Her granddaughter Virginia Jackson could remember only one time when Rebecca went anywhere except to church or work. That was the day she rode in a horse-drawn wagon to the Mineola Fair in neighboring Nassau County, an annual event where farmers purchased and traded produce and livestock and held beautiful baby contests and other events.

Two of Rebecca's surviving quilts reveal something else about her and the rest of her family. Most people sew quilt pieces in straight lines, but the Ballton quilts contain stitches that run off in a dozen different directions, some straight, some seemingly random. Neither Rebecca nor her children took the time to make quilts that told stories or brought to life scenes from the Bible. According to Berenice Easton, another Ballton granddaughter, several family members most likely worked on the quilts together, each one infusing the garments with a different style and energy. Samuel and Rebecca Ballton weren't the only members of this family who could work without patterns and create new traditions from scraps of the past.

In 1911, Samuel and Rebecca celebrated their fiftieth wedding anniversary in a house Samuel had just had built on Boulevard Extension. Since most of the Balltons' furniture hadn't yet been moved in, their guests had plenty of room for dancing. The *Brooklyn Eagle* reporter who interviewed Ballton in 1910 mentioned that he had just "moved into a $5,500 house on which he is putting the finishing touches. On this plot he has erected five houses, all within a short time. His own residence is of cement blocks to the second story, then shingled, and is a substantial structure. It is wired for electric lights." It was a long leap from the days when the family, while waiting for one of Samuel's houses to be built, lived in a shed so small it was later used as a washhouse. That Samuel Ballton had lived in and wrestled with constant pain since the Civil War made his achievements all the more remarkable. After putting in a hard day's work, he sometimes had to spend a day in bed recovering.

In his application for an invalid's pension, he claimed to have chronic diarrhea and rheumatism and cramps "inherited while in service." Such complaints were common among former Civil War soldiers. The pension file for Octave Johnson, another U.S. Colored Troops veteran, noted that he suffered from defective hearing and vision, lung disease, articular rheumatism and hemorrhoids. The surgeon who examined Samuel Ballton wrote that he had "crepitation" in both shoulders, meaning his bones crackled when he moved them. Ballton also found it difficult to raise his arms above his shoulders or to walk with his stiff knees. His other joints, muscles and tendons were apparently normal, according to the doctor. The doctor also noted that Ballton claimed that he had severe hours-long attacks of diarrhea, usually following fatigue and accompanied by muscular pain. His liver was said to be enlarged about half an inch and was sensitive, his stomach distended and tender, tongue coated, breath offensive, spleen and rectum normal. According to the doctor, he had "roughened respiratory murmurs" and "sibilant rales over both lungs."

Yet Ballton never stopped pushing himself or pushing others, including the Commission of Pensions, which he accused in a June 1913 letter of "beating an old soldier out of $5.50 per month for the rest of his life." In a 1982 tape, his granddaughter Virginia Jackson said "he could figure in his head better than I could do it on paper." Despite never attending school a day in his life, he also learned to read and write. He even became literate enough to write letters to the editor, including one published on March 18, 1914, in the Huntington *Long-Islander* newspaper, pointing out how much he had contributed to the hamlet's growth and noting that the place would be further along if more people had done as much.

"Please let me give a little history of Greenlawn, which I think is as nice a locality as there is on this branch of the Long Island Railroad," his letter began.

> What it is to-day, what it was forty-one years ago, when I first came here; how much it has developed in improvements; also what I think is the cause of its not developing more.
>
> When I first came here there was one little grocery store, one little butcher shop, one little hotel, so you can form an opinion of the business of that time. The butcher drove once a week to the farm of Gilbert Carll on the Turnpike to help slaughter a beef, and brought one-half of the carcass home to peddle out. The hotel was paying a rental of about $25 per month; license about $50 per year. There was not a place that had any use for an icebox. If I had not had my few dollars invested I would have got out as quickly as possible. Some of the residents here have bought fine real estate for less than $100 per acre, which they refuse to sell for less than $1,000; yet they won't improve it any.
>
> I, after being here five years, withstood and bought five acres of land; improved it to the best of my ability. After a few years, I sold it with a small profit. I borrowed money and bought 7.5 acres, had it laid out into 33 building lots, built streets and began to build decent cottages which I succeeded in selling with a small profit. This is now the business square of the village.
>
> The Greenlawn Department Store transacts more business in one day than the little one did in two months. There are two thriving butcher shops here now and they are doing a lively business. The Columbia Hotel with its bowling alleys is located on the property at the corner of Gaines and Railroad Avenues,

> and on the opposite corner is a fine ice cream parlor, owned by William B. Gurney. So I form an idea, had they a little more grit and spunk, Greenlawn would be quite a little more advanced than it is.

When Samuel Ballton died on April 30, 1917, he was buried in the black section of the Huntington Rural Cemetery on New York Avenue. After his death, Rebecca applied for his pension, but since they had never married legally she had to collect affidavits from people saying they had been recognized in the community as man and wife. The leading citizens all signed the affidavits. In May 1925, Rebecca died at the home of her daughter, Jessie Easton, in Greenlawn. She was survived by six of her sixteen children. She had been living with her daughter, Mrs. Tina Taylor, in Atlantic City, but had returned to Greenlawn a week before her death, saying she wanted to die there. The death of the pickle industry in Greenlawn soon followed. By the 1920s, a disease called "white pickle blight" turned cucumbers white and hard and stunted their growth at two and a half inches.

The Balltons, however, remain living presences in their adopted hometown. Huntington Township, which includes Greenlawn, remembers them with annual celebrations of Pickle Day, and Huntington saluted them with a special presentation in 2002. Seven of the houses Ballton built still stood in the spring of 2003: a cinder-block and stucco dwelling at 67 Boulevard, the last house Ballton built and the one in which he died in 1917; the house he built in 1894 for blacksmith William Hudson Jr. at 3 Smith Street; the house with clamshell shingles on the gable ends that he built between 1894 and 1900 at 14 Gaines and sold to Joel Barnum Smith in 1903; the house he built at 75 Boulevard Extension and where he and Rebecca celebrated their fiftieth anniversary; the house he built around 1894 for the Howarth family, first owners of the general store, which had been moved twice, most recently to 5 Smith. In 2003, Ballton's eighty-eight-year-old granddaughter Berenice Easton lived in a building her grandfather had put up at 34 Taylor Avenue between 1905 and 1910. He had built it for commercial purposes, but later converted it into a house. Also still standing at 30 Taylor Avenue near Boulevard Extension was the home Ballton built for vaudevillians Charles Gardner and Marie Stoddard.

The Greenlawn-Centerport Historical Association, located in the Oldfield library, evokes the Ballton family's history, too. Its memorabilia includes Samuel's rusty Civil War saber and a mammoth Bible belonging to one of the Balltons' sons, Charles H. Ballton; it recorded the births of two children, one of whom lived only a week and the other who lived less than a year. Like everything else about Samuel and Rebecca Ballton—their escapes, their journeys, their ever-expanding ambitions—the book seems an outsized but appropriate tribute to a family that not only loved in sickness and in health, but in war and peace as well.

Bibliography

Chapter 1: Love in a Time of Hate

"Unsung Heroes of Harpers Ferry." *African American Voices of Triumph: Perseverance.* Alexandria, Va.: Time-Life Books, 1993, pp. 74–75.

Legislative petitions filed in Virginia in the nineteenth century by blacks seeking to remain in the state. www.afrigeneas.com.

Barry, Joseph. *The Strange Story of Harper's Ferry with Legends of the Surrounding Country.* Shepherdstown, W. Va.: The Woman's Club of Harper's Ferry District, 1984. The original is from 1903, copyright by Joseph Barry.

Bennett, Lerone, Jr. *Before the Mayflower: A History of the Negro in America, 1619–1964* (rev. ed.). Baltimore: Penguin Books, 1966.

Berlin, Ira. "The Promised Land," a review of Alan Huffman's book *Mississippi in Africa. The New York Times Book Review*, Sunday, May 2, 2004.

Bibb, Henry. *Narrative of the Life and Adventures of Henry Bibb, an American Slave, written by Himself, with an Introduction by Lucius C. Matlack.* New York: published by the author, 1849.

Blassingame, John W. *The Slave Community.* New York and Oxford: Oxford University Press, 1979. This talks about slave marriages dissolved by their masters. The dissolution of the marriages of Hosea Bidell from his mate of twenty-five years and of Lucy Robinson from her mate of forty-three years is discussed on page 177.

Brown, Stephen D. *Ghosts of Harpers Ferry.* Harpers Ferry, W.Va.: The Little Brown House Publishing Co., 1981, pp. 8–9.

Carr, Peter E. *Guide to Cuban Genealogical Research.* Baltimore: Clearfield Company, Inc., 2000.

Catterall, Helen Tunnicliff, ed. *Judicial Cases Concerning American Slavery and the Negro*, Vol. I. New York: Octagon Books, Inc., 1968, pp. 53–55.

Cauthorn, Henry S. *A History of the City of Vincennes, Indiana, from 1702 to 1901.* Published by Margaret C. Cauthorn, October 15, 1901.

Cohen, Saul B., ed. *The Columbia Gazetteer of the World*, Vol. 2, H to O. New York: Columbia University Press, 1998, p. 1226.

Dalmage, Heather M. *Tripping on the Color Line, Black-White Multiracial Families in a Racially Divided World.* New Brunswick, N.J.: Rutgers University Press, 1965.

Dawson, Joseph G., III, ed. *The Louisiana Governors.* Baton Rouge: Louisiana State University Press, 1990.

Detroit Tribune and Advertiser. February 23, 1875. Obituary for George DeBaptiste. It reads in part: "The most interesting portion of Mr. DeBaptiste's life was while he was connected with the so-called underground railroad which as most of us know was a secret organization formed during the days of slavery to assist slaves in escaping from the slave states into Canada. Mr. DeBaptiste became connected with the underground railroad while living in Madison, Indiana, and has aided hundreds of poor negroes to escape their masters and take refuge in a land of freedom. He used to say that he had walked on the bank of the Ohio river, half the night while the rain was pouring down, intently listening to hear the oars of an expected boat which contained one or more fugitive slaves. It was his custom to pilot these fugitives ten or twelve miles north to the home of a farmer who kept them secreted during the day, and on the next night would send them on to another stopping place. This method of travel was kept up until they arrived at Detroit where they were taken across to Windsor. Mr. DeBaptiste would usually perform these journeys on foot walking sometimes twenty miles during the night, returning to his work the next day, probably to shave the man whose slave he helped escape the previous night."

"Discover Historic Dresden," souvenir visitor's guide.

Drew, Benjamin. *A North-Side View of Slavery. The Refugee: Or the Narratives of Fugitive Slaves in Canada. Related by Themselves with an Account of the History and Condition of the Colored Population of Upper Canada.* Boston: John P. Jewett and Company; Cleveland, Ohio: Jewett, Proctor and Worthington; New York: Sheldon, Lamport and Blakeman, 1856, pp. 213, 221, 222.

Fitzgerald, Ruth Coder. *A Different Story: A Black History of Fredericksburg, Stafford and Spotsylvania.* Virginia: Unicorn, 1979.

Franklin, John Hope, and Loren Schweninger. *Runaway Slaves; Rebels on the Plantation.* New York and Oxford: Oxford University Press, 1999.

Genovese, Eugene D. *Roll, Jordan, Roll: The World the Slaves Made.* New York: Vintage Books, 1976.

Harwood, Michael. "Better for Us to Be Separated." *American Heritage.* New York: American Heritage Publishing Co., Inc., Vol. XXIV, No. 1 (December 1972), p. 55. (Includes the story of slaveholder Joseph Hill's will.)

Kilborn, Peter T. "An All-American Town, A Sky-High Divorce Rate." *The New York Times,* May 2, 2004.

Kotlowitz, Alex. *There Are No Children Here.* New York: Doubleday, 1991.

Lucas, Marion B. *A History of Blacks in Kentucky,* Vol. 1, *From Slavery to Segregation, 1760–1891.* The Kentucky Historical Society, 1992, Prologue, p. xv.

Palmer, Ronald, professor emeritus of The Practice of International Affairs, George Washington University. "Some Useful Things to Know about George DeBaptiste,

Underground Railroad Leader." Speech delivered on August 30, 2002, at the U.S./Canadian History and Genealogy Conference, North Buxton, Ontario.

Pelham, Benjamin B. *Family History,* an undated, handwritten manuscript among the Pelham Papers. Detroit: The Burton Historical Collection of the Detroit Public Library.

Plumb, J. H. "America: Illusion and Reality." *American Heritage.* New York: American Heritage Publishing Co., Inc., Vol. XXVII, No. 5 (August 1976).

Reich, Jerome P. *Colonial America.* Englewood Cliffs, N.J.: Prentice-Hall, Inc., 1984. On page 66 is a definition of "indentured servitude."

Report of John S. Bagg, U.S. Marshal, Detroit, to J. S. Black, Attorney General, Washington, January 16, 1860, for the Senate committee investigating the Harper's Ferry raid.

Ripley, C. Peter, ed. *The Black Abolitionist Papers,* Vol. 2, *Canada, 1830–1865.* Chapel Hill and London: University of North Carolina Press, 1986, p. 276.

Roberts, Nancy. *America's Most Haunted Places.* Orangeburg, S.C.: Sandlapper Publishing Inc., 1974, pp. 13–17, 25, 40–44.

Rogers, J. A. *Sex and Race,* Vol. 11. New York: Margaret Rogers, 1942.

Rossi, Ernest E., and Jack C. Plano. *The Latin American Political Dictionary.* Santa Barbara, Calif., and Oxford, England: ABC-Clio, 1980.

Scheel, Eugene M. *Culpeper: A Virginia County's History Through 1920.* Culpeper, Va.: The Culpeper Historical Society, 1982.

Schwarz, Philip J. *Migrants Against Slavery: Virginians and the Nation.* Charlottesville and London: University Press of Virginia, 2001.

Sexton, Sharon-Elizabeth. "More Historical Errors on Underground Railroad Monument." Press release, December 7, 2001.

Stocking, William. "Underground Railroad; Reminiscences of the Days of Slavery; The Underground Railroad and Its Detroit Agents; Its Efficiency in Abling [*sic*] Fugitives to Escape; Secrecy of Its Workings and Fidelity of Its Operators; Exciting Scenes and Incidents." *The Detroit Post,* May 15, 1870. The interview with DeBaptiste notes that "Of late years, perhaps, the principal manager of the UGRR in this city was George DeBaptiste, our well-known colored fellow citizen. The Secretary of the concern here, for a long period, has been Wm. Lambert, another of our widely known and respected colored fellow citizens. Mr. DeBaptiste began his active career as agent of the road, at Cincinnati, Ohio, in 1837, though he had as early as 1829, while yet a lad, assisted the escape of a fugitive from Richmond, Va. In 1838, he became the station agent at Madison, Indiana. The principal business men of the road at Cincinnati, in those days, were Geo. Cary and James G. Birney, then editor of the *Philanthropist,* a paper whose office was mobbed and its press thrown into the Ohio River, in 1837 or 1838, and Mr. Burnett, the well-known Cincinnati baker and confectioner.

"Mr. DeBaptiste remained in Madison, Indiana for eight years, as station agent of the U.G.R.R. He then moved to Detroit, where he has since resided. During that eight years, he started one hundred and eight fugitives, in his own wagon, for Canada, beside many times that number assisted in other ways and through the employment of other persons."

Thrasher, Albert. *On to New Orleans: Louisiana's Heroic 1811 Slave Revolt.* New Orleans: Cypress Press, 1995, 2nd ed., June 1996.

Will, Thomas E. *Weddings on Contested Ground: Slave Marriage in the Antebellum South*, investigator.netfirms.com/marriage.

Wood, Michael. *Conquistadors.* Berkeley and Los Angeles: University of California Press, 2000.

Woodson, Carter G. *Free Negro Heads of Families in the United States in 1830.* Washington, D.C.: Association for the Study of Negro Life and History, 1925.

www.enlou.com/people/salcedojm-bio.htm. In fall 2003, this website summarized the life of Juan Manuel de Salcedo, the last Spanish governor of Louisiana, but it had become inoperative by September 20, 2004.

www.lapurchase2003.org/history.htm. This website providing eighteenth-century Louisiana history had become inaccessible by September 20, 2004.

Chapter 2: A Love Worth Waiting For

Alderton, David. *Dogs.* Smithsonian Handbooks, New York: Dorling Kindersley, Inc., 2002.

Baughman, A. J. *History of Huron County, Ohio, Its Progress and Development*, Vol. 1. Chicago: S. J. Clarke Publishing Co., 1909.

Bearden, Romare, and Harry Henderson. *A History of African-American Artists from 1792 to the Present.* New York: Pantheon Books, 1993, p. 20. Ohio passed black laws that barred blacks from most skilled occupations and from serving in the militia and as witnesses. In 1830, the president of a trade-oriented association was publicly tried for helping a black youth learn a trade.

Bell, Lyndon Conrad. "The Underground Railroad." Canada was often the final destination for slaves chasing freedom in the North. *African Americans on Wheels*, Vol. 8, No. 3 (June/July 2002).

ben-Jochannan, Yosef. *African Origins of the Major "Western Religions."* New York: Alkebu-Lan Books, 1970.

Blassingame, John W. *The Slave Community.* New York and Oxford: Oxford University Press, Inc., 1979. This describes the Nat Turner and Gabriel Prosser rebellions.

Blockson, Charles L. *The Underground Railroad: First-Person Narratives of Escapes to Freedom in the North.* New York: Prentice-Hall, 1987, pp. 205–12.

Brown, Thomas J., ed. *American Eras: Civil War and Reconstruction. 1850–1877.* Detroit: Gale Research, 1997.

Carter, R. A. "What the Negro Church Has Done." *The Journal of Negro History*, Vol. XI, 1926, pp. 1–2.

Clemens, Samuel Langhorne. *Mark Twain's Autobiography*, Vol. 1. New York and London: Harper & Brothers Publishers, 1924. Copyright by Clara Gabrilowitsch.

Twain talks about his uncle John's farm, four miles from Florida, Missouri, and notes that the local church taught that God approved of slavery and that it was holy.

Daniel 6:7–24 and 3:14–30. Holy Bible (KJV).

Denne, Darrin. "Remembering the Past." *The Windsor Star*, Saturday, October 30, 1999. Describes Labor Day weekend in North Buxton, Ontario, the most successful of Ontario's antebellum black settlements.

Drew, Benjamin. *A North-Side View of Slavery. The Refugee: or the Narratives of Fugitive Slaves in Canada, Related by Themselves with an Account of the History and Condition of the Colored Population of Upper Canada.* Boston: John P. Jewett & Co; Cleveland: Jewett, Proctor and Worthington; New York: Sheldon, Lamport and Blakeman; London: Trubner and Co., 1856, p. 80. "I belonged in Norfolk, Va., from birth until 34 years of age," ex-slave Henry Atkinson told researcher Benjamin Drew. ". . . In regard to religious instruction, I was allowed to go to church on Sunday, to a white clergyman—no colored preacher being allowed in Norfolk. . . . The white clergymen don't preach the whole gospel there. Since I have been here, I have heard the passage about the fact that the Lord hath chose to loose the bands of wickedness, to undo the heavy burdens, to let the oppressed go free, and that ye break every yoke. I never heard that down South. If a colored man were to say it, he'd have the handcuffs put on quick—if a white man were to say it, he'd have to leave, because they'd say he was 'putting too much into the niggers' heads.'" See also pp. 205, 211 (betrayal by friends); p. 234 (description of Chatham).

The Firelands Pioneer, New Series, Vol. V. Norwalk, Ohio: Firelands Historical Society, June 1882, "Reminiscences" by the Honorable H. F. Paden of Clyde, Ohio; "The Underground Railroad of the Firelands" by the Honorable Rush R. Sloane of Sandusky, Ohio; "The Ohio Fugitive Slave Law" by G. T. Stewart, Esq., Norwalk, Ohio; and "Some Experiences in Abolition Times" by Capt. C. Woodruff of Peru, Ohio.

The Firelands Pioneer, New Series, Vol. III. Norwalk, Ohio: Firelands Historical Society, January 1886. This contains an obituary with Lyman Scott's abolitionist activities on page 113.

The Firelands Pioneer, New Series, Vol. XII. Norwalk, Ohio: Firelands Historical Society, 1900. On page 534, the magazine mentions Elvira Dibble, who "assisted many runaway slaves on their way to Canada."

The Firelands Pioneer, New Series, Vol. IX. Norwalk, Ohio: Firelands Historical Society, 1896. This mentions that Sandusky was the end of the UGRR in Ohio.

The Firelands Pioneer, New Series, Vol. XVII. Norwalk, Ohio: Firelands Historical Society, The American Publisher Co., 1909. This includes a paper by Dr. A. Sheldon titled "Reminiscences of Underground Railroads." In it Dr. Sheldon talks about the Society of Quakers, or Friends, in Greenwich and their activities as Underground Railroad conductors. He also mentions the Palmers of Fitchville and a station in Hartland kept by James Lee.

Foskett, Helen R. *History of New London, Ohio, 1815–1941.* New London, Ohio: New London Public Library, 1976.

Franklin, John Hope, and Loren Schweninger. *Runaway Slaves: Rebels on the Plantation.* New York and Oxford: Oxford University Press, Inc., 1999.

Griffin, Paula Porter. *Carved Out of the Wilderness: The History of Fitchville Township, Huron County, Ohio, 1817–1987.* Norwalk, Ohio: Robert T. and Ruth E. Vogt, 1989. This tells the story of Fitchville abolitionists, including Rouse Bly and the Palmer family.

Groene, Janet, and Gordon Groene. *Natural Wonders of Ohio: A Guide to Parks, Preserves & Wild Places.* Castine, Me.: Country Roads Press, 1994.

Hagedorn, Ann. *Beyond the River.* New York: Simon & Schuster, 2003. The story of con artist Robert Russell appears on pages 252–3.

Hayden, Robert C. *Eight Black American Inventors.* Reading, Mass.: Addison-Wesley Publishing Co., Inc., 1972.

Hill, Daniel G. *The Freedom-Seekers.* Toronto: Stoddart Publishing Co., Ltd., 1992. This talks about the population of Sandwich in 1855 and 1861.

Kimmel, Janice Martz. "Break Your Chains and Fly for Freedom." *Michigan History,* January/February 1996, pp. 20–26. The story of Henry Bibb and his slave wife, Malinda.

Klein, Herbert S. *Slavery in the Americas.* Chicago: Quadrangle Books, Inc., 1971, p. 56.

Lustig, Lillie S., S. Claire Sondheim, and Sarah Rensel. *The Southern Cook Book of Fine Old Recipes.* Reading, Pa.: Culinary Arts Press, 1939.

Oickle, Alvin F. *Jonathan Walker: The Man with the Branded Hand.* Everett, Mass.: Lorelli Slater Publisher, 1998.

Paige, Howard. *African American Family Cookery.* Detroit: Harlo Press, 1995. This describes a typical slave diet and the role of slave drivers.

Peacefull, Leonard, ed. *A Geography of Ohio.* Kent, Ohio, and London: Kent State University Press, 1996.

Robinson, Wilhelmena S. *Historical Negro Biographies.* International Library of Negro Life and History. New York: Publishers Company, Inc., 1967. This book contains biographies of Gabriel Prosser, Nat Turner and Denmark Vesey.

Roger, Sharon A. *Slaves No More: A Study of the Buxton Settlement, Upper Canada, 1849–1861,* a dissertation submitted to the faculty of the Graduate School of the State University of New York at Buffalo in partial fulfillment of the requirements for the degree of Doctor of Philosophy, 1995. This talks about Canada's identification with the land of Canaan and how slave owners responded to that by calling Canada a "freezing sort of Hell" where men "had to break the ice with their scythes and with wild geese so numerous and ferocious that they would scratch a man's eyes out" (p. 27). On page 285, Roger mentions that an unknown number of slaves "were severely disciplined and even sold for spreading the word of God." Services, if allowed, were usually supervised or led by white pastors who lauded slavery. Still, as she notes, many slaves blended Christianity with their own traditions and their own reality and prayed in secret.

Sengupta, Somini, and Larry Rohter. "Where Faith Grows, Fired by Pentecostalism." *The New York Times,* Tuesday, October 14, 2003.

Siebert, Wilbur Henry. *The Mysteries of Ohio's Underground Railroad.* Columbus: Long's College Book Co., 1951.

Starobin, Robert S., ed. *Blacks in Bondage: Letters of American Slaves.* New York: New Viewpoints, 1974.

Sydnor, T. Davis, and William E. Cowen. "Ohio Trees." Bulletin 700–00, Ohio State University, 2000.

Timman, Henry. "Just Like Old Times," orig. pub. *The Norwalk Reflector.* Book I, page 19, "Railroad North to Freedom," August 11, 1972. It mentions several underground stations in rural parts of Huron County, including the farm of Quaker Joseph Healy of Greenwich Township, a station agent.

Ullman, Victor. *Look to the North Star: A Life of William King.* Toronto: Umbrella Press, 1994.

Underground Railroad. Official National Park Handbook, No. 156, produced by the Division of Publications, National Park Service, Washington, D.C.: U.S. Department of the Interior, 1998, p. 58. This talks about slave escapes organized by Thomas Tilly.

Voice of the Fugitive, "The Lost Is Found," Sandwich, Canada West, January 15, 1852, Vol. II, No. 4, the first installment of the James Smith story.

Voice of the Fugitive, "The Lost Is Found No. 2," February 26, 1852, the second installment of the James Smith story.

Voice of the Fugitive, "The Lost Is Found No. 3," March 11, 1852, Vol. 2, No. 6, the third installment of the James Smith story.

Voice of the Fugitive, "The Lost Is Found No. 4," April 22, 1852, Vol. II, No. 9, the fourth installment of the James Smith story.

Voice of the Fugitive, "The Lost Is Found No. 5," June 3, 1852, the fifth installment of the James Smith story.

Voice of the Fugitive, December 3, 1851.

Voice of the Fugitive, February 12, 1851. Stories abounded about slaves escaping from drunken slave catchers. This issue of *VOF* contains an account of runaway slave James Madison, about 24, a former slave of John T. Snypes, a Georgia cotton planter. After Snypes and a friend caught Madison, they locked his hands together and chained him to the back part of their buggy, making him walk back to the fields he had fled. However, the men reportedly stopped at numerous taverns along the way to drink and boast about their capture. Madison, who had a nail in his pocket, managed to pick the lock and escape.

Voice of the Fugitive, January 1, 1851, talks about Josiah Henson and the Dawn settlement.

Walton, Jonathan Williams. *Blacks in Buxton and Chatham, Ontario, 1830–1890: Did the 49th Parallel Make a Difference?* Dissertation presented to the faculty of Princeton University in candidacy for the degree of Doctor of Philosophy, recommended for acceptance by the Department of History, June 1979.

Williams, Juan, and Quinton Dixie. *This Far by Faith.* New York: HarperCollins, 2003.

Williams, Stacy. *The Revised History of the Black Preacher and the Black Church.* Series of lectures delivered by Dr. Williams to the Council of Baptist Pastors of Detroit and Vicinity, Detroit, January 26, 1982. The lectures tell the story of Dr. C. T. Walker's sermon on "The Second Coming" (typed manuscript in the author's possession).

———. "The Black Preacher and the Black Church." Lecture #2 on the Black Church, Council of Baptist Pastors, Pleasant Grove Baptist Church, Detroit, September 16, 1980.

Chapter 3: The Special Delivery Package

African Americans, Voices of Triumph: Perseverance. By the editors of Time-Life Books. Alexandria, Va.: Time-Life Books, 1993.

The Archivists' Bulldog. Newsletter of the Maryland State Archives, Vol. 16, No. 15 (August 26, 2002).

Armstead, Myra B. Young, Field Horne, Gretchen Sullivan Sorin, and Cara A. Sutherland, eds. *A Heritage Uncovered: The Black Experience in Upstate New York 1800–1925.* Elmira: Chemung County Historical Society, Inc., 1988. Sorin's piece, "The Black Community in Elmira," talks about the establishment of Elmira's abolitionist church, Park Church, and the sharp divisions in Elmira's white community over slavery before the Civil War. It also capsules the lives of famous black conductors such as John Jones and the growth of the black community itself.

Blockson, Charles L. *The Underground Railroad: First-Person Narratives of Escapes to Freedom in the North.* New York: Prentice Hall Press, 1987, pp. 95–99.

Bourdain, Anthony. "Eating the Best of the Rest." *The New York Times,* June 11, 2003.

Burgess, Robert H., and H. Graham Wood. *Steamboats Out of Baltimore.* Cambridge, Md.: Tidewater Publishers, 1968.

Carruth, Gorton. *The Encyclopedia of American Facts and Dates,* 9th ed. New York: HarperCollins, 1993.

Chalkley, Tom. *Mystery Train.* Baltimore City Paper Online, November 21, 2001.

———. "Native Son: On the Trail of Frederick Douglass in Baltimore." *Baltimore City Paper,* March 15, 2000.

Clayton, Ralph. *Black Baltimore: 1820–1870.* Bowie, Md.: Heritage Books, Inc., 1987. On page 6, Clayton verifies that James Noble's ad for his runaway slave, Lear Green, ran in the *Baltimore Sun* on May 26, 1857.

———. *Cash for Blood.* Bowie, Md.: Heritage Books, Inc., 2002.

———. *Slavery, Slaveholding, and the Free Black Population of Antebellum Baltimore.* Bowie, Md.: Heritage Books, Inc., 1993.

Cohen, Anthony. "A Walk on the Underground Railroad." *American Educator,* Winter 2000–2001.

Cowan, Tom, and Jack Maguire. *Timelines of African-American History: 500 Years of Black Achievement.* New York: Roundtable Press/Perigee Books, 1994.

Curtis, Nancy C. *Black Heritage Sites: The South.* Black Heritage Sites, Vol. 2. New York: The New Press, 1996, pp. 190–91.

Daniel, Nat V. "List of Confederate Soldiers Buried in Woodlawn National Cemetery, Elmira, New York: Emendations to Previously Published Lists, Revised and Corrected Alphabetical List." Elmira: Chemung County Historical Society, 1996.

Dannett, Sylvia G. L. *Profiles of Negro Womanhood, 1619–1900,* Vol. 1. Yonkers, N.Y.: Educational Heritage, Inc., 1964.

Douglass, Frederick. *Narrative of the Life of Frederick Douglass, an American Slave.* Boston: Anti-Slavery Office, 1845.

Elmira City Directories for 1857, 1860 and 1861–62, Elmira, New York.

Federal Census. The 1860 New York Census for Chemung County, image 100 on the Ancestry-Com database and page 492, line 26, of the New York Census for Chemung County lists Wm. H. Adams, age 23, barber, birthplace Maryland and living with Eliza J., age 19, no occupation given, birthplace Maryland, and Elizabeth, age 2, birthplace New York.

Federal Census for City of Baltimore, 1850.

Federal Census for City of Baltimore, 1860.

Foote, Shelby. *The Civil War, A Narrative: Fredericksburg to Meridian,* Vol. 2. New York: Vintage Books, 1986, orig. pub. Random House, 1963. On pages 233–34, Foote remarks that Colonel Charles F. Adams Jr. accused General Joe Hooker of running an army headquarters that was a "combination barroom and brothel. Meanwhile, notes Foote, Hooker's "surname entered the language as one of the many lower-case slang words for prostitute."

Hunsinger, Lou, Jr. "Daniel Hughes: Giant of Freedom Road." *Susquehanna Valley Parent Magazine,* February 2002.

Jensen, Malcolm C. *America in Time.* Boston: Houghton Mifflin Company, 1977.

"John Jones' Friend." *The Daily Advertiser,* April 13, 1898. This obituary of John Smith was reprinted in *The Chemung Historical Journal,* Vol. 43, No. 4 (June 1998), Elmira, N. Y.

Ketter, Frank. "Slabtown Revisited." *The Chemung Historical Journal,* Vol. 5, No. 4 (June 1960), Elmira, N.Y. In this article, Ketter describes the old Slabtown neighborhood and the businesses and personalities that gave it character, including Mr. and Mrs. Jeremiah George and Isaac Collins, on pages 710–11.

Klees, Emerson. *Underground Railroad Tales.* Rochester: Friends of the Finger Lakes Publishing, 1997, pp. 69–70. This account of the Lear Green story claims that Lear's "mother advised her to escape from slavery before she undertook the responsibilities of marriage."

McDonough, Jill. "Elmira's Underground Route to Freedom." *Chemung Historical Journal,* September 1974, Elmira, N.Y.

Merrill, Arch. *The Underground, Freedom's Road, and Other Upstate Tales.* Rochester, N.Y.: American Book–Stratford Press, 1963, pp. 119–25. This tells the story of John W. Jones's early years and his work in Elmira.

Mills, Barbara. *Got My Mind Set on Freedom.* Bowie, Md.: Heritage Books, Inc., 2002.

Owens, Hamilton. *Baltimore on the Chesapeake.* Garden City, N.Y.: Doubleday, Doran & Company, 1941. On pages 45 and 46, Owens has this to say about the possibility that prostitutes were first called "hookers" in Fells Point: "This area was for many years taken over largely by prostitutes. Those who practice that profession are frequently called 'hookers.' . . . Baltimore may or may not be responsible for the spread of this appellation, but it is certain that in Baltimore there is a good reason for it." See also pp. 211–12 (the story of abolitionist Elisha Tyson).

Palmer, Ron, professor emeritus of The Practice of International Affairs, George Washington University, letter to author, September 10, 2002, about George DeBaptiste, Underground Railroad leader. Palmer notes that "George Jr. became a master of barber shop repartee, including later in Madison, Indiana, making a joke out of accusations that he was involved in the Underground Railroad. He would say he certainly supported the UGRR but he wasn't smart enough to do all the things of which he was accused."

Pfiffer, Jim. "Discrimination Kept Many Emancipated Blacks from Getting Educated and Employed, No Matter What Abilities They Had." *Star-Gazette,* February 23, 2003.

———. "In the Path of the Underground Railroad, The Twin Tiers Were a Safe Haven for Some Escaped Slaves." *Star-Gazette,* February 9, 2003.

Polgreen, Lydia. "As Upstate Bleeds, New York's Budget Crisis Rubs Salt in Wound," *The New York Times,* Sunday, May 18, 2003.

Rehbein, Leslie, and Kate E. Peterson, eds. *Beyond the White Marble Steps—A Look at Baltimore Neighborhoods.* Baltimore: Livelier Baltimore Committee of the Citizens Planning & Housing Association, 1979.

Rukert, Norman G. *The Fells Point Story.* Baltimore: Bodine & Associates, Inc., 1976.

Sernett, Milton C. *North Star County: Upstate New York and the Crusade for African American Freedom.* Syracuse: Syracuse University Press, 2002. This relates the story of Elmira's chief Underground Station master John W. Jones.

Shindle, Robert, project archivist, Steamship Historical Society of America, University of Baltimore, Langsdale Library, Special Collections, letter to author, July 22, 2003, about screw propellers that enabled large steamers to travel from Baltimore to Philadelphia.

"The Slave Riot in Elmira Recalled." In the *Wellsboro Advocate,* August 20, 1888, writer unidentified, reprinted in the *Chemung Historical Journal,* Vol. 49, No. 2, December 2003, Elmira, N.Y.

Staples, Brent. "Slaves in the Family: One Generation's Shame Is Another's Revelation." *The New York Times,* June 15, 2003. Staples points out that another Harriet Beecher Stowe sibling, Henry Ward Beecher, helped pressure the Nautilus Insurance Company of New York, the predecessor of New York Life, to quit issuing insurance policies on the lives of slaves in 1848. Among the first 1,000 policies issued, 339 were "upon the lives of negro slaves in Maryland and Virginia," the company's history notes.

Still, William. *The Underground Railroad.* Reprint. Chicago: Johnson Publishing Company, Inc., 1970; orig. pub. Washington, D.C.: William Still, 1871. Still's account of Lear Green's escape appears on pages 289–92. On page 28, the story of William Peel Jones includes vivid details of traveling in a box from Baltimore to Philadelphia on a steamer. See also pp. 632–34 (story of seamstress boxed in straw); p. 28 (story of William Peel Jones); pp. 144–46 (story of Abram Galloway and Richard Eder).

Trager, James. *The People's Chronology: A Year-by-Year Record of Human Events from Prehistory to the Present.* Revised and updated edition. New York: Henry Holt and Company, 1994.

Ullman, Victor. *Look to the North Star.* Orig. pub. Boston: Beacon Press, 1969. Reprint Toronto: Umbrella Press, 1994. "Underground Railroad." Official National Park Handbook. Washington, D.C.: Division of Publications, National Park Service, U.S. Department of the Interior, p. 48.

Williams, Edward. "Waters of Despair, Waters of Hope: Exhibit Showcases Influence of Blacks on the Chesapeake Bay." *New Journal and Guide,* August 16, 2000. The exhibit, which ran from August 2000 to March 2001, included an image of Lear Green. Jeanne Willoz-Egnor, education department, The Mariners' Museum, Newport News, Virginia, said the exhibit, which ended in 2001, featured an original sailor's chest and a replica, both believed to be similar to the one used by Lear Green. The museum had another chest constructed for its exhibit and allowed people to crawl inside. It was about 45 inches long and 22 inches deep.

Williams, Isaac D., and William Ferguson Goldie. *Sunshine and Shadow of Slave Life: Reminiscences Told by Isaac D. Williams to "Tege."* East Saginaw, Mich.: Evening News Printing and Binding House, 1885; copyright 2002 by the Academic Affairs Library, University of North Carolina at Chapel Hill.

Wingate, Dr. Isabel B. *Fairchild's Dictionary of Textiles.* 6th ed. New York: Fairchild Publications, 1984, p. 401, definition of mousseline de laine fabric.

Wright, Abner C. "The Underground Railroad." *Chemung Historical Journal,* August 1985, Elmira, N.Y.

Chapter 4: The Man Who Couldn't Grow a Beard

African Americans, Voices of Triumph: Perseverance. By the editors of Time-Life Books. Alexandria, Va.: Time-Life Books, 1993.

The American Anti-Slavery Almanac. New York: The American Anti-Slavery Society, 1840.

Ballou, Adin. *History of the Hopedale Community.* Philadelphia: Porcupine Press, Inc., 1972. Mentions that Frederick Douglass lectured there and that the utopian community allowed a fugitive slave named Rosetta Hall "to reside at the Community house for an indefinite length of time and work for her board, education, etc. . . . She was made welcome by our people, and treated with all due consideration and kindness while she remained within our borders" (p. 143).

→ Bibliography ←

Blackett, R. J. M. "Fugitive Slaves in Britain: The Odyssey of William and Ellen Craft." *American Studies*, Vol. 12, No. 1, pp. 41–62. Printed in Great Britain, 1978.

Blassingame, John W., ed. *Slave Testimony: Two Centuries of Letters, Speeches, Interviews and Autobiographies.* Baton Rouge: Louisiana State University Press, 1977.

Blockson, Charles L. *African Americans in Pennsylvania, Above Ground and Underground: An Illustrated Guide.* Harrisburg, Pa.: RB Books, 2001.

———. *The Underground Railroad.* New York: Prentice Hall Press, 1987. This book quotes from the "Narrative of Lewis Hayden," which appears in Harriet Beecher Stowe's "Key to *Uncle Tom's Cabin.*" See also p. 229: "Even within the Underground Railroad bigotry was a problem. Fugitives were frequently banned from entering the homes of conductors—burden of anti-slavery work and fugitive aid was carried out by a relatively small contingent of citizens."

Bowditch, Vincent Y. *Life and Correspondence of Henry Ingersoll Bowditch by His Son Vincent Y. Bowditch*, Vol. 1, orig. pub. Cambridge: Riverside Press, 1902.

Buckmaster, Henrietta. *Flight to Freedom: The Story of the Underground Railroad.* New York: Thomas Y. Crowell Company, 1958.

Butler, John C. *Historical Record of Macon and Central Georgia.* Macon, Ga.: J. S. Burke & Co., Printers and Binders, 1879.

Clarke, James Freeman. *Anti-Slavery Days: A Sketch of the Struggle Which Ended in the Abolition of Slavery in the United States.* New York: James Freeman Clarke, 1883, p. 84. In this account Ellen is a nurse with a South Carolina family, forced to leave her "little babe" behind while traveling to the North with her mistress. The author asserts, "So the little babe was left behind and died during its mother's absence. When Ellen got home she made up her mind to escape."

Coggan, Blanche B. "The Underground Railroad . . . and Black-White Cooperation." *Michigan Challenge*, published by the Michigan State Chamber of Commerce, June 1968. She talks about little-known Michigan abolitionists such as Walter Duke in White Lake, Michigan, and W. Q. Atwood in East Saginaw.

Collins, Robert. "Essay on the Management of Slaves." *DeBow's Review and Industrial Resources, Statistics, etc.* Devoted to Commerce, Vol. VII, January/February 1862, p. 154.

Commager, Henry Steele. *Theodore Parker.* Boston: Little, Brown and Company, 1936. On page 218, Commager notes that after passage of the Fugitive Slave Act, "forty Blacks left Boston within a week."

Copeland, Larry. "From a Whisper to a Shout: Museums Teach Black History." *USA Today,* May 15, 2002. Copeland writes about Richard Rusk, a white rental property owner and columnist in Oconee County, Georgia, who discovered two black couples had been lynched in 1946 at a highway ridge near his home. They were shot hundreds of times along the banks of the Apalachee River near Moore's Ford Bridge, but for years nobody talked about the killings. "Rusk learned Georgia was one of the leading states for lynchings: 542 from 1880 to 1930."

Craft, William, and Ellen Craft. *Running a Thousand Miles for Freedom; or, the Escape of William and Ellen Craft from Slavery.* London: William Tweedie, 1860.

Curtis, Nancy C. *Black Heritage Sites: The North.* New York: W. W. Norton, 1996.

Dannett, Sylvia G. L. *Profiles of Negro Womanhood,* Vol. 1, *1619–1900.* Yonkers, N.Y.: Educational Heritage, Inc., 1964. This contains an account of Ellen and William Craft's flight to freedom. See also pp. 135–36. Harriet Tubman was "invited to visit some of Massachusetts' leading literary lights, such as Ralph Waldo Emerson, the Horace Manns and the Bronson Alcotts. She often went to the home of Mrs. Alcott's brother, the Reverend Mr. May, whose home was a station on the railroad."

Decalo, Samuel. *Historical Dictionary of Dahomey (People's Republic of Benin).* African Historical Dictionaries, No. 7. Metuchen, N.J.: The Scarecrow Press, Inc., 1976.

Diggs, Mamie Sweeting, great-granddaughter of Daniel Hughes, Underground Railroad agent and conductor, interview with author, in Loyalsock Township, just outside Williamsport, Pennsylvania, July 1, 2003. Hughes was the father of 16 children, the husband of Annie Rotch, and lived on an Indian reservation in what is now Muncy in Lycoming County. His wife and children helped him. He lived on Freedom Road, originally known as Nigger Hollow.

Douglass, Frederick. "Another Remarkable Escape." *Frederick Douglass' Paper,* Rochester, N.Y., February 25, 1853.

"An Escape from Slavery in America." *Chambers' Edinburgh Journal,* Saturday, March 15, 1851, published by W. & R. Chambers, Edinburgh.

Farrison, William Edward. "William Wells Brown." In Franklin, John Hope, ed., *Negro American Biographies and Autobiographies.* Chicago: University of Chicago Press, 1969.

Federal Union, "Fugitive Slave Law Again," November 5, 1850, Vol. XXI, No. 22, Milledgeville, Ga.

Federal Union, "The Boston Excitement," November 26, 1850, Vol. XXI, No. 25, Milledgeville, Ga.

Federal Union, "The Beginning of the End," December 3, 1850, Vol. XXI, No. 26, Milledgeville, Ga.

Finkelman, Paul, ed. *Articles on American Slavery.* New York and London: Garland Publishing, Inc. In Vol. 6, *Fugitive Slaves,* R.J.M. Blackett writes that Boston's black community was only 2,000 people in 1848 but had four churches and a number of social and benevolent groups. It also, he points out, had a history of uniting against slave catchers and protecting fugitives.

Fox, Jack F., comp. *The 1850 Census of Georgia Slave Owners.* Baltimore: Printed for Clearfield Company, Inc., by Genealogical Publishing Co., Inc., 1999.

Fredrickson, George M. *William Lloyd Garrison.* Englewood Cliffs, N.J.: Prentice Hall Press, 1968. On page 143, Garrison's 1842 speech is quoted: "We affirm that the Union is not of heaven. It is founded in unrighteousness and cemented with blood. . . . Slavery is a combination of Death and Hell and with it the North have made a covenant and are at agreement. . . . Divorced from Northern protection it dies; and with that protection, it enlarges its boundaries, multiplies its victims, and extends its ravages."

Freedman, Florence. *Two Tickets to Freedom: The True Story of Ellen and William Craft, Fugitive Slaves.* New York: Peter Bedrick Books, 1971. She writes that Ellen's new master in Macon owned 62 slaves and 10,000 acres of farmland.

"The Fugitive Slave Bill and Its Effects," in *Five Hundred Thousand Strokes for Freedom, A Series of Anti-Slavery Tracts, of Which Half a Million Are Now First Issued by the Friends of the Negro.* Leeds Anti-Slavery Series, No. 32, orig. pub. 1853. Reprint, Miami: Mnemosyne Publishing Co., 1969.

The Fugitive Slave Law and Its Victims. New York: The American Anti-Slavery Society, 1861. On page 46, a story appears about a fourteen-year-old white girl, daughter of Mr. Samuel Godshall of Downingtown, Chester County, Pa., who was seized by town men and a plaster put upon her mouth. She was taken in a carriage toward Maryland, but the men put her out in a secluded part of the country, threatening to kill her if she made any alarm. The tract notes that "It was supposed the kidnappers mistook her for a mulatto girl, but discovering their blunder, dismissed her." On page 29 is the story of the mistakenly arrested waiter, Patrick Sneed.

Garison, Webb. "The Saga of William and Ellen Craft Still Stirs the Emotions," *The Atlanta Journal and Constitution*, December 25, 1988.

Genovese, Eugene D. *Roll, Jordan, Roll: The World the Slaves Made.* New York: Vintage Books, 1976. The book quotes Ellen's owner, Robert Collins, who claims that Negroes are inherently tyrannical and that without their masters' mediation husbands often would abuse family members.

Georgia: A Guide to Its Towns and Countryside. Compiled and written by workers of the Writers Program of the Work Projects Administration in the State of Georgia. Athens: University of Georgia Press, 1940. The book asserts that the Klan first began operating in Georgia in the spring of 1868, spreading terror by acts of violence.

Georgia Journal and Messenger, "The Fugitive Slave Case in Boston," November 6, 1850, Vol. XXVII, No. 32, Macon, Ga.

Georgia Journal and Messenger, "The Boston Excitement," November 13, 1850, Vol. XXVIII, No. 33, Macon, Ga.

Georgia Journal and Messenger, "Letter from the President," November 20, 1850, Vol. XXVIII, No. 34, Macon, Ga.

Georgia Journal and Messenger, "Letter from Dr. Robert Collins," June 25, 1851, Vol. XXIX, No. 63, Macon, Ga.

Gordon, Asa H. *Sketches of Negro Life and History in South Carolina*, 2nd ed. Columbia, S.C.: University of South Carolina Press, 1971.

Grimé, William Ed. *Ethno-Botany of the Black Americans.* Algonac, Mich.: Reference Publications, Inc., 1979.

Grimke, Archibald. "Anti-Slavery Boston." *The New England Magazine*, New Series, Dec. 1890, Vol. III, No. 4.

Heglar, Charles Joseph. "Rethinking the Slave Narrative: Domestic Concerns in Henry Bibb and William and Ellen Craft," an abstract of a dissertation submitted in partial fulfillment of the requirements for the degree of Doctor of Philosophy, Department of English, University of South Florida, December 1996. Copyrighted by Heglar, 1997.

Hine, Darlene Clark. *Hine Sight: Black Women and the Re-construction of American History.* Brooklyn, N.Y.: New York: Carlson Publishing, Inc., 1994.

Hine, Darlene Clark, Elsa Barkley Brown, and Rosalyn Terborg-Penn, eds. *Black Women in America: An Historical Encyclopedia*, Vol. I, A–L. Brooklyn: Carlson Publishing, Inc., 1993.

Hoffman, Charles, and Tess Hoffman. *North by South: The Two Lives of Richard James Arnold.* Athens, Ga.: The University of Georgia Press, 1988.

Hunsinger, Lou, Jr. "The Underground Railroad in Lycoming County." *The Williamsport Sun-Gazette*, April 24, 2003.

James, Edward T., ed. *Notable American Women, A–F. 1607–1950*, Vol. 1. Cambridge, Mass.: The Belknap Press of Harvard University Press, 1971.

James, Thomas, Rev. "Wonderful Eventful Life of Rev. Thomas James." Rochester, N.Y.: Post Express Printing Company, 1887. This pamphlet includes an account of the Crafts' escape. James describes Ellen Craft as a woman "who had hardly a tinge of African blood in her veins and who could not in color be distinguished from a white person."

Jones, Thomas C., ed. *The Graphic Story of the American Presidents.* Chicago: J. G. Ferguson Publishing Co., 1968.

Kaufman, Polly Welts, et al. *Boston Women's Heritage Trail: Four Centuries of Boston Women.* Gloucester: The Curious Traveller Press, 1999. Gives the address of abolitionists Lewis and Harriet Hayden as 66 Philips Street. The Haydens initially sheltered the Crafts in Boston. It also gives some background on the African Meeting House at 8 Smith Court, where several abolitionists, including the Crafts, spoke.

Kinzer, Stephen. "Leading Charleston to Its Past." *The New York Times*, Tuesday, August 14, 2001.

Lamb, Yvonne Shinhoster. "Epiphany in Savannah." *The Washington Post.* August 3, 1998.

The Liberator, July 27, 1849. Contains an ad for William Craft's Boston furniture store.

The Liberator, June 24, 1851. Letter from William Wells Brown to William Lloyd Garrison about the Crafts in Scotland.

The Liberator, June 24, 1851, contains a letter about the Crafts written by William Wells Brown:

> Dear Mr. Garrison:
>
> I am sure that you will feel an interest in the welfare of our friends, Wm. and Ellen Craft. William has probably already informed you of the safe arrival of himself and wife in England. Although I had been informed by letters from Boston that our friends were coming to this country, I was not

made acquainted with their plans, if indeed they had any. A few days after the arrival of the Crafts in Liverpool, I received information that they were in search of me. I immediately wrote to them, telling that I should be glad to serve them, if I could, in any way, and forthwith made arrangements to give our friends a warm reception at the place where I was then lecturing. But intelligence came that Ellen was very ill, and we had to defer the reception meeting. Ellen, however, so far recovered in a few days as to permit William to leave her and join me, which he did at Newcastle.

I had just been invited by the Smeals, Patons and Wighams to visit Scotland, and I wrote immediately to know if they would like the presence of the Crafts; and was glad to get an affirmative reply.

We came on to Edinburgh, and had the first meeting on Monday evening. It was a meeting of the Edinburgh Emancipation Society, at which William Craft told, for the first time in this country, the story of his escape from slavery. The audience were very deeply interested in the history of our friend and especially the part which related to his escape from Boston. The natural eloquence and simplicity with which Wm. Craft narrated the story of his wrongs, created a deep feeling of hatred against the 'peculiar institution.' . . .

There is a general feeling of hatred here to the Fugitive Slave Bill, and every body, as far as I am able to hear, look upon Mr. Webstor [*sic*] as the originator of this most abominable law, and his connection with and support of it has brought a lasting shame upon him, and I think that the efforts of the friends of the slave in America were never more highly appreciated in this country than at this time. . . .

Yours, right truly.
Wm. Wells Brown,
Commons Hotel,
Edinburgh,
Jan. 3, 1851

Lutz, Tom, and Susanna Ashton. *These "Colored" United States: African American Essays from the 1920s.* New Brunswick: Rutgers University Press. On page 100, historian E. Franklin Frazier notes, in an essay titled "Georgia, or the Struggle Against Impudent Inferiority," that "Georgia, with 414 victims to her shame, led the country in lynching and burning Negroes from 1889 to 1921."

McBride, B. "Directions for Cultivating the Various Crops Grown at Hickory Hill," *Southern Agriculturist and Register of Rural Affairs* (1828–1839), April 1830.

McCaskill, Barbara, associate professor, English, University of Georgia, letter to author, May 17, 2002, about some of the reasons for the appeal of the Crafts' story. They stood out, she pointed out, because their story was so well documented and because people identified with their desire for a Christian marriage and free children.

———. "Yours Very Truly: Ellen Craft—the Fugitive as Text and Artifact," *African American Review*, Vol. 28, No. 4, 1994.

Nutley, Buzz. "Macon, Ga., Is Ripe with Peaches, African-American History." Pittsburgh: *Pittsburgh Post-Gazette*, February 11, 2001. "81 miles south [of Atlanta], on Interstate 75, lies a jewel of Georgia. Its name is Macon." He talks about his visit to the Tubman African-American Museum on Walnut Street, named for Underground Railroad conductor Harriet Tubman. Among other things, the author notes learning about "Ellen Craft, a mulatto who dressed up as a man to smuggle her husband, who posed as her slave, out of Georgia."

Osofsky, Gilbert, ed. *Puttin' on Ole Massa: The Slave Narratives of Henry Bibb, William Wells Brown and Solomon Northup.* New York: Harper & Row, 1969, p. 28. This book's introduction describes men who escaped by making wigs out of horses' manes to disguise themselves as women or who wore false beards, passed for white as did Ellen Craft, tied themselves under trains, escaped on sleighs, or smeared dust from graves or red pepper on themselves to throw off the bloodhounds tracking them. See also pp. 18–21, on which it is pointed out that most slaves on plantations lacked any knowledge of the world outside and "had never heard of Europe, did not know their own states . . . numbers of slaves had been encouraged to believe the Yankees were cannibals who looked upon them as tasty morsels. . . ." Under the circumstances, the Introduction notes, even to dream of escaping called for "imagination, independence, cunning, daring and a sense of self-pride. It required . . . seeming most satisfied at the moment they were most discontented."

Parker, Theodore. *The Trial of Theodore Parker for the "Misdemeanor" of a Speech in Faneuil Hall against Kidnapping, before the Circuit Court of the United States at Boston, April 2, 1855*, with the Defense of Theodore Parker, minister of the Twenty-Eighth Congregational Society in Boston. Orig. pub. Boston, 1855. Reprinted New York: Negro Universities, 1970. On page 147, he tells his version of the Craft story.

Quarles, Benjamin. *Black Abolitionists.* New York: Oxford University Press, 1969. Quarles called Brown's charging admission for talks "an almost unprecedented practice."

Rochester North Star, February 2, 1849. Contains William Wells Brown's quote about the Charleston hotel where the Crafts stayed.

Siebert, Wilbur H. *The Underground Railroad from Slavery to Freedom.* New York: Macmillan, 1898. On page 197, the book notes that "Deacon Allen Sidney, an engineer on his master's boat, which touched at Cincinnati, had a poor opinion of Canada because he had heard that 'nothin' but black-eyed peas could be raised there.' William Johnson, a fugitive from Virginia, had heard the Detroit River was over 3,000 miles wide and a ship starting out in the night would find herself in the morning 'right whar she started from.'"

Smith, Jessie Carney, ed. *Notable Black American Women.* Detroit: Gale Research, Inc., 1992.

Sterling, Dorothy. *Black Foremothers, Three Lives.* Old Westbury, N.Y.: The Feminist Press, 1979.

Still, William. *The Underground Railroad.* Reprint. Chicago: Johnson Publishing Company, Inc., 1970, orig. pub. as *The Underground Rail Road,* Washington, D.C.: William Still, 1871.

Thalimer, Carol and Dan. *Country Roads of Georgia.* Castine, Me.: Country Roads Press, 1995, p. 1.

Tiffany, Nina Moore. "The Escape of William and Ellen Craft." *The New England Magazine,* Vol. 1, No. 5 (January 1890), p. 524.

Volo, James M., and Dorothy Denneen Volo. *Encyclopedia of the Antebellum South.* London and Westport, Conn.: Greenwood Press. On page 4 the book talks about the various means slave women induced miscarriages, including using both the root and seed of the cotton plant.

Young, Ida, Julius Gholson, and Nell Hargrove. *History of Macon, Georgia.* Macon, Ga.: Lyon, Marshall & Brooks, 1950. Sponsored by The Macon Woman's Club.

Chapter 5: Even a Blind Horse Knows the Way

Abstract of Census for Territory of Michigan, 1830, p. 42. Shows a total white population of 21,346, total free colored of 261 and total slave of 32.

"Bethel A.M.E. Church." Pamphlet on Bethel A.M.E. Church, another noted Detroit Underground Railroad stop and haven for both fugitives and activists. The Colored Methodist Society in 1839 founded what became Bethel AME Church, now the oldest African Methodist Episcopal Church in Michigan.

"Blacks in Detroit," a reprint of articles from the *Detroit Free Press,* December 1980. The booklet contains articles about Detroit's premier black abolitionists George DeBaptiste and William Lambert and calls two Detroit churches, Second Baptist and St. Matthews Episcopal, Underground Railroad stops. On page 56, an article titled "Politics and the Pulpit: A Tradition," written by Harry Cook and Joyce Walker-Tyson, says that St. Matthews raised money for antislavery crusades and that the first public school for black youngsters was established in the basement of Second Baptist in 1842.

Casselman, Alexander Clark. *Richardson's War of 1812.* Toronto: Historical Publishing Co., 1902. Information about John Askin.

Catlin, George. *The Story of Detroit.* Detroit: The Detroit News, 1926. Gives the address for the Steamboat Hotel.

Catterall, Helen Tunnicliff, ed. *Judicial Cases Concerning American Slavery and the Negro,* Vol. I, *Cases from the Courts of England, Virginia, West Virginia and Kentucky.* New York: Octagon Books, Inc., 1968, pp. 347–48.

Created for the Ages: A History of Mariners' Church of Detroit. Detroit: Mariners Church of Detroit, 2001. On page 43, this book states that "As many as 5,000 slaves passed through Detroit's Second Baptist church on their way to freedom." On page 444, it states that "The evidence indicating that Mariners' Church, joining the 'freedom ferment' of the 1830s, may have played a role in the struggle to liberate refugee slaves came to light in 1954. Moving the edifice from its original location on Woodward, the C. A. Johnson Company, Detroit contractors, discovered a tunnel leading from the church's lower, or basement, level to the river's edge. The tunnel was spacious enough to enable a grown man to walk upright, according to company officials who later made a verbal report to the Rev. Richard W. Ingalls, Rector beginning in 1965. No written record of the find has appeared."

DeRamus, Betty. "Slaves Met Tricksters, Spies on Freedom's Trail." *The Detroit News*, Tuesday, February 8, 2000. Contains the story of steamboat owner Sylvester Atwood's conversion to abolitionism.

Douglass, The Reverend William. "The Colored People of Detroit: Their Trials, Persecutions and Escapes." A pamphlet containing articles that appeared in the *Detroit Daily Post* January 1 and February 7, 1870.

Farmer, Silas. *The History of Detroit and Michigan, or, The Metropolis Illustrated: Chronological Cyclopaedia of the Past and Present: Including a Full Record of Territorial Days in Michigan and the Annals of Wayne County.* Detroit: S. Farmer & Co., 1884, pp. 345–46. An account of the Blackburn riot.

Fishbaugh, Charles Preston. *From Paddlewheels to Propellers: The Howard Ship Yards of Jeffersonville in The Story of Steam Navigation on the Western Rivers.* Indianapolis: Indiana Historical Society, 1970, p. 4. Talks about the population of Louisville and the steamboat industry in Jeffersonville, Indiana.

Friend, Craig Thompson, ed. *The Buzzel About Kentuck: Settling the Promised Land.* Lexington, Ky.: The University Press of Kentucky, 1999. On pages 243–55, Karolyn Smardz relates the tale of the Blackburns.

Gavrilovich, Peter, and Bill McGraw, eds. *The Detroit Almanac: 300 years of Life in the Motor City.* Detroit: Detroit Free Press, 2000. This is a source for information about Stevens T. Mason.

Glazer, Sidney. *Detroit: A Study in Urban Development.* New York: Bookman Associates, Inc., 1965. Contains information about the black population in early Detroit.

Hall, James. *Notes on the Western States.* Philadelphia: Harrison Hall, 1838.

Hine, Darlene Clark. *Hine Sight—Black Women and the Re-Construction of American History.* Brooklyn, N.Y.: Carlson Publishing, 1994. The book talks about the various reasons for the formation of Detroit's Second Baptist Church, whose original members included many of the Blackburn rioters.

Horton, James Oliver. "Blackburns' Road to Freedom One of Many That Touched Detroit." *Detroit Free Press*, February 25, 2002.

Hudson, Blaine J. *Fugitive Slaves and the Underground Railroad in the Kentucky Borderland*, Jefferson, N.C.: McFarland & Company, Inc., 2002.

Interview with Norman McRae, January 2000.

Journal of the Proceedings of the Common Council of the City of Detroit From the Time of Its First Organization, September 21, A.D. 1824. July 19, 1833.

Journal of the Proceedings of the Common Council, July 24, 1833.

Journal of the Proceedings of the Common Council, July 25, 1833.

Journal of the Proceedings of the Common Council, August 1, 1833.

"Justice at Last—The Great Detroit Riots of 1863." *The Detroit Daily Post*, January 1, 1870.

Kane, Joseph Nathan. *Famous First Facts*. New York: The H. W. Wilson Co., 1964. On page 124, the book talks about the bread riots sparked by Sylvester Graham's advocacy of homemade wheat bread.

Kunnecke, Martina, of the Kentucky Center for African American Heritage, interview with author, Louisville, Kentucky, October 2003.

LaBrew, Arthur. *The Detroit History That Nobody Knew (or Bothered to Remember, 1800–1900)*. Privately printed, Detroit 2001.

Larrie, Reginald. *Makin' Free: African-Americans in the Northwest Territory*. Detroit: Blaine Etheridge Books, 1981, p. 20. Defines the term "boss barber."

A Legacy of Resistance, the online version of records of the Burton Historical Collection of the Detroit Public Library, www.citycom.com/web/heruseye/Textfiles/ALegacyofResistance.html. Articles on the site discuss the Blackburn riot, the Underground Railroad in Detroit, the Fugitive Slave Act of 1850 and John Brown's visit to Detroit in 1859.

Lenox, Leonard. Biography index cards, Burton Historical Collection, Detroit Public Library. Lists Scipio Lenox and Caroline French as the children of Leonard Lenox from Newton, Massachusetts. Scipio Lenox is identified as the son of Cornelius L. Lenox ("colored") "who bought claim 718 in Springwells, formerly the property of John Askin."

Lightfoot, Madison J. Biography index card, Burton Historical Collection, Detroit Public Library. Listed as having a grocery on the corner of Beaubien and Fort.

Lucas, Marion B. *A History of Blacks in Kentucky*, Vol. I, *From Slavery to Segregation, 1760–1891*. Frankfort, Ky.: The Kentucky Historical Society, 1991, pp. 9, 10.

McRae, Norman. "Blacks in Detroit, 1736–1833: The Search for Freedom and Community and Its Implications for Education." A dissertation submitted in partial fulfillment of the requirements for the degree of Doctor of Philosophy (Education) at the University of Michigan, 1982.

———. "A Chronology of the Black Experience in Detroit, 1736–1870. Unpublished. Descriptions of fugitive slave ads in the *Detroit Gazette* in the early 1820s appear on page 7 of this paper.

———. "Thornton and Rutha: Free Blacks North and South, The Blackburn Affair." Draft of an unpublished paper for middle schools, pp. 1–6. Dr. McRae is former head of social studies curriculum for the Detroit Public Schools and has written books and delivered lectures on Detroit history.

"More Historical Errors on Underground Railroad Monument." Press release issued on December 7, 2001, by International Underground Railroad Monument Collaborative headed by Sharon-Elizabeth Sexton. It notes that "Before Michigan became a state, it was the place where fugitives headed before slavery was outlawed in Canada. Even Canadian enslaved blacks came to Michigan for freedom."

"Our New Voters: Past History of the Colored People of Detroit." *Detroit Daily Post*, February 7, 1870. This contains the reference to the blind horse and to Daddy Walker, who is referred to once as Daddy Grace.

Prince, Bryan. *I Came as a Stranger: The Underground Railroad.* New York: Tundra Books, 2004.

Quarles, Benjamin. *Black Abolitionists.* Orig. pub. New York: Oxford University Press, 1969.

Riendeau, Roger, and the staff of the Ontario Ministry of Censorship and Culture. *An Enduring Heritage: Black Contributions to Early Ontario.* Toronto: Dundurn Press Limited, 1984.

Ripley, C. Peter, ed. *The Black Abolitionist Papers*, Vol. II, *Canada, 1830–1865.* Chapel Hill: University of North Carolina Press, 1986.

Robinson, Wilhelmena S. *International Library of Negro Life and History, Historical Negro Biographies.* New York: Publishers Co., Inc., under the auspices of the Association for the Study of Negro Life and History, 1967, 1968, 1969, 1970.

Ruchames, Louis. *The Abolitionists: A Collection of Their Writings.* New York: G. P. Putnam's Sons, 1963, pp. 179–84. Talks about Charles Lenox Remond's campaign against segregated trains.

Runaway slave advertisement for "Thornton." *Louisville Public Defender*, July 7, 1831.

Runyon, Randolph Paul. *Delia Webster and the Underground Railroad.* Lexington, Ky.: University Press of Kentucky, 1996. Describes Calvin Fairbank's arrest in Jeffersonville, Indiana.

"St. John's–St. Luke Evangelical Church of the United Church of Christ." Pamphlet from St. John's–St. Luke Evangelical Church of the United Church of Christ in Detroit about the original German-speaking church's habit of hiding runaway slaves in caskets or having one walk behind the casket in a phony funeral procession. Once the procession reached the Detroit River, the slave would leap into a waiting boat and sail to free Canada.

Second Baptist Advocate, Vol. 6, No. 1, 1957, indicates that the abolitionist church's support for the freedom struggle continued in the twentieth century. A February 18, 1957, letter from Dr. Martin Luther King Jr. to Dr. A. A. Banks Jr., then pastor of the church, noted that the church had contributed more money to the Montgomery Improvement Association than any other American church. Second Baptist 151st anniversary booklet, June 11, 1987, details the story of the church's founding by former members of First Baptist of Detroit.

Second Baptist Advocate, Vol. 4, No. 1 (anniversary ed.), April 1955.

Smardz, Karolyn E. *The Story of Thornton and Lucie Blackburn.* Privately printed, 1991.

Stocking, William. *The Detroit Post*, May 15, 1870. An interview with George DeBaptiste that recounts his early history in Virginia and his subsequent activities as an Underground Railroad agent in Cincinnati, Ohio; Madison, Indiana; and Detroit.

Volgenau, Gerry. "From Here to Freedom." *The Detroit Free Press*, February 9, 2003. In this article Volgenau describes the role of Michigan in the Underground Railroad and talks about slavery being illegal in the Northwest Territory, of which Michigan was a part since 1783. Early fugitives therefore ran to Michigan rather than to

Canada, which didn't become free until 1833, the year of the Blackburns' flight to Canada.

Wheaton, Thomas R., ed. *African-American Archaeology Newsletter of the African-American Archaeology Network*, No. 13, Spring 1995. The url is www.newsouthassoc.com/newsletters/newsletter13.html.

Williams, Stacy, Dr. "The Revised History of the Black Preacher and the Black Church," a series of lectures originally delivered by Dr. Williams to the Council of Baptist Pastors of Detroit and Vicinity, Detroit, between June 10, 1979, and January 26, 1982. This talks about the churches that can trace their origins to Second Baptist.

Winks, Robin W. *The Blacks in Canada: A History*. New Haven: Yale University Press, 1971.

Woodson, Carter G., Ph.D. Free Negro Heads of Families in the United States in 1830 together with a Brief Treatment of the Free Negro, Washington, D.C.: The Association for the Study of Negro Life and History, Inc. Lists Leonard Lenox as a male in Wayne County.

Chapter 6: The Slave Who Knew His Name

Abajian, James de T., comp. *Blacks in Selected Newspapers, Censuses and Other Sources: An Index to Names and Subjects*, Vol. 3, P–Z, Boston: G. K. Hall & Co., 1977. This gives addresses and other sources of information for Still family members.

Ager, Susan. "A Long and Heartbreaking List of Names." *The Detroit Free Press*, April 29, 2004.

Anderson, Matthew. Letter dated January 20, 1907, to his daughters, Helen and Maud, about the death of their grandmother, Letitia Still.

Appiah, Kwame Anthony, and Henry Louis Gates Jr., eds. *Africana, The Encyclopedia of the African and African American Experience*. Basic Civitas Books, 1999, pp. 885–86.

Beck, Henry Charlton. *The Roads of Home: Lanes and Legends of New Jersey*. New Brunswick, N.J.: Rutgers University Press, 1956, pp. 139, 143, 149.

Bedini, Silvio A. *The Life of Benjamin Banneker, the First African-American Man of Science*. Baltimore: Maryland Historical Society, 1972. Talks about the location of the West African region known as Guinea in the seventeenth century and later, pp. 16, 22.

Beech, Wendy. "From Africa to Lawnside." *The Philadelphia Tribune Magazine*, October 1993, pp. 10, 11, 14.

Blockson, Charles L. "The Underground Railroad." *National Geographic*, Vol. CLXVI, No. 1 (July 1984), pp. 3, 9, 10, 11, 13, 29, 30.

———. *The Underground Railroad, First-Person Narratives of Escapes to Freedom in the North*. New York: Prentice Hall Press, 1987, p. 241.

Brathwaite, Edward. *The Development of Creole Society in Jamaica, 1770–1820*. Oxford, England: Clarendon Press, 1971, p. 162.

Chambers, William. *American Slavery and Colour.* New York: Negro Universities Press, 1857. This tells the story of the kidnapping of a freeman, Solomon Northrup, from New York as well as the Peter Still story.

Cohen, David Steven. *Folklore and Folklife of New Jersey.* New Brunswick, N.J.: Rutgers University Press, 1983, pp. 54, 55, 208.

Converry. Frank W.H. "More on the Life of Dr. James Still, 1812–1882." *Mount Holly (N.J.) Herald,* Thursday, April 19, 1962.

Correspondence with Honor Conklin, great-great-great-granddaughter of Miller Conklin, a possible Seth Concklin relative.

Dannett, Sylvia G. L. *Profiles of Negro Womanhood, 1619–1900,* Vol. 1. Yonkers, N.Y.: Educational Heritage, Inc., 1964, p. 217. Profile of Dr. Caroline V. Still Anderson.

Dinwiddie-Boyd, Eliza. *Proud Heritage, 11,001 Names for Your African-American Baby.* New York: Avon Books, 1994, pp. 4–5.

Ellison, Rhonda Coleman. "Propaganda in Early Alabama Fiction." *Alabama Historical Quarterly,* Vol. 7, No. 3 (Fall 1945), pp. 426, 427.

Fisher, Alfred C., grandson of Susan Still Fisher. Email to the author.

Florence Times, July–October 1850. This contains the August 1, 1890, obituary for Major Charles B. McKiernan, born in Nashville, Tennessee, March 15, 1815, but moved with his father to the Spring Hill plantation in Colbert County, Alabama. www.rootsweb.com/~allauder/obits-florencetimes1890.htm.

Fradin, Dennis Brindell. *My Family Shall Be Free.* New York: HarperCollins, 2001.

"The Fugitive Slave Law and Its Victims." Anti-Slavery Tracts, No. 15, New series. New York: American Anti-Slavery Society, 1861, p. 17. This contains the item about the four fugitives' capture.

Graff, Stephen. "A Journey to Springtown." *Philadelphia City Paper,* November 11–19, 1999.

Higgs, Muneerah, producer. *The Best Kept Secret.* Documentary on the history of Lawnside, New Jersey.

Hine, Darlene Clark, Elsa Barkley Brown, and Rosalyn Terborg-Penn, eds. *Black Women in America: An Historical Encyclopedia,* Vol. I, A–L.

James, R. L. "Colbertians." *Alabama Historical Quarterly,* Vol. 7, No. 2 (Summer 1945), p. 369.

Johnston, N. R. *Looking Back from the Sunset Land; or People Worth Knowing.* Oakland, Calif.: published by author, 1898.

"A Journey to the Seaboard Slave States." *National Era,* Vol. X, No. 497 (July 10, 1856).

Kaplan, Justin, and Anne Bernays. *The Language of Names.* New York: Simon & Schuster, 1997, pp. 67–89.

Khan, Lurey. *One Day, Levin . . . He Be Free.* New York: E. P. Dutton & Co., Inc., 1972.

"The Kidnapped and the Ransomed." Classified ad in *New York Daily Times*, June 7, 1856, p. 4.

Knight, Franklin W. *The Caribbean: The Genesis of a Fragmented Nationalism.* New York: Oxford University Press, 1990, p. 93.

Koedel, R. Craig. *South Jersey Heritage: A Social, Economic, and Cultural History.* Washington, D.C.: University Press of America, 1979, pp. 86, 87.

LaBrew, Arthur. *The Afro-American Music Legacy in Michigan: A Sesquicentennial Tribute: Studies in Nineteenth Century Afro-American Music—Series II.* Detroit: Michigan Music Research Center, Inc., 1987. This talks about how people ran notices in the black press as late as 1900 trying to find relatives from whom they'd been separated for decades.

Logan, Rayford W., and Michael R. Winston, eds. *Dictionary of American Negro Biography.* New York and London: W. W. Norton & Co., 1982, p. 573, William Still.

Lucas, Marion B. *A History of Blacks in Kentucky*, Vol. 1, *From Slavery to Segregation, 1760–1891*, The Kentucky Historical Society, 1992, p. 2. Repeats the false story that Peter and Levin Still were kidnapped from Philadelphia and sold into slavery.

Luntta, Karl. *Jamaica Handbook.* Chico, Calif.: Moon Publications, Inc., 1996, pp. 221–22.

Malone, Dumas, ed. *Dictionary of American Biography*, Vol. IX, *Sewell-Trowbridge.* New York: Charles Scribner's Sons, pp. 22–23.

Martin, John Bartlow. *Indiana: An Interpretation.* Orig. pub. Bloomington: Indiana University Press, 1947; reprint, Frances Martin, 1992, pp. 9, 11, 26.

McCloy, James F. "The Black and African Influence on New Jersey Place Names." *Bulletin of Gloucester County Historical Society*, Vol. 14, No. 8 (June 1975), p. 29.

Middleton, Kenneth. "The Manumission of Candas Still." The Central (N.J.) Record, Thursday, April 11, 1974. The author writes about finding a document in the township of Evesham, Burlington County, N.J., documenting that Thomas Wilkins freed the Negro slave Candas Still on March 2, 1787. He speculates that Candas was a relative of Levin Still and her presence in Burlington County drew Levin and his runaway wife to sparsely settled Evesham township. Wilkins was a Quaker.

"Noted Abolitionist Dead—William Still, Author of the Underground Railroad and Clerk of the Pennsylvania Anti Slavery Society Passes Away." *Afro American National Edition*, Maryland, July 16, 1902, Roll 2, January 4, 1902, through August 22, 1903, Wayne State University Kresge/Purdy Library, Newspapers and Periodicals, Detroit.

Paige, Howard. *African-American Family Cookery.* Southfield, Mich: Aspects Publishing Co., 1995, p. 94. Aletha Tanner's story.

Pickard, Kate E. R. *The Kidnapped and the Ransomed, Being the Personal Recollection of Peter Still and His Wife "Vina," after Forty Years of Slavery.* Syracuse: William T. Hamilton, 1856. The Appendix contains a profile of Seth Concklin written by Dr. William Furness.

"Recollections of Peter Still." From the *Syracuse Journal*, reprinted in *National Anti-Slavery Standard*, Vol. XVII, No. 7, Saturday, July 5, 1856.

Ripley, C. Peter, ed. *The Black Abolitionist Papers*, Vol. II, *Canada, 1830–1865.* Chapel Hill: The University of North Carolina Press, 1986, pp. 205 and 519 (mentions Letitia Still).

Robinson, Wilhelmena S. *International Library of Negro Life and History, Historical Negro Biographies.* New York: Publishers Co., Inc., under the auspices of the Association for the Study of Negro Life and History, 1967, 1968, 1969, 1970.

Sellers, James Benson. *Slavery in Alabama.* Tuscaloosa, Ala.: University of Alabama Press, 1950, p. 29. Talks about the plantation of John Peters of Florence, Alabama.

Sharif, Dara N. *Scholastic News*, January 17, 2003.

"Slaves Liberated—A Family United—Story of Two Kidnapped Boys," *Cincinnati Columbian*, January 4, 1855.

Smith, Jessie Carney, ed. *Notable Black American Women.* Detroit: Gale Research, Inc., 1992.

"Still Family Bibliography," compiled by Bonita Still Austin, great-great-granddaughter of Dr. James Still.

Still Family Reunion Banquet program, Saturday, August 9, 1986, Best Western Hotel, Bellmawr, New Jersey. The program includes music by William Grant Still.

Still, Clarence, Jr., grandson of Charles Still, one of Sidney and Levin Still's 18 children, interview with author, Peter Mott House, 26 Kings Court, Lawnside, New Jersey, October 11, 2003.

Still, Gloria Tuggle. *Still Family Keepsake, 2002.* Lawnside, N.J.: GTS Communications, 2003. This is a family reunion booklet prepared by the Still family.

Still, Kierra, interview with author, June 29, 2003, at Still Family Reunion.

Still, Mary. *An Appeal to the Females of the African Methodist Episcopal Church.* Philadelphia: Publication Society of AME Church of Philadelphia, 1857.

Still, William. "An Address on Voting and Laboring." Delivered at Concert Hall, Tuesday, March 10, 1874. Philadelphia: Jas. B. Rodgers Co., 1874.

———. *The Underground Rail Road.* Philadelphia: Porter & Coates, 1872.

———. Letter to Mr. J. M. McKim. *The Pennsylvania Freeman*, Philadelphia, August 22, 1850, p. 2, telling the story of Still's first meeting with his brother, Peter.

Stormont, Gil R. *History of Gibson County, Indiana: Her People, Industries and Institutions.* Indianapolis: B. F. Bowen & Co., 1914. On page 225 there is a letter dated February 18, 1851, from Seth Concklin to William Still. See also p. 231 (description of Stormont's house and his vigilance in watching out for the slave hunters who shadowed him).

Switala, William J. *Underground Railroad in Pennsylvania.* Mechanicsburg, Pa.: Stackpole Books, 2001. Tape produced by Lawnside Historical Society, Lawnside, N.J., 1992.

Thrasher, Albert. *On to New Orleans: Louisiana's Heroic 1811 Slave Revolt,* 2nd ed. New Orleans: Cypress Press, June 1996.

Washington, Booker T. *The Story of the Negro: The Rise of the Race from Slavery,* Vol. 1. New York: Negro Universities Press, 1909, pp. 218–21.

Washington, Linn, Jr. "The Chronicle of an American First Family." *Philadelphia Enquirer Magazine,* October 11, 1987.

White, White & Taulane, Philadelphia law firm. Letter to Mrs. William Still, July 15, 1902, expressing condolences on the death of William Still.

"Wm Still to B. McKiernon, Philadelphia, Aug 16th, 1851." *Journal of Negro History,* Vol. XI, 1926.

The Women's Project of New Jersey, Inc. *Past and Promise: Lives of New Jersey Women.* Metuchen, N.J.: The Scarecrow Press, Inc., 1990.

The WPA Guide to Kentucky. Compiled and written by the Federal Writers' Project of the Works Projects Administration for the State of Kentucky. Lexington: The University Press of Kentucky, orig. pub. 1939, Harcourt, Brace and Company, under the title *Kentucky: A Guide to the Bluegrass State;* reprinted 1996, The University Press of Kentucky.

The WPA Guide to 1930s New Jersey. Compiled and written by the Federal Writers' Project of the Works Progress Administration for the State of New Jersey. New Brunswick: Rutgers University Press; orig. pub. 1939, Viking Press.

Chapter 7: Footprints in the Snow

African Americans, Voices of Triumph: Perseverance. By the editors of Time-Life Books. Alexandria, Va.: Time-Life Books, 1993, p. 98. This describes the mass westward movement of blacks to Kansas in 1879.

Barfknecht, Gary W. *The Michigan Book of Bests.* Davison, Mich.: Friede Publications, 1999.

Bennett, Lerone, Jr. "10 Biggest Lies about Black History." *Ebony,* May 2001, www.findarticles.com. One of the myths Bennett dispels is that nineteenth-century blacks lacked the ability to run businesses, including barbershops.

Blacks in Detroit. Detroit: Detroit Free Press, December 1980. A reprint of articles from *The Detroit Free Press.*

Coggan, Blanche. "The Underground Railroad . . . and Black–White Cooperation." *Michigan Challenge,* official publication of Michigan State Chamber of Commerce, Vol. III, No. 9 (June 1968), p. 52. Story of the Bongas.

Crittendon, Denise. "The Secret Corridors of Black History." *African American Parent Magazine,* February/March 2000.

DeRamus, Betty. "Adrian House Opened a Window to Freedom." *The Detroit News,* Tuesday, February 1, 2000.

———. "Black Pioneers Tackle Northern Wilderness." *The Detroit News,* Tuesday, February 15, 2000.

———. "History, Humanity, Horror and Happiness All Flow Along the Region's Watery Lifeline." *The Detroit News*, February 6, 2003.

———. "Slaves Met Tricksters, Spies on Freedom's Trail." *The Detroit News*, Tuesday, February 8, 2000.

———. "A Testament to Freedom." *The Detroit News*, Thursday, October 18, 2001.

———. "Younger People Keep Spirit of Black Combat Pilots Alive." *The Detroit News*, November 8, 2000.

Detroit Tribune and Advertiser, February 23, 1875, obituary for George DeBaptiste.

1860 Federal Census records for a study of the Underground Railroad in Michigan's Upper Peninsula.

1880 Federal Census records for black residents of Marquette, Michigan.

1860 Marquette County census data base with blacks and mulattos listed.

Gaines, Cherie A. Letter to the Marquette Historical Society, Marquette, Michigan, November 3, 1998, concerning her family's legacy.

"Gaines Rock." *Harlow's Wooden Man*, Vol. 31, No. 2 (Spring 1995). Published by the Marquette County Michigan Historical Society, Inc.

Grove, Noel. "The Two Worlds of Michigan." *National Geographic*, Vol. 155, No. 6 (June 1979).

Gutsche, Andrea, and Cindy Bisaillon. *Mysterious Islands: Forgotten Tales of the Great Lakes.* Toronto: Lynx Images, Inc., 1999.

Hobart, Henry. *Copper Country Journal: The Diary of Schoolmaster Henry Hobart, 1863–1864.* Detroit: Wayne State University Press, 1991.

LaBrew, Arthur. *The Afro-American Music Legacy in Michigan: A Sesquicentennial Tribute.* Detroit: Michigan Music Research Center, Inc., 1987.

Magnaghi, Russell, director of Northern Michigan University's Center for Upper Peninsula Studies. Email, January 17, 2000, about early black settlers.

———. Email, February 7, 2000, about racism in the Upper Peninsula.

———. Email, February 1, 2000, about Munising.

———. Unpublished paper on blacks in the Upper Peninsula, a study of federal census data for 15 counties.

———. "African Americans in the History of the Upper Peninsula of Michigan." Draft of an unpublished study, p. 15. Information on Joseph L. Smith.

———. Ibid., pp. 2–8. Information about slavery under the French and British and about the Bonga family.

Magnaghi, Russell M., and Michael T. Marsden, eds. *A Sense of Place: Michigan's Upper Peninsula.* Marquette: Northern Michigan University Press in conjunction with the Center for Upper Peninsula Studies, 1997.

Marquette Daily Mining Journal, August 7, 1903. Obituary for William Washington Gaines, 80, who was said to have died from "old age and a complication of troubles."

Marquette (Mich.) city directories for 1886–87, 1889, 1891, 1894, 1895, 1908, 1910, 1912, recorded by Marquette County Historical Society, October 1956.

McRae, Norman. A Chronology of the Black Experience in Detroit, 1736–1870, unpublished.

Monette, Clarence J. *The History of Eagle Harbor, Michigan.* Lake Linden, Mich.: first printing 1977, second printing 1978.

Palmer, Ronald, professor emeritus of The Practice of International Affairs, George Washington University. "DeBaptiste Underground Railroad Leader," a speech delivered on August 30, 2002, at the U.S./Canadian History and Genealogy Conference, North Buxton, Ontario.

———. "Some Useful Things to Know about George DeBaptiste."

Piljac, Pamela A., and Thomas M. Piljac. *Mackinac Island: Historic Frontier, Vacation Resort, Timeless Wonderland.* Portage, Ind.: Bryce-Waterton Publications, 1988, 1989.

Polaczek, John, Dossin Great Lakes Museum, Detroit. Letter to author about slaves escaping on boats that ran from Buffalo to Sandusky, then came on to Toledo and Detroit.

Powers, Tom. *Natural Michigan.* Davison, Mich.: Friede Publications, 1987, p. 165. Description of Munising.

Prosek, James. "Making Tracks in a World Gone Silent." *The New York Times*, Friday, February 6, 2004, p. D1.

Rogers, Julia Ellen. *The Nature Library. Trees.* Garden City, N.Y.: Doubleday, Doran & Co., Inc., 1917, 1926. Describes white pines on p. 222 and hemlocks on p. 260.

Sabin, Jan M. *Riding the Runners: The Annual Heartbeat of Marquette, Michigan.* Marquette, Mich.: Oak River Publishing, 2003.

Seton, Ernest Thompson. The Nature Library. *Animals.* New York: Doubleday, Doran & Co., Inc., 1909, 1925, 1926, p. 181. Talks about difference between huskies' tails and wolves' tails.

Sexton, Sharon-Elizabeth, and Nathaniel Leach. "More Historical Errors on Underground Railroad Monument," press release issued on December 7, 2001.

Smith, Eric. "The History of Black Barbers and Barbershops, 1820–1900." Afro-American Genealogical & Historical Society of Chicago Newsletter, Vol. 23, No. 3 (March 2003).

Stocking, Kathleen. *Lake Country.* Ann Arbor: University of Michigan Press, 1994.

Stocking, William. *The Detroit Post*, May 15, 1870. Interview with George DeBaptiste, identified as "perhaps the principal manager of the UGRR in this city."

Thurner, Arthur W. *Calumet Copper and People: History of a Michigan Mining Community, 1864–1970*, pp. 24–25.

"Upper Peninsula Business Register & Guide, 2004." In *Upper Peninsula Business Today* (undated pamphlet), pp. 11–12. Climate and annual snowfall information.

Vielmetti, Douglas B. "Memories of Bygone Era Return with Visit to City of Four in Gaines Family." *Marquette Daily Mining Journal*, July 30, 1959, p. 14. This story talks about four members of the Gaines family receiving a copy of the city planning book from city manager George T. Meholick Jr. during a visit to Marquette, which they had left 42 years earlier.

Walch, Diane, boarder of Siberian and Alaskan huskies and a dogsledder, interview with author, at her home near Negaunee, Michigan, March 6, 2004.

"Winter Very Hard on Negro Colony." *Pioneer Tribune of Manistique, Manistee Tribune*, January 21, 1927.

Chapter 8: Chased by Wolves

Agreement signed by the heirs of Sarah and Hugh Gordon on September 26, 1834: "Know all men by these presents: that we the heirs of Hugh Gordon, deceased, do bind ourselves, our heirs, assigns, Executors or Adminis., personally and jointly, to make a Division of the Estate of the above said Hugh Gordon, Real & personal among the heirs, Equally Share And Share alike, Except Frances Gordon. We, the other heirs, do obligate ourselves to give the above said Frances Gordon, one Slv Woman named Charlotte over and above an Equal Share in the Estate to her and her heirs forever. We further obligate ourselves to Give to Frances Gordon the plantation on which she now lives, over and above an Equal Share During her natural life. We do bind ourselves, our heirs, assigns and (an . . . s) to Defend against all Claim or Claims that may be made on the Estate of the above said Hugh Gordon, deceased (should there be any) forever. In Testimony Whereof we Do hereby duly affix our names this 26th day of September, 1834."

Beals, June Lowe, comp. *The 1856 State Census of Lee County Iowa.*

Bergmann, Leola Nelson. *The Negro in Iowa.* Iowa City, Iowa: State Historical Society of Iowa, February 1969, pp. 32, 35, 50, 53.

Bivins, Larry. "Street-Smart Kids Discover Wisdom at Rural Academy." *Detroit News*, May 22, 1997. Describes the curriculum at Piney Woods.

Blockson, Charles L. *Hippocrene Guide to the Underground Railroad.* New York: Hippocrene Books, 1995, pp. 235–40.

———. *The Underground Railroad: First-Person Narratives of Escapes to Freedom in the North.* New York: Prentice Hall Press, 1987, pp. 187–91.

Boris, Joseph J., ed. *Who's Who in Colored America: A Biographical Dictionary of Notable Living Persons of Negro Descent in America*, Vol. I. New York: Who's Who in Colored America Corp., 1927, p. 111.

Brown, Hallie Q., ed. *Homespun Heroines and Other Women of Distinction.* Xenia, Ohio: Aldine Publishing Co., 1926, p. 22.

Brown, Mabel E. "Dusky Lading." *The Palimpsest* (a publication of the State Historical Society of Iowa), Vol. IX (July 1928), pp. 242–48.

Brown, Tony. "Publisher's Statement: In Historical Perspective." *Tony Brown's Journal.* New York: Tony Brown Productions, Inc., 1984, p. 3. Description of the lynching of Jeff Brown.

Byrkit, Christian S. "A Derailment on the Railway Invisible." *Annals of Iowa*, Series 3, Vol. XIV (October 1923), pp. 95–100.

Clarkson, J. S., letter on Civil Rights. In Albert Fried, ed. *Annals of Iowa*, Series 3, Vol. XXXV, No. 3 (Winter 1960). Clarkson wrote to General James B. Weaver on January 16, 1907, countering Weaver's argument favoring the return of blacks to Africa. He noted that his mother kept an Underground station on Melrose Farm in Grundy County and that he operated a section of the road.

Coggan, Blanche B. *Prior Foster: First Afro-American to Found and Incorporate an Educational Institution in the Northwest Territory*. Self-published, 1969.

Cohen, Saul B., ed. *The Columbia Gazeteer of the World*, Vol. 1, A–G. New York: Columbia University Press, 1952, 1962, p. 263. Bardstown, Kentucky.

———. *The Columbia Gazeteer of the World*, Vol. 2, H–O. New York: Columbia University Press, 1998, p. 1536. Keokuk City.

———. *The Columbia Gazeteer of the World*, Vol. 3, P–Z. New York: Columbia University Press, p. 3005. Information about Lincoln's parents.

Connor, James. "The Antislavery Movement in Iowa." *Annals of Iowa*, Series 3, Vol. 40 (Fall 1970), pp. 450–79.

Cooper, Arnie. "A Stony Road: Black Education in Iowa, 1838–1860." *Annals of Iowa*, Series 3, Vol. XLVII (Winter/Spring 1986), pp. 113–34.

Curtis, Nancy, Ph.D. *Black Heritage Sites: The North*. New York: The New Press, 1996, pp. 68–72.

Dahl, Linda. *Stormy Weather: The Music and Lives of a Century of Jazzwomen*. Orig. pub. New York: Pantheon Books, 1984; second Limelight Edition, December 1992, pp. 53–57.

Day, Beth. *The Little Professor of Piney Woods*. New York: Julian Messner, a division of Simon & Schuster, Inc., 1955.

Dykstra, Robert. "Dr. Emerson's Sam: Black Iowans Before the Civil War." *The Palimpsest* (a publication of the State Historical Society of Iowa), Vol. 63, No. 3 (May/June 1982), pp. 66–68.

Ellerbe, Alma, and Paul Ellerbe. "Inchin' Along: The Story of the Piney Woods School in the Black Belt of Mississippi." *McClure's Magazine*, Vol. 54, No. 2 (April 1922), pp. 7, 8.

Erickson, Lori. *Iowa Off the Beaten Track*. Chester, Conn: The Globe Pequot Press, 1990.

Fort Madison Plain Dealer, May 27, 1857. An editorial noting that "To the disgrace of the County and State, Denmark has the name of being the rendezvous of men, who occasionally engage in negro-stealing, at the same time professing the religion of the gospel. Men of less shrewdness have been hanged—have received their just desserts—for engaging in practices of which respectable citizens of Denmark had been accused."

Garrison, Ramond. *Tales of Old Keokuk Homes*. Hamilton, Ill.: Hamilton Press, 1959, p. 76.

The Gate City, Keokuk, Iowa, February 25, 1869. Item about Frederick Douglass's visit to the city.

Gibson, Robert A. "The Negro Holocaust: Lynching and Race Riots in the United States, 1880–1950." Yale-New Haven Teacher Institute, www.yale.edu/ynhti/curriculum/units1979.

Gorden, Thomas. Letter to author, Boston, Massachusetts, February 15, 2004, " . . . The Rev. Joel and William . . . kidnapped Benjamin to literally sell him 'down the river' in a slave market that had dollar-inflated by triple between the 1830s and 50s," according to Thomas C. Gorden, the great-great-great-great-grandson of the Reverend Joel Gordon. (There is no evidence that Hugh Gordon could read or write and in his various court, tax and census papers his name is most often spelled Gordon, but also is written as Gorden, Gordan or Gordin. His sons who could sign their name used the spelling Gorden.)

———. Letter to author, Boston, Massachusetts, February 21, 2004.

———. Letter to author, Boston, Massachusetts, February 22, 2004.

———. Letter to author, Boston, Massachusetts, February 23, 2004.

Grinnell, Josiah Bushnell. *Men and Events of Forty Years.* Boston: D. Lothrop Co., 1891, p. 211.

Handy, Robert W., and Gertrude Handy. "The Remarkable Masters of a First Station on the Underground Railroad." *Iowan* 22 (Summer 1974), pp. 45–50.

Harnack, Curt. "The Iowa Underground Railroad." *Iowan* 4 (June/July 1956), pp. 20–23, 44, 47.

Hawley, Charles Arthur. "For Peace and Freedom." *The Palimpsest* (a publication of the State Historical Society of Iowa), Vol. XVI, No. 11 (November 1935).

Hine, Darlene Clark, Elsa Barkley Brown, and Rosalyn Terborg-Penn, eds. *Black Women in America: An Historical Encyclopedia*, Vol. I, A–L. Bloomington and Indianapolis: Indiana University Press, 1993, pp. 615–16.

Inventory and appraisement of Hugh Gordon Estate, 1834, Book F, p. 4424. Lists twenty slaves, including "Sharlet."

Iowa Census, 1856, Lee County: " 'Julyiannn Piles,' 36, William, 15; George, 10, Ruan, 5; Josephus, 7, all born in Kentucky, J.W. Piles, 8, Daniel, 7, James, 4, Frances Gordon, 83; Walker Catline?, 24, husband of Emily; 'Henry Pills,' 70; 'Charlotte Piles,' 57, Barnun, 27, Ellen, 24, Pelina, 19; Elisabeth, 13, Henry, 10, Mary A., 8, Emily, 32."

Iowa Census, 1860.

Jones, Charisse. "Owning the Airwaves." *Essence*, October 1998.

Jones, Laurence Clifton, 1884–1975, www.africanpubs.com.

Jones, Laurence C., comp. *Little Journeys to Piney Woods.* Mississippi: Piney Woods School, 1956. The story of Jones's near hanging appears on page 32.

Jones, Mrs. Laurence C. "The Desire for Freedom." *The Palimpsest* (a publication of the State Historical Society of Iowa), Vol. VIII, No. 5 (May 1927), pp. 154–61.

Keokuk City Directory, 1887. Lists Barney Pyles, driver, residing at 1426 Bank.

Keokuk Public Library, information on deaths and burial places of Charlotta and Harry Pyles.

Lee County, Iowa, GenWeb Project, 1879. Keokuk, Iowa, Biographies, Index of Names. Barney Pyles, teamster, is listed as son of Charlotta and Harry Pyles, p. 5, www.rootsweb.com/ialee/data/bios/keobiodx.html.

Let's Travel: Pathways Through Iowa. Pamphlet. St. Paul, Minn.: Clark & Miles Publishing, Inc., 1996.

Lopez, Barry Holstun. *Of Wolves and Men.* New York: Charles Scribner's Sons, 1978.

Lucas, Marion B. *A History of Blacks in Kentucky,* Vol. 1, *From Slavery to Segregation, 1760–1891.* The Kentucky Historical Society, 1992, p. 4. Description of hemp farming.

Lustig, Lillie S., S. Claire Sondheim, and Sarah Rensel, eds. *The Southern Cook Book of Fine Old Recipes.* Reading, Pa.: Culinary Arts Press, 1939, pp. 5, 6.

Matlack, Lucius C. *The History of American Slavery and Methodism from 1780 to 1849; and History of the Wesleyan Methodist Connection of America.* In two parts, with an Appendix. New York: No. 5 Spruce Street, 1849.

McLaughlin, Lillian. "Brave Black Women in an Intrepid Family." *Des Moines Tribune,* Wednesday, May 14, 1975.

McLeister, Ira Ford, and Roy Stephen Nicholson. *History of the Wesleyan Methodist Church of America,* rev. ed. Marion, Ind.: The Wesley Press, 1959.

Mid-American Frontier, Gazetteer of the State of Missouri. New York: Arno Press, 1975. Talks about the physical landscape of Howard, Monroe and Shelby counties.

Mills, George. "The Crusade of John Brown." *Annals of Iowa,* Series 3, Vol. XXXV, No. 1 (Fall 1959).

Missouri: A Guide to the Show Me State, compiled by Workers of the Writers' Program of the Work Projects Administration in the state of Missouri, American Guide Series, copyrighted 1941, the Missouri State Highway Department, pp. 478, 479. Describes Waverly and the Missouri River.

Moulton, Candy. *The Writer's Guide to Everyday Life in the Wild West from 1840–1900.* Cincinnati: Writer's Digest Books, 1999, pp. 160, 259.

Newhall, J. B. *A Glimpse of Iowa in 1846; or the Emigrant's Guide, and State Directory; with a Description of the New Purchase: Embracing Much Practical Advice and Useful Information to Intending Emigrants. Also, the New State Constitution,* 2nd ed. Burlington, Iowa: W. D. Skillman, 1846, p. 91.

Notes from National Public Radio tribute to the International Sweethearts of Rhythm, broadcast on public radio stations nationwide on March 25, 2004, and including an interview with Helen Jones Woods.

Parkman, Francis. *The Oregon Trail.* New York: Dodd, Mead & Co., Inc., 1964.

Pierson, Dudley. "A Home Away from Home." *African American Family Magazine* (Southfield, Mich.: Metro Parent Publishing Group, Inc.), November 2002.

The Pine Torch (Piney Woods, Miss.), Vol. XVII, No. 6 (April 1928), p. 4.

Purcell, Leslie Harper. *Miracle in Mississippi: Laurence C. Jones of Piney Woods.* New York: Comet Press Books, 1956.

Redford, The Reverend A. H. *The History of Methodism in Kentucky,* Vol. I. Nashville: Southern Methodist Publishing House, 1868, pp. 18–27. Talks about early Methodist preachers in Kentucky.

Ricketts, S. P., and Grace L. Ricketts. "The Underground Railroad of Southwestern Iowa," from the Papers of Elvira Gaston Platt, 1853–1974, Iowa Women's Archives. Iowa City: University of Iowa.

Rydjord, John. *Indian Place Names.* Norman, Okla.: University of Oklahoma Press, 1968. Contains information about Chief Keokuk.

Sernett, Milton C. *North Star County, Upstate New York and the Crusade for African American Freedom.* Syracuse: Syracuse University Press, 2002, p. 77.

Siebert, Wilbur H. *The Underground Railroad from Slavery to Freedom.* New York: MacMillan, 1898, pp. 42–43.

Silag, Bill, ed. *Outside In: African-American History in Iowa, 1838–2000.* Iowa City, Iowa: State Historical Society of Iowa, 2001, Chapter 3.

Simon, F. Kevin, ed. *The WPA Guide to Kentucky.* Compiled and written by the Federal Writers' Project of the Work Projects Administration for the State of Kentucky. Lexington: The University Press of Kentucky, 1996.

"Slavery at Farmington," a brochure produced by Farmington Historic Home, a historic museum home in Louisville, Kentucky, owned and operated by Historic Homes Foundation, Inc.

Smith, Frederic C. *One Hundred Ten Years of Public Education in Keokuk.* Keokuk: Keokuk Community School District, 1961.

Smith, Warren Thomas. *John Wesley and Slavery.* Nashville: Abingdon Press, 1986, p. 94. Quote from John Wesley.

Staples, Brent. "The Black Seminole Indians Keep Fighting for Equality in the American West." *The New York Times,* November 18, 2003.

Styron, William. *Sophie's Choice.* New York: The Modern Library, 1999.

Todd, John. *Early Settlement and Growth of Western Iowa; or Reminiscences.* Des Moines: Historical Department of Iowa, 1906, pp. 152–53.

Turton, Cecil Marie. *The Underground Railroad in Kansas, Nebraska and Iowa.* Columbus: Ohio State University, 1935.

Van Ek, Jacob. "Underground Railroad in Iowa." *The Palimpsest* (a publication of the State Historical Society of Iowa), Vol. II, No. 5 (May 1921).

Varhola, Michael J. *Everyday Life During the Civil War: A Guide for Writers, Students and Historians.* Cincinnati: Writers Digest Books, 1999, pp. 10, 11.

Washington County (Kentucky) Court, Deed Book N, p. 107, transcribed-edited, Thomas K. Gorden, Boston, Massachusetts, 2000.

Washington County (Kentucky) Court records of the seizure of Frances Gordon's slaves on October 22, 1853, sworn to by James R. Parrott, March 14, 1854, and copied from Washington County Court records by Willis Gorden, Cedar Rapids, Iowa.

Washington County, Kentucky, Bicentennial History, 1792–1992. Paducah, Ky.: Turner Publishing Company, p. 282. Contained in the archives of the Family History Library, Salt Lake City, Utah.

Washington County, Kentucky, tax list, 1819.

Williams, Ora. "Underground Railroad Signals." *Annals of Iowa*, Series 3, Vol. XXVII (April 1946), pp. 297–303.

Wubben, Hubert H. *Civil War Iowa and the Copperhead Movement.* Ames: Iowa State University Press, 1980.

Wundram, Bill, Tricia DeWall, Jeffrey Bruner, Tom Thoma, and Bill Zahren. *Iowa Celebrating the Sesquicentennial.* American & World Geographic Publishing, 1995.

Yanak, Ted, and Pam Cornelison. *The Great American History Fact-Finder.* Boston and New York: Houghton Mifflin Company, 1993, p. 49.

Chapter 9: The Woman on John Little's Back

Bolden, Tonya. *Strong Men Keep Coming: The Book of African American Men.* New York: John Wiley & Sons, Inc., 1999.

Drew, Benjamin. *A North-Side View of Slavery. The Refugee: or the Narratives of Fugitive Slaves in Canada. Related by Themselves, with an account of the History and Conditions of the Colored Population of Upper Canada.* Boston: John P. Jewett and Company, 1856.

Hill, Daniel G. *The Freedom-Seekers: Blacks in Early Canada.* Toronto: Stoddart Publishing Co., Ltd., 1992.

Chapter 10: Angeline's Blues

Adams, Virginia M., ed. *On the Altar of Freedom: A Black Soldier's Civil War Letters from the Front.* New York: Warren Books, 1992.

Bingham, Millicent Todd. *Emily Dickinson's Home, Letters of Edward Dickinson and His Family with Documentation and Comment by Millicent Todd Bingham.* New York: Harper & Brothers Publishers, 1955, pp. 3–8.

Blockson, Charles L. *The Underground Railroad, First-Person Narratives of Escapes to Freedom in the North.* New York: Prentice Hall Press, 1987, pp. 34–37. Contains Rachel and Elizabeth Parker's stories.

Cohen, Saul B., ed. *The Columbia Gazeteer of the World,* Vol. 1, A–G. New York: Columbia University Press, 1998, p. 700. Description of Colrain in Franklin County.

Copage, Eric V. *Kwanzaa: An African-American Celebration of Culture and Cooking.* New York: William Morrow and Company, Inc., 1991.

Cornish, Dudley Taylor. *The Sable Arm: Black Troops in the Union Army, 1861–1865.* Lawrence, Kan.: University Press of Kansas, 1987.

Curtis, Nancy C. *Black Heritage Sites: The North.* New York: The New Press, 1996, pp. 76–77. The Elizabeth Freeman story.

DeRamus, Betty. "Some of Us Are Brave." *Essence,* February 1998, p. 86.

Gladstone, William A. *Men of Color.* Gettysburg, Pa.: Thomas Publications, 1993.

History of the Town of Amherst, Massachusetts, 1731–1896. Compiled and published by Carpenter & Morehouse, Amherst, Massachusetts, 1896.

Hitchcock, Frederick H., preparer and publisher. *The Handbook of Amherst, Massachusetts,* 1891.

McClellan, Charles H. *The Early Settlers of Colrain, Massachusetts.* Greenfield, Mass.: W. S. Carson, printer, 1885, pp. 16, 25.

Packard, the Reverend Theophilus, Jr. *A History of the Churches and Ministers and of Franklin Association in Franklin County, Massachusetts, and an Appendix Respecting the County.* Boston: S. K. Whipple and Company, 1854, p. 80.

Palmer, Robert. *Deep Blues,* orig. pub. Viking Press, 1981; Penguin Books, 1982.

Patrie, Lois McClellan. *A History of Colrain Massachusetts with Genealogies of Early Families.* Self-published, copyrighted 1974 by Lois McClellan Patrie.

Pronouncing Gazetteer of the World. Philadelphia: Lippincott, 1905.

Smith, James Avery. *The History of the Black Population of Amherst, Massachusetts, 1728–1870.* Boston: New England Historic Genealogical Society, 1999, pp. 22–36.

Thomas, Velma Maia. *Freedom's Children.* New York: Crown Publishers, Inc., 2000.

www.arps.org/amhersthistory/HenryJackson/abolition/index.htm

Chapter 11: Suspicious Lynchings, Passing for White, Passing for Black and Mixed Marriages in Deadly Times: A Chronology

African Americans Voices of Triumph: Perseverance. By the editors of Time-Life Books. Alexandria, Va.: Time-Life Books, 1993, pp. 206–7.

Asbury, Herbert. *The Gangs of New York: An Informal History of the Underworld.* New York: Thunder's Mouth Press, 2001.

Bauerlein, Mark. *Negrophobia: A Race Riot in Atlanta, 1906.* San Francisco: Encounter Books, 2001, p. 57.

Clements, John. *Virginia Facts: A Comprehensive Look at Virginia Today, County by County.* Dallas: Clements Research II, Inc., 1991.

Coffin, Levi. *The Reminiscences of Levi Coffin.* Cincinnati: Western Tract Society, 1876, chapter 12. Story about abolitionist John Fairfield helping mulattos and quadroons escape to Detroit by using powder and wigs to make them look white.

Cose, Ellis. *Bone to Pick: Of Forgiveness, Reconciliation, Reparation and Revenge.* New York: Atria Books, 2004.

Curry, George E. "The Death That Won't Die." *Emerge,* Vol. VI, No. 9 (July/August 1995), pp. 24–27. A retelling of the Emmett Till story.

Dalmage, Heather M. *Tripping on the Color Line: Black-White Multiracial Families in a Racially Divided World.* New Brunswick, N.J., and London: Rutgers University Press, 1965.

"Five Generations Gather for Estes-Stark Reunion." Gulf Islands Driftwood, Wednesday, August 10, 1994. The article describes the first Estes–Stark reunion.

Gettleman, Jeffrey. "Strom Thurmond's Child: Old Times There Are Not Forgotten." *The New York Times,* Sunday, December 21, 2003.

Giese, James R., and Laurel R. Singleton. *U.S. History: A Resource Book for Secondary Schools,* Vol. 1, 1450–1865. Santa Barbara, Calif., and Oxford: ABC-CLIO, Inc., 1989.

Herbert, Bob. "Stolen Kisses." *The New York Times,* March 1, 2004. Talks about the *Loving v. Virginia* case.

Higginbotham, A. Leon, Jr. *In the Matter of Color, Race and the American Legal Process: The Colonial Period.* New York: Oxford University Press, Inc., 1978.

Holiday, Billie, and William Duffy. *Lady Sings the Blues.* New York: Lancer Books, 1956.

Hudson, J. Blaine. *Fugitive Slaves and the Underground Railroad in the Kentucky Borderland.* Jefferson, N.C., and London: McFarland & Co., Inc., 2002. Interracial escapes are described on page 63 and interracial romances leading to escapes on pages 79 and 80.

Irby, Charles C. "The Black Settlers on Saltspring Island, Canada." *The Yearbook of the Pacific Coast Geographers,* Vol. 36. Corvallis, Ore.: Oregon State University Press, 1974. This piece provides a decade-by-decade count of the blacks who moved to the island, talks about intermarriage on Saltspring and explains why blacks on the island developed no social cohesion.

Irons, Peter, and Stephanie Guitton, eds. *May It Please the Court.* New York: The New Press, 1993.

Janofsky, Michael. "Thurmond Kin Acknowledge Black Daughter." *The New York Times,* Tuesday, December 16, 2003.

Johnson, Oakley C. "The Negro-Caucasian Club: A History, The American Students' First Inter-racial Organization." *Negro History Bulletin,* February 1970.

Katz, William Loren. *The Black West.* Seattle: Open Hand Publishing, 1987. This talks about Sylvia Stark firing through the roof to run off Indians. See also p. 152. Talks about California's passage of its own fugitive slave law.

———. *Black People Who Made the Old West.* New York: Thomas Y. Crowell, 1977.

Knappman, Edward W., ed. *Great American Trials.* Detroit: Visible Ink Press, copyright ©1994, New England Publishing Associates, Inc., pp. 109–13.

Kristof, Nicholas D. "Lovers Under the Skin." *The New York Times*, Wednesday, December 3, 2003. This mentions the 1958 poll and the 1959 ban on interracial marriage in Virginia.

Levy, Paul. "Lime Jell-O Marshmallow Cottage Cheese Surprise." *The New York Times*, Sunday, April 18, 2004.

"*Life* Goes to the Movies," Wallaby edition. New York: Pocket Books, 1977, orig. pub. Time-Life Books, 1975, pp. 105, 137.

Lightblau, Eric, and Andrew Jacobs. "U.S. Revives Emmett Till Case Based on New Details in Films." *The New York Times*, Tuesday, May 11, 2004.

Overmyer, James E. *Effa Manley and the Newark Eagles.* Metuchen, N.J., and London: The Scarecrow Press, Inc., 1993, pp. 6, 8.

Synnestvedt, Sig. *The White Response to Black Emancipation.* New York: Macmillan, 1974, pp. 52, 53. See also p. 63 (the story of William Donegan's murder).

Chapter 12: Hound Dogs Hate Red Pepper

Ager, Susan. "Memories: The Apple of His Eye." *The Detroit Free Press*, October 8, 2000.

Barber, David L. "Santa, Settlers and Science." *Pioneer East*, September 27, 1999, Big Rapids, Michigan.

Bernauer, Barbara, assistant archivist, Church of Jesus Christ of Latter-day Saints. Letter to author. "I checked several sources and found no membership record for Solomon Millard, sorry."

Brown, Dee. *The Westerners.* New York, Chicago, San Francisco: Holt, Rinehart and Winston, 1974.

Brown, Patricia Leigh. "Dixie Redesign: Fun and Fancy Without the Dust." *The New York Times*, Thursday, July 6, 2000.

Browning, Janisse, coordinator. *Some Johnson Family Stories: From Slavery to the Present.* Amherstburg, Ontario: The North American Black Historical Museum, 1993.

Carbone, Elisa. *Stealing Freedom.* New York: Alfred A. Knopf, 1998.

Catlin, George. *The Story of Detroit.* Detroit: The Detroit News, 1926.

Census Population Schedule 1, 1850. "Free Inhabitants in Livingston Co., Kentucky, Sept. 4, 1850." This reveals that Uriah G. Berry, in 1850, was 33, a merchant and had real estate valued at $8,000. However, dwellings around him were worth a lot less—$2,000, $300, $1,700, $4,300, $1,500, $2,000, $150, $250, $3,500, $500, $400, $500, $500. On August 19, 1850, Uriah owned a 16-year-old female slave, a 28-year-old female, a 10-year-old male, an 8-year-old male, a 14-year-old female mulatto and a 21-year-old black male, presumably Isaac Berry.

City of Detroit, Mi, 1701–1922, Vol. 1. Detroit-Chicago: S. J. Clarke Publishing Co., 1922, pp. 476–78. The book tells the story of Erastus Hussey, a Quaker in Battle Creek, Michigan, who helped 1,300 fugitives escape.

Clemens, Samuel L. *Mark Twain's Autobiography*, Vol. 1. Copyright 1924 by Clara Gabrilowitsch. New York and London: Harper & Brothers Publishers, pp. 124, 125. He notes that the local church taught that God approved slavery, that it was holy. To blacks and whites in the area, the Southern plantation was "simply hell; no milder name could describe it. If the threat to sell an incorrigible slave 'down the river' would not reform him, nothing would—his case was past cure."

Crittendon, Denise. "The Secret Corridors of Black History." *African American Parent Magazine*, February/March 2000.

Cross, Jim. Interviews, Mecosta County, Michigan, February, June and September 2000.

Cross, Marie Loretta Berry. Interviews, Mecosta County, Michigan, February, June and September 2000.

A Descriptive and Historical Guide. Compiled and written by the Federal Writers' Project of the Work Projects Administration for the State of Illinois. Chicago: A. C. McClurg & Co., 1939.

Dedmon, Emmett. *Fabulous Chicago.* New York: Random House, 1953.

DeRamus, Betty. "Important Lessons to Learn from Slavery." *The Michigan Chronicle*, February 5–11, 1997.

———. "Adrian House Opened a Window to Freedom." *The Detroit News*, February 1, 2000.

Diehl, Lorraine B. "Skeletons in the Closet." *New York Magazine*, October 5, 1992. This talks about the gangs that kidnapped black children and sold them to Southerners.

Dorson, Richard M., ed. *Negro Folktales in Michigan.* Cambridge, Mass.: Harvard University Press, 1956. This collection includes Katy Pointer's account of the escape of her father, Isaac Berry. Dorson makes no attempt to distinguish between true and made-up tales in his collection, saying only that the people who told the tales believed they were true and that they could have happened.

1850 Federal Census for Michigan, p. 346. This shows Solomon Millard, 42; wife, Diana, 38; daughter Clarissa, 13; daughter Lucy E., 11; son, Ransom H., 10; daughter Sarah, 4; and son Solomon, four months living in Nankin Township in Wayne County, Michigan. Only son Solomon lists his birthplace as Michigan. The other residents of the household list New York as their birthplace. According to the census, the elder Solomon was born in 1808 in New York; Diana was born November 1812 in New Hampshire and died January 5, 1853, in Michigan; Clarissa Millard was born 1837 in New York; Lucy E. Millard was born in 1839 in New York; Ransom was born in 1840 in New York; Sarah was born in 1846 in New York; Solomon Jr. was born in June 1850 in Nankin, Wayne Co., Michigan; and William Millard died in Michigan. The elder Solomon lists his occupation as farmer.

Essex County Genealogical Society. Transcriptions of marriage registrations, 1859, 1860. J. B. Huffman of the British Methodist Episcopal Church of Windsor solemnized a marriage on April 30, 1859, between Isaac Berry, 30, a resident of Windsor born in Kentucky, and Lusea Millon, 18. Huffman also solemnized a subsequent marriage on January 16, 1860, between "Lucy Miller" and Isaac Berry.

Lucy's religion is identified as Latter-day Saint, but she is called of African origin for the first time.

Freeman, Roland L. *A Communion of the Spirits: African American Quilters, Preservers and Their Stories*. Nashville: Rutledge Hill Press, 1996. Quilter Marguerite Berry Jackson tells the story of her grandparents.

Gibson, Robert A. "The Negro Holocaust: Lynching and Race Riots in the United States, 1880–1950." Yale-New Haven Teacher Institute, www.yale.edu/ynhti/curriculum/units1979.

A Guide to the Hoosier State. Compiled by workers of the Writers' Project of the Work Projects Administration in the State of Indiana. New York: Oxford University Press, 1941.

Gutman, Herbert G. *The Black Family in Slavery and Freedom, 1750–1925*. New York: Vintage Books, 1977, p. 349. This tells the story of a black couple who committed suicide, reported in 1746 in the *Boston Evening Post*. The woman was about to be sold. They were in a garret; the man cut the woman's throat and then shot himself. See also pp. 3–37 (Send Me Some of the Children's Hair).

Hill, Daniel G. *The Freedom-Seekers: Blacks in Early Canada*. Toronto: Stoddard Publishing Co., Limited, 1992. Orig. pub. The Book Society of Canada, Limited, 1981. This book contains information on John "Daddy" Hall and his five wives.

Hu, Winnie. "In Upstate New York: A Tourist Chapter to the Book of Mormon." *The New York Times*, Wednesday, December 20, 2000.

Hudson, J. Blaine. *Fugitive Slaves and the Underground Railroad in the Kentucky Borderland*. Jefferson, N.C., and London: McFarland & Co., Inc., 2002. Interracial escapes are described on page 63 and interracial romances leading to escapes on pages 79 and 80.

Interview with abolitionist William Lambert. *Detroit Tribune*, January 17, 1886.

Jackson, Marguerite Berry. *Finding a Home*, an unpublished memoir about black settlers in central Michigan. In this unpublished memoir, Jackson, a retired teacher of Afro-American history and granddaughter of Isaac and Lucy Berry, talks about pioneers Thomas Cross, Granderson Norman, Daniel Pointer, Joseph Cummin, James Guy and the Berry family's first encounter with the Chippewas.

———. Videotaped interviews, Mecosta County, Michigan, May and October 1991. In these videos, Jackson recounts the story of her grandparents, Isaac and Lucy Berry. She mentions the names of free blacks who aided Isaac, including Albert Campbell in Quincy, Illinois, and the Purdues in Coloma, Indiana.

Jackson, Ronald Vern, ed. *Federal Census Index, Missouri 1850 Slave Schedules*. Published by Genealogical Services.

Jackson, Ronald Vern, and David Schaefermeyer, eds. *Kentucky 1850 Census Index*. Bountiful, Utah: Accelerated Indexing Systems, Inc.

Kirkland, Caroline. *Chicago Yesterdays*. Chicago: Daughaday & Co., 1919.

Larrie, Reginald. *Makin' Free: African-Americans in the Northwest Territory*. Detroit: Blaine Etheridge Books, 1981. On page 28, the book notes that the papers carried by free blacks "gave a description of the person who was supposed to carry them at all times. Yet in many instances, the description was inaccurate. For example, Jack James was a black man who happened to be married to a white woman of German descent. Regardless of this fact, his wife's papers described her as Indian. Frequently, white people who married blacks carried 'free papers which classified them as Indian.'"

Lippincott's Gazetteer. Philadelphia: J. B. Lippincott & Co., 1883, p. 1689. This lists twenty-six places called Palmyra.

Lustig, Lillie, S. Claire Sondheim, and Sarah Rensel, eds. *The Southern Cook Book of Fine Old Recipes.* Reading, Pa.: Culinary Arts Press, 1939.

McGraw, Bill. "Slavery Is a Quiet Part of City's Past." *Detroit Free Press,* February 22, 2001.

McRae, Norman, Ph.D. Interview, Detroit, January 2000.

———. *Black Participation in the Civil War: The Underground Railroad in Michigan.* Detroit: unpublished social studies unit.

Missouri 1860 slave schedule. Ronald Vern Jackson, ed. North Salt Lake, Utah: Accelerated Indexing Systems International (no date).

Schedule 1—Free inhabitants in Palmyra in the County of Marion, state of Missouri, enumerated on the 21st day of August, 1850, Ronald Vern Jackson, ed. This shows a Gridley Pratt, stagecoach driver, living in Palmyra.

Schedule 1—Free Inhabitants in Palmyra in the County of Marion, state of Missouri, enumerated on the 21st day of August, 1860, Ronald Vern Jackson and Gary Ronald Teeples (sic), eds. Bountiful, Utah: Accelerated Indexing Systems International (no date). This shows a James Pratt in Marion County.

Schedule 1, First Ward, City of Hannibal, state of Missouri, 1860, Ronald Vern Jackson, ed. North Salt Lake, Utah: Accelerated Indexing Systems International (no date).

Missouri 1860, Census Index Vol. II. This shows Solomon N. Millard living in Knox County, Missouri, and other Millards in Missouri, including James Millard in Marion County, Daniel and William in Sullivan, G.B. in Texas County, Lawrence in Perry County, Samuel in Lewis County and Selden in Lewis County.

Missouri, A Guide to the "Show Me" State. Compiled by workers of the Writers' Project of the Works Project Administration in the state of Missouri. New York: Duell, Sloan and Pearce, 1941.

Missouri, State of, Official Manual, *The Role of the Negro in Missouri History,* www.umsl.edu/services/library/blackstudies/slavery.htm. "The purchase of the Louisiana Territory by the United States in 1803 . . . offered slave owners a potential new world, spreading from the Mississippi to the Rockies. . . . Part of that new world was Upper

Louisiana, containing the present states of Missouri and Arkansas. Upper Louisiana was not as conducive to cotton growing geographically as Lower Louisiana, but there still existed possibilities for slave labor in tobacco and hemp production, as well as in the cultivation and production of grain and live stock. This caused an influx of slaveholders and their chattel into Missouri. A majority of these slaveholders came from the worn out lands of Kentucky, Tennessee, North Carolina and Virginia. . . . In 1860, top male slaves brought about $1,300 each, and female slaves about $1,000. Since Missouri was largely agricultural, most slaves were employed in the fertile bottom lands which bordered the Mississippi and Missouri rivers and their tributaries. Without a single staple crop, Missouri never developed large plantations as did the cotton states. . . . In general, most of the Missouri slaveowners held only one or two slaves. . . . They were employed as valets, butlers, handy men, field hands, maids, nurses and cooks. Masters often hired out their slaves during periods when the slave was otherwise likely to be unemployed. The person hiring the slave was responsible for the sustenance of the slave, in addition to an amount of money paid to the slaveowner for the services of his chattel. During the 1850s, the crews of river boats on the Mississippi and Missouri rivers were generally black. Aboard the boats, hired out slaves served as deck hands and cabin boys or as stevedores. . . . Many slaves became skilled laborers—blacksmiths, carpenters, masons, bricklayers, horticulturists, as well as general all-around trouble-shooters for the entire farm. In fact, the slave and his family and the master and his family were, more often than not, a team, sharing the burden of work together in the field. . . . Missouri's institutions, both social and legal, constantly reminded the black man he was property not a human being."

The Old Settlers: A World Unto Themselves. Mecosta County, Mich.: The Old Settlers Family Reunion Committee, 1987. This book was compiled by descendants of the original black settlers in Michigan's Mecosta, Isabella and Montcalm counties. It includes the genealogy of the Isaac and Lucy Berry family, the Stephen Todds and the Guy and Sleet families.

Our Untold Stories. Compiled and written by members of the Fred Hart Williams Genealogical Society. Detroit: Fred Hart Williams Genealogical Society, 2001. This contains the story of black inventor George Thompson.

Paige, Howard. *African American Family Cookery.* Southfield, Mich.: Aspects Publishing Co., 1995. On page 88, Paige gives a recipe for the kind of cornbread that gave Harriet Tubman and others the strength to rescue slaves. He calls the bread "Harriet Tubman's Fat Cornbread."

Pierson, Dudley. "An Ode to Michigan's Forgotten Trailblazers." *African American Parent Magazine,* February/March 2001.

Pointe to Pointe: A Tour of East Jefferson-Lakeshore Road from Windmill Pointe to Gaukler Pointe. Grosse Pointe, Mich.: Grosse Pointe Historical Society, 1987. This describes the road from Detroit to Grosse Pointe in the nineteenth century.

Pointer, Raymond, Sr. Interview, Mecosta County, Michigan, February 2001. As a child, Raymond Pointer lived with his great-grandmother, Lucy Berry. He tells stories about her pipe smoking, her pretending to be a witch, her quilting and her strength.

Pointer, Ray, telephone interview and emails to author, great-great-grandson of Isaac and Lucy Berry. "As far as I can recall," he wrote in an email on July 24, 2000, "there were five slaves, Isaac's mother, Harve, Louis, a sister whose name I don't recall and Isaac. My father may be able to give you the details you are seeking. . . . My father is 79, he attended that school which was built in 1901 to replace the original log school built by Isaac Berry. Lucy, my great, great grandmother was the first teacher in the area, and both Isaac and Lucy were members of the school board for many years."

In a July 25, 2000, email Pointer said: "As I know about Jim Pratt, his ownership of the Berry slaves was through Juliann's inheritance from her father, Uriah. I never knew that Jim owned any property of consequence, not to say that he wouldn't have had slaves. But according to what I heard, Jim and Juliann lived on a rather shabby farm. I don't know what crop they raised, if they did raise anything at all. I do understand that Jim rented the slaves out to German immigrant farmers, as I told you on the phone. Considering that Jim was a compulsive gambler, I now wonder how Juliann fared with Jim after he sold all the other slaves and let Isaac go."

Poremba, David Lee. *Images of America: Detroit, 1860–1899.* Charleston: Arcadia Press, 1998. On page 10, the author talks about billboard advertisements next to the Michigan Central Railroad depot at Third and Woodbridge; they directed passengers to the terminals of the Grand Trunk Railroad of Canada. The book's introduction mentions that Detroit had a population of some 45,000 in 1860.

Preliminary Report on the Eighth Census 1860 by Jos. C. G. Kennedy, superintendent. Washington, D.C.: Government Printing Office, 1862. Figures for the state of Michigan show that in 1860, the "free colored population" in Mecosta County, Michigan, included one male in the 20-and-under-30 category, one male 30 and under 40, one male and one female in the 40-and-under-50 category.

Rawick, George P., ed. *The American Slave: A Composite Autobiography,* Vol. 4, orig. pub. 1941; reprint, Westport, Conn.: Greenwood Publishing Co., 1974. On pages 10 and 206 are descriptions of slave dances. See also Vol. 6, Alabama and Indiana narratives. This contains the story of an overseer supposedly torn to pieces by his own hounds after climbing a tree after a slave and then falling. See also Vol. 4, Texas narratives. Page 27 features a reference to rubbing salt and pepper on wounds. See also Vol. 7, Oklahoma, p. 66.

Roger, Sharon A. "Slaves No More: A Study of the Buxton Settlement, Upper Canada, 1849–1861." A dissertation submitted to the faculty of the Graduate School of the State University of New York at Buffalo in partial fulfillment of the requirements for the degree of Doctor of Philosophy, 1995. On pages 208–11, the book talks about biracial couples in Buxton.

Shockley, Robert, and Charles K. Fox. *Survival in the Wilds.* New York: A. S. Barnes and Co., 1970. The book talks about the various ways in which lost persons can orient themselves in the wild and about the North Star that guided runaway slaves.

Sommers, Laurie Kay. "Herb Woman of Mecosta." *Michigan National Resources Magazine,* September/October 1989. This profile of Marie Berry Cross talks about the herbal lore Marie gained from her grandmother, Lucy Berry. It includes Marie's account of how Lucy Millard found Isaac Berry in Canada after hearing his violin.

Thomas, Jo. "Tallgrass Prairie to Be Preserved." *Detroit Free Press,* Wednesday, May 2, 2001.

Thompson, George. *Prison Life and Reflections*, orig. ed., Missouri: James M. Fitch, 1847; reprint, New York: Negro Universities Press, 1969. This book includes the story of the abolitionists who called their church in Quincy, Illinois, The Lord's Barn and defended it from a proslavery mob.

Todd, Stephen. His file on his request for a pension for Civil War injuries, National Archives, Washington, D.C. The file includes an affidavit signed by Isaac Berry Sr. and his son, William, saying that the two men witnessed Todd's marriage to Caroline Kahler in 1874 in Windsor, Canada.

Tyree, Marion Cabell. *Housekeeping in Old Virginia.* Louisville: John P. Morton & Co., 1879.

Underground Railroad. Official National Parks Handbook, produced by the Division of Publications, National Park Service, U.S. Department of the Interior, Washington, D.C., 1998, pp. 39, 40.

Voice of the Fugitive, January 1, 1851, Sandwich, Canada West. Henry Bibb talks about two letter writers fearful that blacks and whites will intermarry in Canada.

Walls, Bryan. *The Road That Led to Somewhere.* Windsor: Olive Publishing Co., 1980. This "documented novel" tells the story of Walls's ancestors, Jane and John Freeman Walls, an interracial couple who ran away together from North Carolina.

Warren, Francis H. *Michigan Manual of Freedmen's Progress*, orig. pub. Detroit: 1915; reprint, Detroit: John M. Green, 1985.

Yanak, Ted, and Pam Cornelison. *The Great American History Fact-Finder.* Boston and New York: Houghton Mifflin Co., 1993.

Chapter 13: The Schoolteacher Had to Duck Dead Cats

Barnett, Glenn Warren, II. *Lett-Banneker-Banna Ka Family Kinship, 2003.* Columbus, Ohio: Barnett Family Enterprises.

Bedini, Silvio A. *The Life of Benjamin Banneker, the First African-American Man of Science.* Baltimore: Maryland Historical Society, 1972, p. 72.

Bernikow, Louise. *The American Women's Almanac.* New York: Berkley Books, 1997, p. 127. Story of Prudence Crandall's school for black girls.

British Columbia Geography Manual. Victoria, British Columbia, Canada: Province of British Columbia Department of Education, 1954.

Brown, Tony. "In Historical Perspective." *Tony Brown's Journal.* New York: Tony Brown Productions, Inc., January/March 1984.

"Cal Davis One of Four Awarded Oak Leaf Cluster." *Manistee News and Advocate*, June 2, 1944.

Carruth, Gorton. *The Encyclopedia of American Facts and Dates*, 9th ed. New York: HarperCollins, 1993.

Coffin, Levi. *The Reminiscences of Levi Coffin.* Cincinnati: Western Tract Society, 1876, chapter 12. Story about abolitionist John Fairfield helping mulattos and quadroons escape to Detroit by using powder and wigs to make them look white.

Cose, Ellis. *Bone to Pick: Of Forgiveness, Reconciliation, Reparation and Revenge.* New York: Atria Books, 2004.

DeRamus, Betty. "The Color of Courage: The Calvin Clark Davis Story." Unpublished.

———. "Duty, Not Race, Defined War Hero." *The Detroit News,* February 5, 2002.

———. "Younger People Keep Spirit of Black Combat Pilots Alive." *The Detroit News,* November 8, 2000.

———. "Neil Loving's Story Will Inspire the Democratic Convention." *The Detroit News,* July 25, 2002.

The 8th Air Force Museum. Letter to Calvin Murphy, December 13, 2001.

Flesher, John. "Fallen Pilot Honored." Associated Press article reprinted in the *Detroit Free Press,* Tuesday, February 19, 2002.

Foner, Philip S., and Josephine F. Pacheco. *Three Who Dared: Prudence Crandall, Margaret Douglass, Myrtilla Miner—Champions of Antebellum Black Education.* Westport, Conn., and London: Greenwood Press, 1984.

Gavrilovich, Peter, and Bill McGraw, eds. *The Detroit Almanac: 300 Years of Life in the Motor City.* Detroit: Detroit Free Press, 2000.

Grabowski, Ken. "Bear Lake Man Seeks Congressional Medal of Honor for Uncle." *Manistee News and Advocate,* Tuesday, May 1, 2001.

———. "World War II Veterans a Special Breed." *Manistee News and Advocate,* Wednesday, May 2, 2001.

Gutman, Herbert G. *The Black Family in Slavery and Freedom, 1750–1925.* New York: Vintage Books, 1977, p. 389. Story of Bill Wyrnosdick.

Hayden, Robert C. *Seven Black American Scientists.* Reading, Mass.: Addison-Wesley Publishing Company, Inc., 1972.

Herberg, Ruth M. "We Are a Free People and This Is Our Island." *Seattle Post-Intelligencer,* Sunday, June 24, 1979.

Hill, Daniel G. *The Freedom-Seekers: Blacks in Early Canada.* Toronto: Stoddart Publishing Co., Ltd., 1992; second printing, 1995, pp. 212–13. Story of John "Daddy" Hall.

Hoekstra, Pete, and John Conyers, Jr. Letter to Thomas E. White, secretary of the Army, from U.S. Rep. Hoekstra, and U.S. Rep. John Conyers Jr., asking for the Army's assistance in determining Calvin C. Davis's eligibility for various medals, written February 13, 2002.

Kroeger, Brooke. *Passing: When People Can't Be Who They Are.* New York: Public Affairs, 2003.

Levin, Carl. Letter to John W. Martin, Frankenmuth, Michigan, from U.S. Senator Levin about the loss of 75 to 80 percent of World War II Army and Air Force records in a 1973 fire at the National Personnel Records Center.

Louisiana, A Guide to the State. Compiled by workers of the Writers' Project of the Work Projects Administration in the State of Louisiana. New York: Hastings House, first printing, 1941.

Martin, John W. *History of District No. 2, Wass-Malcolm School, 1867–1957, Pleasanton Township, Manistee County, Michigan.* Self-published, 1985.

McCloy, James F. "The Black and African Influence on New Jersey Place Names." Bulletin of the Gloucester County Historical Society, Vol. 14, No. 8.

McFarlin, Jim. "A Choice of Colors." *African American Family Magazine,* March 2004, p. 32.

McGhee, Scott, and Susan Watson, eds. *Blacks in Detroit.* A reprint of articles from the *Detroit Free Press,* December 1980.

McNamara, Robert P., Maria Tempenis, and Beth Walton. *Crossing the Line: Interracial Couples in the South.* Westport, Conn., and London: Greenwood Press, 1999.

"Michigan's 83 Counties: Manistee." *Michigan History,* Vol. 70, No. 5 (September/October 1986).

Murphy, Calvin, cousin of Calvin Clark Davis. Interviews with author, January 2000 and December 2001.

———. Interview with author, Bear Lake, Michigan, August 2001.

———. Letters to author, December 6, 2001; December 13, 2001; January 28, 2002.

Murphy, Shelley. "A Special Tribute to Calvin Clark Davis." Unpublished article.

———. "George W. Marsh." Unpublished article.

Murphy, Verna. Telephone interview with Calvin Clark Davis's cousin, January 2002.

New York: A Guide to the Empire State. Compiled by workers of the Writers' Project of the Work Projects Administration in the State of New York. New York: Oxford University Press, 1947, 3rd printing, p. 577. Information about Fishkill, New York.

Our Untold Stories: A Collection of Family History Narratives. Compiled and written by members of the Fred Hart Williams Genealogical Society, Detroit, 2001, p. 144. Story of George and Elizabeth Thompson; pp. 1–3. Story of Charles Storeman. See also pp. 155–57 (story of William Webb).

Owens, Mitchell. "Surprises in the Family Tree." *The New York Times,* Thursday, January 8, 2004. Showcases genealogist Paul Heinegg's research on colonial African-American and biracial families descended from white women and African slaves, freedmen or indentured servants.

Palmer, Robert. *Deep Blues.* New York: Penguin Books, 1982. The book describes the Wolof people.

Pitts, Leonard, Jr. "Appreciation for Generation of True Heroes." *Detroit Free Press,* Friday, May 28, 2004.

"Poll Finds Improved Race Relations in America," aolsvc.news.aol.com/news/article, April 9, 2004.

Raleigh Register, February 23, 1802. Advertisement for a runaway.

"The Road That Led to Somewhere," a flyer promoting Bryan Walls's book about his ancestors.

Rogers, J. A. *Sex and Race: A History of White, Negro and Indian Miscegenation in the Two Americas,* Vol. II, *The New World.* New York: Helga M. Rogers, 1942.

———. Vol. I, *The Old World.* New York: Helga M. Rogers, 1967.

Ruchames, Louis. *The Abolitionists: A Collection of Their Writings.* New York: G. P. Putnam's Sons, 1963, p. 64. Novelist Lydia Maria Childs talks about the rumors that dogged Prudence Crandall's school.

Schwarz, Philip J. *Migrants Against Slavery: Virginians & The Nation.* Charlottesville, Va., and London: University Press of Virginia, 2001, pp. 150–58. Talks about Henry and Elsey Newby.

"Sgt. Davis, Cited for Heroism at Rabaul, Visits Home for Well-Earned Rest." *Bear Lake Beacon,* April 11, 1944. This article talks about how much servicemen enjoyed the movies and contains the quote in which Sergeant Davis talks about feeling let down after a flight.

Smith, Warren Thomas. *John Wesley and Slavery.* Nashville: Abingdon Press, 1986, p. 41. Talks about the practice of giving young white children slaves their own age.

Synnestvedt, Sig. *The White Response to Black Emancipation.* New York: The Macmillan Company, 1974, pp. 52, 53.

"T. Sgt. Calvin Davis, Pleasanton Hero Ace, Reported Missing in Action over Germany." *The Bear Lake Beacon,* January 9, 1945.

Tucker, Cynthia. "One Month Can't Erase Ignorance." *The Atlanta-Journal Constitution,* February 20, 2002.

U.S. Census Office. Population of the United States in 1860, p. 359. Gives the number of free Negroes of mixed blood in North Carolina.

Vollers, Maryanne. *Ghosts of Mississippi.* Boston: Little, Brown and Company (Back Bay Books), 1995.

Walls, Bryan. *The Road That Led to Somewhere.* A documented novel published by the Walls family, 1980.

Whitehill, Walter M., and Norman Kotker. *Massachusetts: A Pictorial History.* New York: Charles Scribner's Sons, 1976, p. 194. A description of whaling.

Williams, Michael W., ed. *The African American Encyclopedia,* Vol. 4. New York: Marshall Cavendish Corp., 1993, pp. 1086–88.

Wingfield, Marshall. *History of Caroline County, Virginia.* Richmond: Trevvet Christian and Co., Inc., 1924.

Yanak, Ted, and Pam Cornelison. *The Great American History Fact-Finder.* Boston and New York: Houghton Mifflin Company, 1993.

Chapter 14: Guns and Pickles

African Americans, Voices of Triumph: Perseverance. By the editors of Time-Life Books. Alexandria, Va.: Time-Life Books, 1993.

Bibliography

The Arcata Union, Arcata, California, Saturday, January 21, 1899. This article claims Lucy Nichols escaped from slavery with her husband and a little girl, but there is no other evidence that she had a husband before the Civil War.

Ball Blue Book of Canning and Preserving Recipes. Muncie, Ind.: Ball Brothers Glass Manufacturing Company, 1938.

Ballton, Samuel. Letter to the editor. *The Long-Islander*, March 18, 1914.

Berlin, Ira, and Leslie Rowland, eds. *Families & Freedom, A Documentary History of African-American Kinship in the Civil War Era.* New York: The New Press, 1998.

Bernikow, Louise, in association with the National Women's History Project. *The American Women's Almanac.* New York: Berkley Books, 1997. The section headed "Civil War Spies" talks about how a white spy named Elizabeth Van Lew of Richmond, Virginia, smuggled freed slave Mary Elisabeth Bowser into the home of Jefferson Davis, president of the Confederacy. Bowser reported whatever she overheard to Van Lew, who passed it on to Union officers. On page 15, Bowser is discussed, and Harriet Tubman's role as a spy is described on page 13.

Blackett, R.J.M., ed. *Thomas Morris Chester, Black Civil War Correspondent: His Dispatches from the Virginia Front*, with a biographical essay and notes. New York: Da Capo Press, Inc., 1991, pp. 109, 202, 295.

Blassingame, John, ed. *Slave Testimony: Two Centuries of Letters, Speeches, Interviews and Autobiographies.* Baton Rouge: Louisiana State University, 1977.

Blockson, Charles L. *African Americans in Pennsylvania, Above Ground and Underground: An Illustrated Guide.* Harrisburg, Pa.: RB Books, 2001.

———. *The Underground Railroad, First-Person Narratives of Escapes to Freedom in the North.* New York: Prentice Hall Press, 1987.

Bowman, John S., ed. *The Civil War Day by Day: An Illustrated Almanac of America's Bloodiest War.* Greenwich, Conn.: Dorset Press, 1989.

Boyd, Herb, ed. *Autobiography of a People: Three Centuries of African American History Told by Those Who Lived It.* New York: Anchor Books, 2001.

Brown, Thomas J., ed. *American Eras: Civil War and Reconstruction, 1850–1877.* Detroit: Gale Research, 1997, p. 329. It mentions that General Rosecrans was a Catholic and kept a rosary in his pocket.

Buckley, Gail. *American Patriots: The Story of Blacks in the Military from the Revolution to Desert Storm.* New York: Random House, 2001.

Burns, Ken, and Ric Burns, producers. *The Civil War: 1863—the Universe of Battle.* Florentine Films. This 1990 video, Episode 5 in the acclaimed PBS series, describes the Battle of Gettysburg, the fall of Vicksburg, the use of black troops and the battles at Chickamauga and Chattanooga.

Cooper, Desiree. "Group Keeps Black Troops' History Alive." *Detroit Free Press*, July 31, 2003.

Crozier, William Armstrong, ed. *Virginia County Records*, New Series, *Westmoreland County Wills*, Book II.

DeRamus, Betty. "Slaves Met Tricksters, Spies on Freedom's Trail." *The Detroit News*, February 8, 2000.

Dorwart, Bonnie Brice, M.D., medical staff, Lankehau Hospital, Wynnewood, Pa. "Rheumatism During the U.S. Civil War." A speech delivered at the 11th Annual Conference of the National Museum of Civil War Medicine, October 2003.

Dougher, Louise, and Carol Bloomgarden. *Images of America: Greenlawn, A Long Island Hamlet.* Charleston, S.C.: Arcadia Publishing, 2000.

Douglass, Frederick. *Life and Times of Frederick Douglass.* New York: 1962, p. 199.

Easton, Berenice, granddaughter of Samuel and Rebecca Balton. Interview with author in the Harborfield Library, Greenlawn, New York, May 9, 2003.

Farmer, Alice G. "The Long Island Rail Road . . . Ties That Bind." Greenlawn-Centerport Historical Association, undated.

Fitzgerald, Ruth Coder. *A Different Story.* Fredericksburg: Unicorn, 1979.

Foote, Shelby. *The Civil War, A Narrative: Red River to Appomattox.* New York: Vintage Books, 1974.

Ford, Worthington Chauncey, ed. *A Cycle of Adams Letters, 1861–1865,* Vol. II. Boston and New York: Houghton Mifflin Company, 1920. This volume includes letters from Charles Francis Adams Jr. to his mother, father and Henry Adams about the Civil War, particularly his command of the 5th Massachusetts Cavalry.

Fothergill, Augusta B. *Wills of Westmoreland County, Virginia, 1654–1800.* Richmond, Va.: Appeals Press, 1925.

Franklin, John Hope, and Loren Schweninger. *Runaway Slaves: Rebels on the Plantation.* New York, Oxford: Oxford University Press, 1999, pp. 56, 64.

Funkhouser, Darlene. *Civil War Cookin', Stories, 'n Such,* self-published, 2000.

Garrison, Webb. *Civil War Trivia and Fact Book.* Nashville: Rutledge Hill Press, 1992. Garrison reveals that there were 519 battles between Union and Confederate troops in Virginia compared to 298 in Tennessee, 244 in Missouri, 186 in Mississippi, 167 in Arkansas, 138 in Kentucky, 118 in Louisiana, 108 in Georgia, 85 in North Carolina, 70 in West Virginia, 78 in Alabama, 60 in South Carolina, 32 in Florida, 30 in Maryland, 19 in New Mexico, 17 in Indian Territory, 14 in Texas, 11 in Dakota Territory, 9 in Pennsylvania, 7 in Kansas, 6 in California, 6 in Minnesota, 4 in Oregon, 4 in Arizona, 4 in Colorado, 4 in Indiana, 2 in Nebraska, 2 in Nevada, 1 in Washington, 1 in the District of Columbia, 1 in Utah, 1 in New York, 1 in Idaho, 1 in Illinois.

Gladstone, William A. *United States Colored Troops—1863–1867.* Gettysburg, Pa.: Thomas Publications, 1990.

Glueck, Grace. "Expressions of Hope and Faith, Inspired by the Work of a Freed Slave." *The New York Times*, Friday, January 30, 2004.

"Greenlawn Pickle King: His Life Story Interesting." *The Brooklyn Eagle*, September 8, 1910.

Hargrove, Hondon B. *Black Union Soldiers in the Civil War.* Jefferson, N.C.: McFarland & Company, Inc., 1998.

Hine, Darlene Clark, Elsa Barkley Brown, and Rosalyn Terborg-Penn, eds. *Black Women in America: An Historical Encyclopedia*, Vol. II, M–Z. Bloomington and Indianapolis: Indiana University Press, 1994.

"The History of Centerport and Greenlawn—A Brief Outline." Compiled and written by the Greenlawn-Centerport Historical Association.

Jackson, Thelma. *African Americans in Northport: An Untold Story.* Huntington, N.Y.: Maple Hill Press, Ltd., 2000.

Lain & Healy's Brooklyn & Long Island Business Directory, 1896, which contains an ad for Samuel Ballton's real estate.

Leech, Margaret. *Reveille in Washington, 1860–1865.* New York: Carroll & Graf Publishers, Inc., 1986; orig. pub. 1941, M. L. Pulitzer.

LeGaye, E. S. "Rocky," ed. *Authentic Civil War Battle Sites, Land & Naval Engagements.* Houston: Western Heritage Press, 1982.

The Long-Islander, May 22, 1925. Contains an obituary for Rebecca Ballton.

Long Island Genealogies. Albany, N.Y.: Joel Munsell's Sons, 1895.

Mackay, Robert B., Geoffrey L. Rossano and Carol A. Traynor, eds. *Between Ocean and Empire: An Illustrated History of Long Island.* Northridge, Calif.: Windsor Publications, 1988.

Main, Edwin M. *The Story of the Marches, Battles and Incidents of the Third United States Colored Cavalry.* Louisville, Ky.: Globe Printing Company, 1908; reprint, New York: Negro Universities Press, 1970.

Mallin, Robert, M.D., retired plastic and reconstructive surgeon. "Patent (Proprietary) Medicines in the Civil War," a speech delivered at the 11th Annual Conference of the National Museum of Civil War Medicine, October 2003.

McGrath, Charles. "The Civil War Without All the Sepia Tint." *The New York Times*, Sunday, December 21, 2003.

The National Archives, Soldier's certificate No. 975436, Lucy Nichols, nurse, medical department, U.S. Volunteers.

"Negro Woman Given Membership in G.A.R.," *The Atlanta Constitution*, January 31, 1915. This is an obituary for Lucy Nichols, who died in 1915 in New Albany, Indiana. According to the article, she joined the 23rd Indiana Regiment in Tennessee in 1861 and was the only Negro woman honored with membership in the Grand Army of the Republic.

New Albany Weekly Ledger, February 3, 1915. This contains an article that notes that Aunt Lucy Nichols was taken to the county asylum to be cared for but was not a pauper. It also states that she would be "buried with military honors in the colored cemetery beside her husband," though in 2003 it was unclear where she was actually buried.

New Albany Weekly Tribune, February 5, 1915. This contains another short death notice for Lucy Nichols.

"Only Woman Ever Member of G.A.R. Dies in Asylum." *New Albany Daily Ledger*, January 29, 1915. This article claims that Lucy Nichols died at age 72.

Pension records for Octave Johnson, USC Inf., certificate no. 942746, National Archives.

The Pickle Industry in Greenlawn, Including Old Family Recipes. A pamphlet compiled and written by the Greenlawn-Centerport Historical Association, 4th ed., 1993.

Public Press, February 2, 1915. Death notice for Lucy Higgs Nichols, who died at the county asylum at the age of 69 in 1915.

Record Group 15: Records of the Veterans Administration: Civil War Pension: "Samuel Ballton, Co. H, 5th Mass. Cav., 1885 Oct. 12: Invalid Application; 1917 Aug. 1 Widow's Application."

Robertson, James I., Jr. *Civil War Sites in Virginia: A Tour Guide.* Charlottesville, Va.: The University Press of Virginia, 1982. This book states that all of Fredericksburg and much of Richmond were in ashes and more than 17,000 dead from fighting or sickness by April of 1865. It describes Petersburg as the scene of more fighting than any Virginia community other than Richmond, and notes that Richmond and Washington, the two capitals at the heart of the conflict, were only 110 miles apart.

Roger, Sharon A. "Slaves No More: A Study of the Buxton Settlement, Upper Canada, 1849–1861." A dissertation submitted to the faculty of the Graduate School of the State University of New York at Buffalo in partial fulfillment of the requirements for the degree of Doctor of Philosophy, 1995. The book states on page 3 that "During the Civil War, many of Buxton's able-bodied men . . . volunteered for service in the Federal army and performed active military duty for a country they had fled." She further states on page 392 that about 35,000 Canadians, many black, joined the Union, and that of the 8 black surgeons in the Union Army, two once were residents of Buxton, Ontario.

Rogers, J. A. *Africa's Gift to America: The Afro-American in the Making and Saving of the United States.* Revised and enlarged Civil War Centennial Edition, copyright 1961. St. Petersburg, Fla.: Helga M. Rogers, copyright renewed 1989. This includes information on the heroics of black Medal of Honor winners at the battle of Chaffins Farm.

Schneider, Ben. "Trampled, Forgotten and Lost." *New Albany Tribune*, March 8, 1998. This article speculated that Lucy Nichols was buried in New Albany's original colored black cemetery in Floyd County, but can offer no proof.

Schwarz, Philip J. *Migrants Against Slavery: Virginians & The Nation.* Charlottesville and London: University Press of Virginia, 2001, p. 62. Tells the story of Garland White, who returned from Canada to fight.

Sernett, Milton C. *North Star Country: Upstate New York and the Crusade for African American Freedom.* Syracuse, N.Y.: Syracuse University Press, 2002. On page 125, the author notes that John Quincy Adams was remembered affectionately for his efforts to release the Africans who had mutinied on the Spanish ship *Amistad* in 1839.

"She Belongs to the G.A.R." *The Sandusky Star*, Wednesday, January 18, 1899. Talks about Lucy Nichols being granted a $12 per month pension by special order of Congress for participating in 28 battles, nursing, cooking and washing.

Starobin, Robert S., ed. *Blacks in Bondage: Letters of American Slaves.* New York: New Viewpoints, 1974, p. 113. George Moses Horton story.

Thompson, Benjamin F. *History of Long Island,* Vol. 1, 3rd ed., rev. New York: Robert H. Dodd, 1918. This describes the soil and topography of the region.

Ullman, Victor. *Look to the North Star: A Life of William King.* Toronto: Umbrella Press, 1994. The book contains information about fugitives who returned from Canada to fight in the Civil War on pages 212 and 229.

U.S. Federal Census for 1880, which lists Ballton as 39 years old and a farm laborer and Ann R. as his wife and her occupation as keeping house.

Weidman, Jane "Budge." "Medical Stories from U.S. Colored Troops." An address delivered at the National Museum of Civil War Medicine's 8th Annual Conference, August 4–6, 2000.

Wright, T.R.B. *Westmoreland County, Virginia, 1653–1912,* parts I and II. Richmond, Va.: Whittet & Shepperson, 1912.

INDEX

Page numbers in *italics* refer to illustrations.

Printed in the United States
By Bookmasters